Better Homes and Gardens®

1985 BEST-RECIPES YEARBOOK

© Copyright 1985 by Meredith Corporation, Des Moines, Iowa.
All Rights Reserved. Printed in the United States of America.
First Edition. Second Printing, 1985.
ISSN: 8755-3090
ISBN: 0-696-02105-6

Our seal assures you that every recipe in the *1985 Best-Recipes Yearbook* has been tested in the Better Homes and Gardens® Test Kitchen. This means that each recipe is practical and reliable, and meets our high standards of taste appeal.

CONTENTS

Every month, *Better Homes and Gardens*® magazine makes your life easier with recipes and ideas to suit your family's needs. We update you on nutrition, convenience cooking, and entertaining ideas. But don't worry about clipping and storing all that timely information; we've done it for you. In this durable, easy-to-use book, you'll rediscover the recipes we published for you in 1984.

JANUARY

"Learning about and improving your family's eating habits should be an ongoing process." —Dottie Hagan

(Right) Old favorites **Raisin-Apple Cake** (front) and **Hot Fruit Compote** (back) use less sweetener than in the past, yet still satisfy the family's taste for dessert.
(Opposite) **Seasoned Torsk** (front) gains everybody's acceptance because it's a mild-tasting fish topped with a favorite cheese.
Fruited Rice Pilaf (back right) is a fiber-rich meal accompaniment. When an entrée such as **Slimming Beef Burgundy** (left) highlights dinner, a lean meat cut and modest portions are the house rule.
Dottie's Wheat Bread (back) is tasty served with low-sugar **Rhubarb Spread** (center). In the summer, the Hagans make **Bread and Butter Pickles** (back); an extra rinse removes excess salt from the pickles.

Photographs: Mike Dieter

Putting More Nutrition In Family Meals

BY JOY TAYLOR
More and more families have changed their eating habits because they're convinced that well-being starts with good nutrition. The surprise for many of them is that altering what and how they eat is relatively easy—wholesome meals rely on nutrient-packed ingredients and nutrient-preserving cooking methods. Recently, we visited four families who changed their cooking for better health. Let their wellness strategies and newfound recipes (each nutritionally analyzed) guide your family to more healthful eating, too.

I'd like my children to be just as fired-up about health as I am," confides Don Hagan, an orthodontist in Des Moines, Iowa. Nine years ago, when he was overweight and inactive, that aspiring thought would have been foreign to Don. However, a doctor's advice to lose weight and a family history of vascular disease jolted him to count calories and jog.

Don's 30-pound weight loss and commitment to physical fitness changed his family's nutritional awareness. Dottie, his wife, was already attuned to wholesome eating, but "with Don's enthusiasm, we made a concentrated effort to supply our family with good food," she explains.

Today, the Hagans' revitalized diet emphasizes whole grains and made-from-scratch meals. To reduce fat intake, fish and poultry are the mainstays of their menus. But convincing the meat-loving children, Christy, Cindy, Doug, and Jeff, of the value of this action isn't always easy. Don admits, "If I had my way, I'd push for a more drastic change, but this might turn off the children."

The Hagans' approach to cooking is relaxed and encourages the family to try new foods. Here and there in recipes, they reduce or eliminate some ingredients to cut calories, sodium, or fat. "For instance, we spray pans with a nonstick coating rather than greasing them," says Dottie. "And in entrées we replace salt with spices. The little changes we make in our cooking every day add up to a big improvement overall."

Exercise is an integral part of the Hagans' life-style. Don and Dottie take a vigorous walk every day, and the entire family bikes. Don leads the troupe in distance; he bicycles across Iowa every summer.

"We have the best of both worlds—really good-for-you health foods that taste wonderful, too!" —Donna Gahwiler

*(Right) Vegetable juice, parsnip, celery, and potato give a vitamin lift to the Gahwilers' **Veal Stew** (left). **Oven-Fried Chicken** (right) gets its crispness from whole wheat flour and sesame seed. **Falafel Patties** (center) are based on protein-rich beans.*

*(Opposite) For holidays, the Gahwilers enjoy honey-sweetened **Carob Fudge** and **Whole Grain Pecan Cookies** (front). Birthday celebrations include **Good-for-You Carrot Cupcakes** (back) enriched with tofu. Year round, the Gahwilers' refrigerator houses **Mock Sangria** (far back), plus the makings (cottage cheese, milk, and fruit) for **Thick and Creamy Milkshakes** (center). For a yogurt-capped, cheesy concoction, try **Ricotta Sundae** (right).*

Photographs: Hedrich-Blessing

A few years ago, Donna and Carl Gahwiler of Zionsville, Indiana, began to read countless nutrition books and consult with their pediatrician about children's diets. After recognizing that their meals included too many processed foods, salt, and sweets, Donna and Carl became convinced that a change was needed for everyone's well-being. They restocked the kitchen with whole grains, legumes, tofu, dried fruits, nuts, and fresh produce, then embarked on a whole new way of cooking. "We experimented constantly to create satisfying meals and healthful versions of 'no-no' foods. With time, we've learned new cooking habits that would now be difficult to break," reflects Donna.

The Gahwilers' meals are more nutritious than ever and, best of all, they're pleasing, too. The Gahwilers never use salt but do use small amounts of soy sauce, lemon juice, herbs, and cheese as seasonings. Fried foods are avoided; instead, most foods are steamed, broiled, or roasted. Desserts are less sweet and usually feature fruits.

Breaking poor nutrition habits was especially hard for the children, Christy, Carla, Lisa, and Paul. But Donna's education in child development helped her introduce foods to replace the ones the kids seemed to like. "Children eat almost anything if you present the new food in the right way," explains Donna. Now favorite family snacks include natural cheese, nuts, popcorn, and vegetable sticks.

Donna was so successful with her four children that she volunteers at schools to teach students about food. "Nutrition education at home or in the classroom must be fun; it shouldn't be a lecture," she stresses.

"Providing nutritious, good-tasting meals for your family is a labor of love. It says: 'I want you to be healthy and to enjoy life.'" —Judith Curland

Tofu, mixed with other protein-rich foods such as grains, nuts, and milk products, enables the Curland and Corsetti families to reduce their meat consumption.

The Curlands use tofu as a meat stretcher (opposite) in entrées like **Chicken and Tofu Stir-Fry** (front left) and **Beef-Tofu Loaf** (left). **Kasha with Vegetables** (back left) is a quick whole grain alternative to potatoes or rice.

(Right) **Italian-Style Tripe** served atop **Polenta** and accompanied by **Our-Kids-Love-It Eggplant** (on platter) makes a nourishing meal that reflects Sandra's ethnic heritage. The Corsettis plan for up to four meatless dinners a week. Family specialties like **Cheesy Beans and Brown Rice** (in bowl) offer high-quality protein and are low cost.

Field editor: Estelle Bond Guralnick
Photographs: Hedrich-Blessing

N Nathan Curland and Sandra and Bill Corsetti share the same food philosophy as well as nutritious recipes, pots of stew, and garden surpluses. After they met five years ago, both families developed an interest in food and health. The Corsettis' resolution to raise children with good eating habits and lower Bill's high blood pressure motivated them to learn more about healthful cooking. At that same time, the Curlands' concern was to create recipes that satisfied both Judith's vegetarian preference and steak-and-salad-loving Nathan. "The more we shared our beliefs, the more encouraged each family was to explore new nutritional avenues," reflects Judith.

Knowing the source of their food is important for the Curland and Corsetti families. Both wives buy fruits, vegetables, dairy products, whole grains, honey, and tea from the food co-op where they work. During the summer, a garden in each yard provides produce. "Typically, dinner for us consists of two or three vegetables and a small serving of protein-rich food," explains Sandra.

Both families confirm that their time and energy aimed at good eating are well spent. The Curlands boast that their 3-year-old daughter, Rebecca, requests oatmeal for breakfast and tofu sandwiches for lunch; 10-year-old Christopher Corsetti's favorite after-school snack is tossed salad! The Corsettis note that nutritious foods have resulted in noticeable health benefits. "During the past two winters," Sandra reports, "neither of my sons has had a cold or flu, and Bill's blood pressure has gone down. Hopefully, there are long-term benefits of nutritious eating as well."

Note: To obtain the nutrition analysis of each recipe, the following guidelines were used:

When ingredient options appear in a recipe, the analysis was calculated using the first ingredient choice.

Optional ingredients were omitted in the analyses.

The nutrition analyses for recipes calling for fresh ingredients were calculated using the measurements for raw fruits, vegetables, and meats.

If a recipe gives two serving sizes (such as "Makes 6 to 8 servings"), the nutrition analysis was calculated using the first choice.

Note: Microwave recipes were tested in countertop microwave ovens that operate on 600 to 700 watts. Cooking times are approximate since microwave ovens vary by manufacturer.

The Hagans

RHUBARB SPREAD

The Hagan family enjoys this thick sauce as a topping for pancakes and waffles and as a spread for bread.

  ¼ **cup water**
  2 **to 3 tablespoons sugar**
  1 **tablespoon cornstarch**
1½ **pounds fresh *or* frozen rhubarb, cut into 1-inch pieces (about 4 cups)**
  2 **to 3 tablespoons honey**

In a saucepan stir together the water, sugar, and cornstarch. Add the rhubarb and honey. Bring to boiling, stirring constantly; reduce heat. Cover and simmer 5 to 10 minutes or till rhubarb is tender and mixture is thickened; stir occasionally. Makes about 2½ cups.

Per tablespoon: 10 calories, 0.1 g protein, 2 g carbohydrate, 0 g fat, and 0.4 mg sodium.

HOT FRUIT COMPOTE

During the warm-weather months, substitute fresh pineapple and peaches for the canned variety.

  3 **tablespoons butter *or* margarine**
  ¼ **cup packed brown sugar**
  1 **tablespoon cornstarch**
  1 **cup dry white wine**
  1 **20-ounce can pineapple chunks (juice pack), drained**
  1 **16-ounce can peach halves (juice pack), drained**
  2 **large pears, cored and sliced**
  1 **cup halved and seeded red *and/or* green grapes**

For sauce, in a saucepan melt the butter or margarine. Stir in the brown sugar and cornstarch. Add the wine. Cook and stir over medium heat till mixture is thickened and bubbly.

In a 2-quart casserole arrange the pineapple chunks, peach halves, pear slices, and grape halves. Pour the sauce over fruit. Bake, covered, in a 350° oven for 40 minutes or till heated through. Serve warm. Makes 6 to 8 servings.

Per serving: 241 calories, 1 g protein, 42 g carbohydrate, 6 g fat, and 79 mg sodium.

Microwave directions: For sauce, in a 4-cup glass measure micro-cook the butter or margarine, uncovered, on 100% power (HIGH) for 30 to 40 seconds or till melted. Stir in the brown sugar and cornstarch. Stir in the wine. Micro-cook, uncovered, for 3 to 4 minutes or till mixture is thickened and bubbly, stirring after every minute.

Combine fruits in a 2-quart nonmetal casserole. Add sauce. Micro-cook, covered, for 6 to 7 minutes or till heated through, stirring once. Serve warm.

RAISIN-APPLE CAKE

  2 **cups unbleached flour**
  2 **teaspoons baking soda**
  2 **teaspoons ground cinnamon**
  ½ **teaspoon salt**
  ¼ **teaspoon ground nutmeg**
  2 **eggs**
  ½ **cup honey**
  ½ **cup butter *or* margarine**
  ¼ **cup sugar**
  2 **teaspoons vanilla**
  4 **cups chopped, peeled apples**
  1 **cup raisins**
  1 **cup chopped walnuts**

Stir together flour, baking soda, cinnamon, salt, and nutmeg. In a mixer bowl beat together eggs, honey, butter or margarine, sugar, and vanilla. Stir dry ingredients into egg mixture. Stir in chopped apple and the raisins.

Spread mixture in an ungreased 13x9x2-inch baking pan. Sprinkle the nuts atop. Bake in a 350° oven for 35 to 40 minutes. Cool in pan on wire rack. Cut into bars. Makes 12 servings.

Per serving: 339 calories, 5 g protein, 49 g carbohydrate, 15 g fat, and 380 mg sodium.

FRUITED RICE PILAF

  ½ **cup apple juice**
  1 **cup regular brown rice**
  1 **tablespoon butter *or* margarine**
  1 **tablespoon honey**
  2 **medium apples, coarsely chopped**
  ¾ **cup sliced celery**
Celery leaves (optional)
Apple slices (optional)

Combine the apple juice and enough *water* to equal the amount of liquid called for on rice package directions. In a medium saucepan bring liquid to boiling. Stir in rice, butter or margarine, and ½ teaspoon *salt.* Reduce heat. Cover tightly and cook over low heat for 30 to 35 minutes or till most of the liquid is absorbed. Stir in the honey, chopped apples, and celery. Cover and cook for 10 to 15 minutes more or till all of the liquid is absorbed and rice is tender. Serve warm. If desired, garnish with celery leaves and apple slices. Serves 8.

Per serving: 133 calories, 2 g protein, 27 g carbohydrate, 2 g fat, and 168 mg sodium.

DOTTIE'S WHEAT BREAD

You'll need less unbleached flour if you add soy grits. Gluten flour has a high proportion of gluten (the protein that gives bread its structure) and produces a superior texture in baked bread.

2¼ cups warm water (110° to 115°)
¼ cup honey
2 packages active dry yeast
3 cups whole wheat flour
¾ cup nonfat dry milk powder
½ cup gluten flour
½ cup toasted wheat germ
1 tablespoon brown sugar
2 teaspoons salt
⅓ cup cooking oil
½ cup soy grits (optional)
1½ to 2½ cups unbleached flour

Stir together the warm water, *1 table-spoon* of the honey, and the yeast; set aside. In a large mixer bowl stir together *2 cups* of the whole wheat flour, the milk powder, gluten flour, wheat germ, brown sugar, and salt. Add the yeast mixture, the remaining honey, and the oil. Beat on low speed of electric mixer for 30 seconds, scraping sides of bowl constantly. Beat for 3 minutes on high speed. Stir in soy grits, if desired, and the remaining whole wheat flour. Using a spoon, stir in as much of the unbleached flour as you can.

Turn out onto a lightly floured surface. Knead in enough of the remaining unbleached flour to make a moderately stiff dough that is smooth and elastic (6 to 8 minutes). Shape into a ball. Place in a lightly greased bowl; turn once to grease surface. Cover; let rise in warm place till double (about 1 hour).

Punch dough down; divide in half. Cover; let rest for 10 minutes. Shape dough into two loaves; place in two greased 8x4x2-inch or 9x5x3-inch loaf pans. Cover; let rise in warm place till nearly double (about 30 minutes). Bake in a 375° oven for 35 to 40 minutes, covering with foil the last 10 minutes of baking to prevent overbrowning. Remove from pans; cool on wire racks. Makes 2 loaves; 18 slices per loaf.

Per slice of bread: 103 calories, 4 g protein, 17 g carbohydrate, 2 g fat, 127 mg sodium.

BREAD AND BUTTER PICKLES

Serve these pickles year-round just as the Hagans do.

1 gallon medium-size cucumbers (5 pounds)
6 to 12 large onions (about 3¼ pounds)
2 large green peppers, chopped (1½ cups)
½ cup pickling salt
5 cups sugar
4 cups vinegar
2 tablespoons mustard seed
1½ teaspoons ground turmeric *or* allspice
1½ teaspoons celery seed
½ teaspoon ground cloves

Thinly slice the cucumbers and onions. In a large bowl combine cucumbers, onions, green peppers, and pickling salt; mix well. Cover and chill the mixture for 3 hours. Drain vegetables. Rinse well in cold water; drain well.

In a large kettle or a Dutch oven combine the sugar, vinegar, mustard seed, turmeric or allspice, celery seed, and cloves. Bring to boiling. Add the vegetables; return to boiling. Pack the vegetables and hot liquid in hot, clean pint or half-pint jars, leaving a ½-inch headspace. Wipe jar rims; adjust lids. Process in a boiling water bath 5 minutes for pints or half-pints (start timing when water boils). Makes 10 pints.

Per serving (½ cup): 123 calories, 1 g protein, 32 g carbohydrate, 0.1 g fat, 711 mg sodium.

Note: Nutrition analysis was determined by assuming that *half* of the salt is rinsed off the chilled vegetable mixture before processing.

SLIMMING BEEF BURGUNDY

This rendition of the popular wine-based stew reduces the calories in each serving by about 75 calories. To control the calorie count, use a lean meat, a minimum of oil, and allow only ½ cup of cooked noodles per serving.

2 pounds boneless beef chuck steak, cut into ¾-inch cubes
2 tablespoons cooking oil
1 cup water
½ cup chopped onion
3 tablespoons all-purpose flour
1 10½-ounce can condensed beef broth
16 whole fresh mushrooms, halved
¾ cup dry red wine
2 tablespoons tomato paste
1 teaspoon Kitchen Bouquet (optional)
1 bay leaf
⅛ teaspoon pepper
16 frozen *or* canned small whole onions
4 cups hot cooked noodles
Sliced green onion (optional)

In a Dutch oven brown meat, half at a time, in hot oil. Drain off fat. Set meat aside. Add the water and chopped onion to Dutch oven. Bring to boiling; reduce heat. Simmer, uncovered, for 8 to 10 minutes or till water evaporates.

Stir the flour into condensed beef broth; stir into Dutch oven. Stir in mushrooms, wine, tomato paste, Kitchen Bouquet (if desired), bay leaf, and pepper. Return meat to Dutch oven. Bring to boiling, stirring occasionally. Bake, covered, in a 350° oven for 1 to 1¼ hours or till meat is almost tender. Add whole onions; bake about 30 minutes more or till meat and vegetables are tender. Remove bay leaf. Toss noodles with green onion, if desired. Serve meat over noodles. Makes 8 servings.

Per serving: 498 calories, 28 g protein, 31 g carbohydrate, 27 g fat, and 334 mg sodium.

SEASONED TORSK

The Hagan children prefer this entrée when the poached fish is flaked, then topped with the seasonings and cheese, before baking.

- 1 **pound fresh *or* frozen torsk *or* cod fillets**
- 1 **bay leaf**
- 1 **tablespoon lemon juice**
- 2 **tablespoons dry white wine**
- 2 **teaspoons lemon juice**

Dash garlic powder
Dash salt
Dash pepper

- 2 **tablespoons grated Parmesan cheese**
- 1 **tablespoon snipped parsley**

Lemon slices (optional)

Thaw fish, if frozen. Cut into four portions. In a skillet bring 1 inch of *water* to boiling. Add the bay leaf and the 1 tablespoon lemon juice. Add the fish; simmer, covered, about 10 minutes or till fish is nearly done and flakes when tested with a fork. Transfer fish to a 10x6x2-inch baking dish; leave in portions or flake.

Pour the wine and the 2 teaspoons lemon juice over all. Sprinkle fish with the garlic powder, salt, and pepper. Sprinkle Parmesan cheese and snipped parsley over fish. Bake in a 350° oven for 5 to 10 minutes or till the cheese is light brown. Transfer fish to a serving platter. Garnish with lemon slices, if desired. Makes 4 servings.

Per serving: 180 calories, 27 g protein, 1 g carbohydrate, 6 g fat, and 156 mg sodium.

Microwave directions: Combine 1 cup *water*, the bay leaf, and 1 tablespoon lemon juice in a 12x7½x2-inch nonmetal baking dish. Arrange the fish fillets in dish, turning under any thin ends. Micro-cook, covered with vented plastic wrap, on 100% power (HIGH) for 3 to 4 minutes or till fillets flake easily when tested with a fork. Remove fish with slotted spatula; discard cooking liquid. Return fish to baking dish. Pour the wine and 2 teaspoons lemon juice over all. Sprinkle with the garlic powder, salt, and pepper. Sprinkle with Parmesan cheese and parsley. Micro-cook, uncovered, for 1 minute more.

The Gahwilers

CAROB FUDGE

- 1⅓ **cups nonfat dry milk powder**
- ¼ **cup butter *or* margarine**
- ⅔ **cup carob powder**
- ⅓ **cup honey**
- 2 **teaspoons vanilla**
- 1 **cup chopped sunflower nuts**

In a small mixer bowl beat together the milk powder and butter or margarine till mixture is crumbly. Add the carob powder, honey, and vanilla; beat till almost smooth. Knead in sunflower nuts till fudge is shiny. Shape mixture into two 10-inch-long rolls. Wrap in clear plastic wrap. Chill till firm. To serve, cut into ½-inch-thick slices. Store in refrigerator. Makes 40 slices.

Per serving (1 slice): 51 calories, 2 g protein, 6 g carbohydrate, 3 g fat, 27 mg sodium.

RICOTTA SUNDAE

- 1 **small banana**

Lemon juice

- ¼ **cup ricotta cheese**
- 1 **teaspoon toasted wheat germ**
- 1 **teaspoon miller's bran**

Dash ground cinnamon

- ¼ **cup halved and seeded red *or* green grapes**
- 3 **tablespoons plain *or* fruit yogurt (strawberry, raspberry, *or* cherry)**
- 1 **tablespoon chopped pecans**
- 1 **whole strawberry, halved (optional)**
- 1 **small bunch red grapes (optional)**

Peel and cut banana in half lengthwise; brush with lemon juice. Place in banana-split dish or small, shallow dessert dish. In a bowl combine ricotta, wheat germ, miller's bran, and cinnamon; stir in the halved grapes. Using an ice-cream scoop, form mixture into one scoop. Place ricotta mixture in the center of the banana strips. Drizzle desired yogurt over all; top with pecans. If desired, garnish with a halved strawberry and grapes. Divide for 2 servings.

Per serving: 153 calories, 6 g protein, 21 g carbohydrate, 6 g fat, and 53 mg sodium.

THICK AND CREAMY MILKSHAKES

For extra banana flavor, use four bananas and omit the second fruit.

- 1¼ **cups cold milk**
- 2 **medium bananas, frozen and cut up**
- 1 **cup fresh *or* frozen chopped peaches, strawberries, *or* blueberries**
- ½ **cup cream-style cottage cheese**
- 4 **pitted dates**
- 2 **teaspoons honey**
- 5 **large ice cubes**

In a blender container combine milk, frozen bananas, desired chopped fruit, cottage cheese, dates, honey, and ice cubes. Cover and blend till smooth. Makes 4 (8-ounce) servings.

Per serving: 179 calories, 8 g protein, 31 g carbohydrate, 4 g fat, and 104 mg sodium.

WHOLE GRAIN PECAN COOKIES

- 1 **cup butter *or* margarine, softened**
- ½ **cup honey**
- 2 **teaspoons vanilla**
- 1¾ **cups whole wheat flour**
- ½ **cup toasted wheat germ**
- 1½ **cups finely chopped pecans**

In a mixer bowl beat together the butter or margarine, honey, and vanilla. Beat in the whole wheat flour and wheat germ. Stir in the nuts. Divide dough into thirds. Place each portion between two pieces of waxed paper; roll to ⅜-inch thickness. Lay dough flat on baking sheets in freezer for 10 minutes.

Working with one portion of dough at a time, remove waxed paper. Cut dough into desired shapes with 2-inch cookie cutters. Transfer cutouts to a well-greased cookie sheet. Repeat with remaining dough. Reroll, freeze, and cut out dough scraps. Bake in a 325° oven about 10 minutes or till brown. Cool for 1 minute. Transfer to a wire rack. Makes about 48 cookies.

Per cookie: 88 calories, 1 g protein, 7 g carbohydrate, 7 g fat, 47 mg sodium.

MOCK SANGRIA

1½ cups boiling water
1 teaspoon dried mint leaves
½ cup honey
1 cup orange juice
1 cup grape juice
¾ cup lemon juice
2 cups chilled carbonated water
   or water
Ice cubes
Lemon and orange slices (optional)

Combine the boiling water and the mint leaves; let stand for 5 minutes. Stir in the honey. Stir in the orange juice, grape juice, and lemon juice. Cover and chill. Before serving, strain the mixture through several thicknesses of cheesecloth; stir in the chilled water. Add ice cubes. If desired, garnish with fruit slices. Makes 8 (7-ounce) servings.

Per serving: 105 calories, 0.5 g protein, 28 g carbohydrate, 0.1 g fat, 2 mg sodium.

SEASONED COATING MIX

Brewers' yeast is rich in iron, thiamine, and niacin.

1 cup sesame seed, toasted
2 cups whole wheat flour
¼ cup toasted wheat germ
2 tablespoons paprika
1 tablespoon brewers' yeast
   (optional)
1 tablespoon onion powder
1 tablespoon ground sage
1 tablespoon poultry seasoning
½ teaspoon garlic powder

Place the sesame seed in a blender container. Cover and blend till coarsely ground. In a small bowl stir together the sesame seed, whole wheat flour, wheat germ, paprika, brewers' yeast (if desired), onion powder, sage, poultry seasoning, and garlic powder. Use for Oven-Fried Chicken (see the recipe at right). Store mix, tightly covered, in the refrigerator. Makes about 3 cups.

Per tablespoon: 37 calories, 1 g protein, 4 g carbohydrate, 2 g fat, and 2 mg sodium.

GOOD-FOR-YOU CARROT CUPCAKES

The unusual ingredient in these cupcakes is bean curd, also called tofu. It is available in most large supermarkets.

2 eggs
1 cup honey
½ cup cooking oil
8 ounces fresh bean curd
   (tofu), drained
2 teaspoons baking soda
2 teaspoons ground cinnamon
2 teaspoons lemon juice
2 teaspoons vanilla
2 cups whole wheat flour
1 cup finely shredded carrot
1 cup chopped walnuts
1 recipe Cream Cheese Frosting

In a blender container or a food processor bowl combine the eggs, honey, oil, bean curd, baking soda, cinnamon, lemon juice, and vanilla. Cover and blend or process till smooth. Pour the mixture into a large mixing bowl. Beat in the whole wheat flour and carrot. Stir in the walnuts.
Grease 2½-inch muffin pans or line with paper bake cups; fill ⅔ full. Bake in a 325° oven about 20 minutes or till done. Cool thoroughly on a wire rack. Spread with Cream Cheese Frosting. For a decorative frosting, use a cake comb to spread. Store cupcakes, covered, in refrigerator. Makes 22.

Cream Cheese Frosting: In a mixer bowl beat together one 8-ounce package *cream cheese*, softened; 2 tablespoons *honey;* and 2 teaspoons *vanilla.*

Per frosted cupcake: 224 calories, 5 g protein, 24 g carbohydrate, 14 g fat, 135 mg sodium.

OVEN-FRIED CHICKEN

Chicken thighs oven-fry as deliciously as the chicken breasts and drumsticks.

2 whole large chicken
   breasts, skinned, halved
   lengthwise, and boned
6 chicken drumsticks
Milk
⅓ cup Seasoned Coating Mix
   (see recipe at left)
2 tablespoons butter or margarine,
   melted
Carrot and turnip curls (optional)
Carrot tops (optional)

Place each chicken breast half between two pieces of clear plastic wrap. Using the flat side of a meat mallet, lightly pound each piece to ¼-inch thickness. Remove the plastic wrap. Roll up chicken breasts jelly-roll style; secure with wooden toothpicks. If desired, remove skin from chicken legs. Brush chicken with milk, then toss with the Seasoned Coating Mix, coating well.
Place chicken in a shallow baking pan. Drizzle melted butter or margarine over chicken. Bake in a 375° oven about 45 minutes or till tender. (Do not turn chicken while baking.) Remove toothpicks from chicken breasts. Transfer chicken to a serving platter. If desired, garnish with carrot and turnip curls and carrot tops. Makes 6 servings.

Per serving: 244 calories, 32 g protein, 4 g carbohydrate, 11 g fat, and 48 mg sodium.

Microwave directions: Coat the chicken with coating mix as directed above. Place chicken breast halves and drumsticks in an ungreased 12x7½x2-inch nonmetal baking dish; drizzle with the melted butter or margarine. Micro-cook, covered, on 50% power (MEDIUM) for 15 to 18 minutes or till tender, rotating the dish a quarter-turn after every 5 minutes.

FALAFEL PATTIES

Purchase tahini, a paste made from sesame seed, at a specialty food shop.

      1 egg
      3 tablespoons snipped parsley
      2 tablespoons olive *or* cooking oil
      1 tablespoon brewers' yeast
         (optional)
      1 tablespoon water
      1 tablespoon soy sauce
      2 to 4 cloves garlic, minced
      1 teaspoon ground cumin
      1 teaspoon ground coriander
      1 teaspoon chili powder
      1 teaspoon lemon juice
    ¼ teaspoon ground celery seed
      2 cups cooked garbanzo beans
    ¾ cup toasted wheat germ
    ¼ cup tahini (sesame paste)
      2 tablespoons cooking oil
    Lettuce leaves (optional)
    Alfalfa sprouts (optional)
    Pita bread rounds, halved
         (optional)
    Plain yogurt
    Chopped green onion
    Chopped tomato *and/or* tomato
         wedges

In a blender container or a food processor bowl combine the egg, parsley, 2 tablespoons olive or cooking oil, brewers' yeast (if desired), water, soy sauce, garlic, cumin, coriander, chili powder, lemon juice, and celery seed. Cover and blend till smooth. Add the beans, wheat germ, and tahini; blend till smooth, stopping and scraping sides of container as necessary. Shape the mixture into six ½-inch-thick patties.

In a 12-inch skillet cook patties in 2 tablespoons cooking oil over medium heat about 5 minutes on each side or till brown. To serve, arrange patties on a plate lined with lettuce leaves and alfalfa sprouts, or put into pita bread halves, if desired. Serve with yogurt, green onion, and tomato pieces and/or wedges. Makes 6 main-dish servings.

Per serving: 287 calories, 11 g protein, 25 g carbohydrate, 17 g fat, and 250 mg sodium.

VEAL STEW

Use either veal or beef stew meat for this hearty stew.

    ¾ pound veal *or* beef stew meat,
         cut into ¾-inch cubes
      1 large onion, chopped (1 cup)
      1 clove garlic, minced
      1 tablespoon cooking oil
      2 12-ounce cans (3 cups) vegetable
         juice cocktail
    ¼ cup dry lentils
      1 bay leaf
      2 teaspoons lemon juice
    ½ teaspoon dried basil, crushed
      2 small potatoes, cut into 1-inch
         chunks
      1 large stalk celery, sliced
      1 parsnip, sliced
      1 cup sliced fresh mushrooms
      1 cup coarsely chopped cabbage

In a Dutch oven or a large saucepan cook the veal or beef stew meat, the chopped onion, and minced garlic in hot cooking oil till meat is brown. Drain off fat. Add the vegetable juice cocktail, lentils, bay leaf, lemon juice, and basil. Bring the mixture to boiling. (If using the beef stew meat, reduce heat; cover and simmer for 30 minutes.)

Add potato chunks, sliced celery, sliced parsnip, sliced mushrooms, and chopped cabbage. Reduce heat. Cover and simmer over low heat for 50 to 60 minutes or till the meat and vegetables are tender. Before serving, remove the bay leaf from the stew. Serve in bowls. Makes 6 servings.

Per serving: 219 calories, 16 g protein, 21 g carbohydrate, 8 g fat, and 302 mg sodium.

The Curlands and Corsettis

MISO SOUP

A favorite of the Curlands is this soup, which uses the Oriental flavoring, miso (fermented soybean paste).

Slice 1 medium *onion* and separate into rings. Cut 2 medium *carrots* into 2-inch strips. Cut 1 small *turnip* into 2-inch strips. In a 2-quart saucepan cook onion, carrot, and turnip in 2 tablespoons hot *cooking oil* for 6 to 8 minutes or till tender but not brown. Drain off fat. Add 2½ cups *water* and 2 *vegetable bouillon cubes*. Bring to boiling; reduce heat. Cover and simmer for 10 minutes. Gradually stir about ½ cup of the liquid into 1 tablespoon *miso*. Add the miso mixture and 2 cups chopped *spinach* or *Chinese cabbage* to the saucepan; heat through for 1 minute. Serve immediately. Makes 4 to 6 side-dish servings.

Per serving: 102 calories, 3 g protein, 8 g carbohydrate, 7 g fat, and 531 mg sodium.

KASHA WITH VEGETABLES

      4 large carrots, cut into
         matchstick-size strips
      1 large onion, thinly sliced and
         separated into rings
      1 tablespoon cooking oil
    ¾ cup buckwheat groats (kasha)
         or 1 cup bulgur wheat
      1 beaten egg
      1 vegetable bouillon cube
      1 tablespoon butter *or* margarine

In a 10-inch skillet cook carrots and onion in hot oil about 10 minutes or till crisp-tender. Remove from skillet; set aside. Drain any liquid from skillet.

In the same skillet stir together groats or bulgur wheat and egg. Cook and stir over medium heat about 4 minutes or till kernels are separate and dry. Add bouillon cube, 2 cups hot *water,* and ½ teaspoon *salt*. Simmer, covered, for 10 to 15 minutes or till grain is tender; stir once. Stir in vegetables and butter; heat through. Serves 6 to 8.

Per serving: 175 calories, 5 g protein, 27 g carbohydrate, 6 g fat, and 398 mg sodium.

OUR-KIDS-LOVE-IT EGGPLANT

    Cooking oil
2 beaten eggs
2 teaspoons olive *or* cooking oil
1 medium eggplant, peeled and sliced ¼ inch thick
1⅓ cups Cheese- and Herb-Seasoned Crumbs (see recipe below)
    Shredded mozzarella *or* Monterey Jack cheese (optional)

Brush unheated broiler pan with oil. Beat together eggs and the 2 teaspoons oil. Dip eggplant slices into egg mixture; coat with Cheese- and Herb-Seasoned Crumbs. Place on greased pan. Broil 4 inches from heat for 2 minutes or till golden. Turn; broil 1 to 2 minutes more. Top with cheese. Broil 1 minute more or till cheese is melted. Serves 8.

Per serving: 89 calories, 4 g protein, 8 g carbohydrate, 5 g fat, and 145 mg sodium.

CHEESE- AND HERB-SEASONED CRUMBS

5 slices dry whole wheat bread
⅓ cup grated Romano *or* Parmesan cheese
1 teaspoon dried oregano, crushed
1 teaspoon dried basil, crushed
1 teaspoon dried thyme, crushed
1 teaspoon dried marjoram, crushed
1 teaspoon dried parsley flakes
½ teaspoon salt
½ teaspoon dried rosemary, crushed
½ teaspoon dried savory, crushed
½ teaspoon celery seed
½ teaspoon fennel seed
½ teaspoon paprika
½ teaspoon ground sage
¼ teaspoon garlic powder

Place 2½ slices bread in a blender container. Cover and blend to fine crumbs. Remove crumbs. Repeat with remaining bread. Stir together all of the bread crumbs and the remaining ingredients. Store seasoned crumbs, covered, in the refrigerator. Makes 2½ cups.

Per tablespoon: 12 calories, 1 g protein, 2 g carbohydrate, 0.3 g fat, 52 mg sodium.

MINESTRONE SOUP

The Corsettis have experimented and found that almost any vegetable can be added to this soup.

1 large onion, chopped
2 stalks celery, chopped
1 clove garlic, minced
2 tablespoons olive *or* cooking oil
4 tomatoes, finely chopped, *or* one 15-ounce can tomatoes, cut up
2 tablespoons snipped parsley
1½ teaspoons dried basil, crushed
½ teaspoon dried oregano, crushed
⅛ teaspoon pepper
1 bay leaf
2½ to 3 cups vegetable *or* beef broth
2 cups desired vegetables (cubed potatoes, sliced green beans, sliced zucchini, chopped broccoli, *and/or* sliced carrots)
½ cup broken thin spaghetti
¾ cup cooked *or* canned red kidney beans, drained
⅓ to ½ cup grated Romano *or* Parmesan cheese

In a large Dutch oven cook the onion, celery, and garlic in hot oil till onion is tender but not brown. Add the fresh or *undrained* canned tomatoes, parsley, basil, oregano, pepper, and bay leaf. Add the vegetable or beef broth. Bring to boiling; reduce heat. Cover and simmer for 50 minutes.

Add the desired vegetables *except* zucchini. Cover and simmer about 15 minutes more or till the vegetables are just tender. Add the spaghetti, zucchini, and the cooked or canned beans. Cook about 15 minutes more or till the spaghetti is done. Remove bay leaf. Sprinkle *1 tablespoon* of the grated cheese over *each* serving. Makes 6 to 8 main-dish servings.

Per serving: 201 calories, 10 g protein, 26 g carbohydrate, 7 g fat, 483 mg sodium.

ITALIAN-STYLE TRIPE

2 pounds beef tripe
1 stalk celery, cut into 1-inch pieces
1 onion, quartered
1 small onion, chopped
1 clove garlic, minced
2 tablespoons cooking oil
1 28-ounce can tomato puree
1 stalk celery, sliced
1 tablespoon snipped parsley
1 teaspoon dried basil, crushed
½ teaspoon dried oregano, crushed
¼ teaspoon salt
¼ teaspoon pepper
¼ teaspoon bottled hot pepper sauce
1 recipe Polenta
    Cooked green beans (optional)
½ cup grated Parmesan cheese

Rinse the tripe in warm water twice, then in cold water. Put tripe into a Dutch oven; cover with cold water. Add the first cut-up celery stalk and quartered onion. Bring to boiling; reduce heat. Simmer, covered, about 1 hour or till tripe is very tender. Drain, rinse, and cool. Discard the celery and onion. Remove fat from tripe. Cut the tripe into bite-size strips.

In the same Dutch oven cook the chopped onion and garlic in hot oil till tender but not brown. Add tripe. Cook and stir over medium heat for 8 minutes. Add the tomato puree, the sliced celery, parsley, basil, oregano, salt, pepper, and hot pepper sauce. Cover and simmer about 30 minutes or till vegetables are tender. Serve with Polenta and beans, if desired. Sprinkle *1 tablespoon* of cheese atop *each* serving. Serves 8.

Polenta: In a large saucepan bring 4½ cups *water* to boiling. Stir together 1½ cups *yellow cornmeal*, 1½ cups cold *water*, and 1 teaspoon *salt*; add to the boiling water. Reduce heat. Simmer for 20 minutes, stirring frequently. Serve immediately.

Per serving: 393 calories, 42 g protein, 29 g carbohydrate, 12 g fat, and 912 mg sodium.

BEEF-TOFU LOAF

      1 **beaten egg**
      2 **tablespoons water**
     ¼ **cup rolled oats**
     ¼ **cup soft whole wheat bread crumbs**
      3 **tablespoons snipped parsley**
      1 **teaspoon dried oregano, crushed**
     ½ **teaspoon salt**
     ¼ **teaspoon pepper**
      1 **pound ground beef**
      8 **ounces fresh bean curd (tofu), mashed**
      1 **medium onion, finely chopped**
     ¾ **cup shredded carrot**
     ¼ **cup shredded turnip**
     ¼ **cup shredded zucchini**
      2 **tablespoons water**
    Cherry tomatoes (optional)
    Italian parsley (optional)

In a bowl stir together the egg, the first 2 tablespoons water, the oats, bread crumbs, parsley, oregano, salt, and pepper. Add the ground beef, bean curd, and onion; mix well. Spoon *half* of the mixture into the bottom of a 9x5x3-inch or 8x4x2-inch loaf pan. Place *half* of the carrot and all of the turnip and zucchini down the center of the meat to within ½ inch of edges. Spoon remaining meat mixture over all, lightly pressing meat layers together. Bake in a 350° oven for 1 to 1¼ hours or till done.

Meanwhile, place reserved carrot in a small saucepan with the last 2 tablespoons water. Cover and cook over medium-high heat for 3 to 5 minutes or till crisp-tender; drain. Drain fat from meat loaf. Transfer the loaf to a serving platter; top with the cooked carrots. Garnish with cherry tomatoes and Italian parsley sprigs, if desired. Makes 6 to 8 servings.

Per serving: 275 calories, 19 g protein, 7 g carbohydrate, 19 g fat, and 258 mg sodium.

CHEESY BEANS AND BROWN RICE

    1½ **cups regular brown rice**
    1½ **cups water**
      1 **large onion, chopped**
      1 **medium carrot, chopped**
      1 **stalk celery, chopped**
     ⅓ **cup snipped parsley**
      1 **tablespoon dried basil, crushed**
     ½ **teaspoon dried oregano, crushed**
      1 **clove garlic, minced**
      3 **tablespoons olive *or* cooking oil**
     ¾ **cup cooked *or* canned red kidney beans, drained**
      1 **large tomato, chopped**
     ¼ **teaspoon salt**
     ⅛ **teaspoon pepper**
     ½ **cup shredded Monterey Jack *or* grated Parmesan cheese**
      2 **tablespoons butter *or* margarine**

In a heatproof bowl combine the brown rice and the water. Place bowl, uncovered, on a rack in a large Dutch oven. Add 2 to 3 inches *water* to Dutch oven. Bring water in Dutch oven to boiling. Reduce heat. Cover and steam rice for 45 to 60 minutes or till done.

Meanwhile, in a medium saucepan cook the onion, carrot, celery, parsley, basil, oregano, and garlic, covered, in hot oil about 8 minutes or till onion is tender but not brown. Add beans, tomato, salt, and pepper; heat through. Stir Monterey Jack or Parmesan cheese and butter or margarine into rice; stir in vegetable mixture. Serve immediately. Makes 5 main-dish servings.

Per serving: 415 calories, 10 g protein, 55 g carbohydrate, 17 g fat, and 252 mg sodium.

Note: To prepare and cook dry red kidney beans, first rinse 1 pound beans with water to remove dirt or residue. In a Dutch oven combine the beans with 6 cups *water*. Let the beans stand, covered, at room temperature for 6 to 8 hours. Do not refrigerate. (*Or*, bring the beans to boiling. Reduce heat; simmer for 2 minutes. Remove from heat. Cover; let beans stand for 1 hour.) Drain and rinse beans. Return beans to Dutch oven. Add 6 cups *water*. Simmer, covered, 1 hour or till tender. Store, covered, in the refrigerator up to five days or in moisture- and vaporproof containers in the freezer up to six months.

CHICKEN AND TOFU STIR-FRY

      1 **pound fresh bean curd (tofu), cut into ¾-inch cubes**
      2 **tablespoons soy sauce**
      1 **tablespoon dry sherry**
      1 **tablespoon cornstarch**
      1 **whole large chicken breast, skinned, boned, and cut into bite-size strips**
      3 **tablespoons cooking oil**
      8 **ounces broccoli, cut into bite-size pieces (about 3 cups)**
      1 **medium onion, cut into wedges**
      1 **cup fresh bean sprouts**
      2 **cloves garlic, halved**
      2 **tablespoons oyster sauce *or* soy sauce**
    Hot cooked brown rice (optional)

Marinate the bean curd in the 2 tablespoons soy sauce for 10 minutes. Drain well, reserving soy sauce. Combine reserved soy sauce, the sherry, and cornstarch. Marinate the chicken in soy mixture for 15 minutes.

Heat a wok or a large skillet over high heat. Add *1 tablespoon* of the cooking oil. Stir-fry bean curd for 1 to 2 minutes or till light brown; remove from wok with a slotted spoon. Add another tablespoon cooking oil to wok. Stir-fry the broccoli for 3 minutes. Add the onion to wok; stir-fry for 2 minutes more. Add bean sprouts; stir-fry for 1 minute more. Remove vegetables from wok.

Add another tablespoon cooking oil to wok, if necessary. Add garlic to wok; stir-fry for 1 minute. Discard garlic. Stir the chicken and marinade mixture; add to wok. Cook and stir for 2 to 3 minutes or till bubbly. Add the oyster sauce or soy sauce, vegetables, and bean curd cubes; heat through. Serve with hot cooked brown rice, if desired. Makes 6 servings.

Per serving: 220 calories, 21 g protein, 9 g carbohydrate, 12 g fat, and 893 mg sodium.

FEBRUARY

Better Homes and Gardens

February 1984 • $1.50

100 IDEAS UNDER $100

BRAND-NEW PROJECTS TO BUILD, CRAFT, STITCH FOR HOME AND FAMILY
NEW TREATMENTS FOR HIGH BLOOD PRESSURE
HOMEMADE SOUPS • MICROWAVE COOKING

GREAT SOUPS
From Homemade Mixes

By Nancy K. Wall

Soup's on! You can cook up a homemade potful more easily and quickly than starting from scratch, with the help of two versatile soup mixes. Make up recipe-size bundles of the soup mixes in assembly-line fashion to keep on hand in your pantry. When it's soup-making time, simmer one bundle of mix with two or three of your favorite ingredients.

BEAN Choose-a-Bean Soup Mix allows you to select which kinds of dried beans or peas you'd like to combine with wheat berries, pearl barley, and seasonings. Use the mix to make the trio of soups shown here or create your own delicious soup combinations.

(Counterclockwise from back left) For *Spicy Bean Pot,* cook the mix with ground beef, tomatoes with peppers, and chili powder; serve your creation in tortilla bowls. *Meaty Vegetable Soup* is chock-full of tomatoes, carrots, and pork hocks. *Cheese and Bean Soup* gets its flavor from smoked cheese.

PASTA From a light and elegant first course to a healthful and hearty main dish, each of these savory soups gets its start from the versatile *Pick-a-Pasta Soup Mix*. It's a made-to-order combination of pasta, lentils, Parmesan cheese, dried onions, and seasonings.

(Clockwise from back right) *Pea Pod Appetizer Broth* is a superb start for a special dinner. Minutes before serving, simply add frozen pea pods and soy sauce to the cooked pasta soup mix. To punctuate the soup's Oriental style, mild enoki mushrooms and coriander garnish each serving. Evaporated milk imparts richness to *Indonesian-Style Chicken Chowder*. Either cooked chicken you have on hand or canned chicken can be added to this main-dish soup that's delicately spiced with curry. For pizza flavor without the pizza crust, serve *Pepperoni and Vegetable Soup*. Vegetable juice cocktail adds zest to the soup base. For a flavor-filled change of pace, you can substitute smoked sausage links for the pepperoni.

Food stylist: Fran Paulson. Photograph: Mike Dieter

Note: Each soup mix yields enough for one recipe of prepared soup. To make up multiples of a mix to keep on hand, measure the ingredients, assembly-line fashion, and put them into separate storage containers. If you try to make and store either of the mixes in bulk, the seasonings will separate and settle to the bottom of the container.

CHOOSE-A-BEAN SOUP MIX

- ¼ **cup dry garbanzo beans**
- ¼ **cup dry navy beans** *or* **lima beans**
- ¼ **cup dry red kidney beans** *or* **pinto beans**
- ¼ **cup dry split** *or* **whole green peas**
- 3 **tablespoons minced dried onion**
- 2 **tablespoons whole wheat berries**
- 2 **tablespoons pearl barley**
- 2 **tablespoons dried celery flakes**
- 2 **teaspoons instant beef bouillon granules**
- ½ **teaspoon dried basil, crushed**
- 1 **bay leaf**

In a plastic bag or airtight container combine all ingredients. Seal tightly and store till needed.

To cook Choose-a-Bean Soup Mix: In a 3-quart saucepan combine 1 recipe Choose-a-Bean Soup Mix and 7 cups *water.* Bring to boiling; reduce heat. Cover; simmer for 2 minutes. Remove from heat. Cover; let stand 1 hour. (*Or,* soak soup mix in the water overnight in a covered pan.) *Do not drain.*

Bring beans and liquid to boiling; reduce heat. Cover and simmer for 1½ to 2 hours or till beans are tender. Remove bay leaf. Season to taste with salt. Ladle the soup into soup bowls. Makes 6 to 8 side-dish servings.

SPICY BEAN POT

For the pepper flower garnish shown on page 20, use a sharp knife to cut small fresh jalapeño peppers lengthwise into 8 strips, leaving the strips attached at the stem end. Remove and discard seeds. Place peppers in a bowl of ice water till strips curl and separate to form "flower petals."

- 1 **recipe Choose-a-Bean Soup Mix**
- ½ **pound ground beef**
- 1 **teaspoon chili powder**
- 1 **10-ounce can tomatoes and green chili peppers, cut up**
- 1 **recipe Tortilla Bowls (optional)**
Jalapeño chili pepper flowers (optional)

Prepare and cook Choose-a-Bean Soup Mix as directed, *except* reduce the water to 5½ cups. Remove the bay leaf.

Meanwhile, in a small skillet cook the ground beef till brown. Drain off fat. Stir in the chili powder and cook for 1 minute. Add the beef mixture to the bean mixture along with *undrained* tomatoes and green chili peppers. Heat through, stirring occasionally. Season to taste with salt. Ladle the soup into Tortilla Bowls, if desired, or soup bowls. If desired, garnish each serving with a jalapeño chili pepper flower. Makes 6 to 8 main-dish servings.

Tortilla Bowls: In a large skillet warm six to eight 10-inch flour tortillas over low heat just till warm and pliable. Place each warm tortilla in an ovenproof soup bowl, fluting the tortilla as necessary to fit the bowl. Place soup bowls on a baking sheet. Bake tortillas in a 350° oven for 15 minutes.

MEATY VEGETABLE SOUP

Eliminate seasoning with salt if you use the smoked pork hocks in this recipe.

- 1 **recipe Choose-a-Bean Soup Mix**
- 1 **pound smoked pork hocks** *or* **beef shank crosscuts**
- 1 **16-ounce can tomatoes, cut up**
- 1 **medium carrot, chopped**

Prepare Choose-a-Bean Soup Mix as directed through the soaking step. To the soaked bean mixture add smoked pork hocks or beef shank crosscuts. Bring to boiling; reduce heat. Cover and simmer 1 hour for pork hocks or 1½ hours for beef shank crosscuts.

Remove meat from pan. When cool enough to handle, remove meat from bones and coarsely chop. Discard bones. Remove and discard bay leaf.

Return the chopped meat to pan. Add *undrained* tomatoes and carrot. Cover and simmer for 30 minutes more. Season to taste with salt. Ladle the soup into soup bowls. If desired, tie a bone and bay leaves together for a garnish. Makes 4 to 6 main-dish servings.

CHEESE AND BEAN SOUP

- 1 **recipe Choose-a-Bean Soup Mix**
- 2 **cups milk**
- 1 **6-ounce link cheese food** *or* **cheese food with hickory smoke flavor**
Snipped parsley (optional)

Prepare and cook Choose-a-Bean Soup Mix as directed, *except* reduce water to *4 cups.* Remove bay leaf. In the same saucepan mash beans slightly. Add milk and cheese. Cook and stir till cheese is melted and soup is heated through. Ladle into soup bowls. If desired, garnish each serving with parsley. Makes 4 to 6 main-dish servings.

PEA POD APPETIZER BROTH

The tiny, white enoki mushrooms are available in the produce section of some large grocery stores. Use sliced fresh mushrooms if you can't locate these mild-flavored specialties.

    1 recipe Pick-a-Pasta Soup Mix
 3½ cups water
    ½ of a 6-ounce package frozen pea
      pods, halved crosswise
    2 teaspoons soy sauce
Enoki mushrooms (optional)
Fresh coriander sprigs (optional)

In a 2-quart saucepan combine Pick-a-Pasta Soup Mix and the water. Bring to boiling, then reduce heat. Cover and simmer about 35 minutes or till the lentils are tender, stirring the mixture occasionally during cooking.

Stir the frozen pea pods and the soy sauce into the hot mixture. Cover and cook the soup for 2 to 3 minutes more or till pea pods are tender. Ladle the soup into soup bowls. If desired, garnish each serving with enoki mushrooms and fresh coriander. Makes 3 or 4 side-dish servings.

PEPPERONI AND VEGETABLE SOUP

    1 recipe Pick-a-Pasta Soup Mix
    3 cups water
    1 12-ounce can (1½ cups)
      vegetable juice cocktail
    1 cup frozen mixed vegetables
    4 ounces sliced pepperoni,
      halved, *or* ½ of a 12-ounce
      package fully cooked smoked
      sausage links, sliced (4 links)
Shredded Parmesan cheese

In a 2-quart saucepan combine Pick-a-Pasta Soup Mix, the water, vegetable juice cocktail, and frozen mixed vegetables. Bring to boiling, then reduce heat. Cover and simmer about 35 minutes or till the lentils are tender, stirring the mixture occasionally during cooking.

Stir the sliced pepperoni or sausage into the hot mixture. Cover and cook the soup for 5 minutes more. Ladle the soup into soup bowls. Garnish each serving with shredded fresh Parmesan cheese. Makes 4 or 5 main-dish servings.

INDONESIAN-STYLE CHICKEN CHOWDER

Round out a meal of this spicy soup with a savory vegetable stir-fry or pita bread rounds.

    1 recipe Pick-a-Pasta Soup Mix
    2 cups water
    1 13-ounce can (1⅔ cups)
      evaporated milk
    ¾ cup diced cooked chicken *or*
      one 5-ounce can chunk-style
      chicken, cut up
 1½ to 2 teaspoons curry powder
Apple slices (optional)
Fresh mint leaves (optional)

In a 2-quart saucepan combine the uncooked Pick-a-Pasta Soup Mix and the water. Bring the mixture to boiling, then reduce the heat. Cover and simmer about 35 minutes or till the lentils are tender, stirring the mixture occasionally during cooking.

Stir in the evaporated milk, diced cooked chicken or canned chunk-style chicken, and the desired amount of curry powder. Cover and cook the soup for 5 minutes more. Ladle the soup into soup bowls. If desired, garnish each serving with some apple slices and fresh mint leaves. Makes 3 or 4 main-dish servings.

PICK-A-PASTA SOUP MIX

If you add the dried mushrooms, expect them to be very dark. You'll find the mushrooms in the Oriental or specialty section of your supermarket.

    ½ cup medium shell macaroni *or*
      other small pasta*
    ¼ cup dry lentils
    ¼ cup dried chopped mushrooms
      (optional)
    2 tablespoons grated Parmesan
      cheese
    1 tablespoon minced dried onion
    1 tablespoon instant chicken
      bouillon granules
    1 teaspoon dried parsley flakes
    ½ teaspoon dried oregano,
      crushed
Dash garlic powder

In a plastic bag or airtight container combine shell macaroni or other pasta, lentils, dried mushrooms, Parmesan cheese, dried onion, bouillon granules, parsley flakes, oregano, and garlic powder. Seal tightly and store till needed.

To cook Pick-a-Pasta Soup Mix: In a 2-quart saucepan combine 1 recipe Pick-a-Pasta Soup Mix and 3 cups *water*. Bring to boiling; reduce heat. Cover and simmer about 40 minutes or till lentils are tender, stirring occasionally. Ladle the soup into soup bowls. Makes 3 side-dish servings.

Note: Try using different pasta shapes for a new look each time you make Pick-a-Pasta Soup Mix. Choose from any of the following small pastas: farfalle (bows), route (wagon wheels), rotell (corkscrews), cavatelli (open fluted clam shells), or elbow macaroni.

MICROWAVE COOKING

Nancy K. Wall

One of today's best answers to preparing home-cooked meals quickly is your microwave oven. You can speed-cook your favorite recipes solely in the microwave oven or team your microwave and conventional oven to streamline cooking steps. Explore some of the possibilities by sampling these recipes. We've also included conventional cooking alternatives for families without a microwave.

Converting Favorite Recipes

Prepare these family-pleasing recipes with ease—Pea- and Cheese-Stuffed Steak, Zesty Chicken Bites, Shortcut Gumbo, and Apple and Spice Upside-Down Cake.

Photographs:
Mike Dieter
Food stylist: Fran Paulson

Saucy main dishes and high-moisture foods such as poultry, vegetables, and fruits make ideal candidates for microwave redos.

One big plus of micro-cooking *Pea- and Cheese-Stuffed Steak (center front)* is the succulent, juicy result. Another plus lies in cleanup; there's no messy broiler pan to wash!

Zesty Chicken Bites (center back) make a first-rate appetizer version of oven-fried chicken. A nonmetal rack (to elevate the chicken pieces over their juices) plus the nut and sesame seed coating, promise crisp results.

Southerners say that the color and flavor of great Gumbo lies in the preparation of the roux. This thickening mixture of flour and fat takes 35 to 40 minutes to cook. In this spicy-hot *Shortcut Gumbo (back right)* you can prepare the traditional thickener in 20 minutes.

For a dessert that's ready in minutes and just as tasty when cooked in the microwave as when cooked in the conventional oven, choose *Apple and Spice Upside-Down Cake (back left)*. Generally, micro-cooked cakes lack a golden brown color when compared to conventionally baked cakes. A fancy swirl of paper-thin apple slices serves as a decorative and delicious finish.

MICROWAVE COOKING

Teaming Microwave and Conventional Ovens

These eye-catching foods benefit from combination cooking— Winter Parsnip Puff, Biscuit-Topped Turkey Pie, Swirl Breakfast Loaf, and Pear Meringue Tarts.

Using your conventional oven, range top, or broiler along with your microwave oven often offers best results. Combined cooking methods create appealing, delicious foods in the shortest time with a minimum of effort.

Micro-cooking brings out the natural flavor of foods, especially vegetables. Micro-cooking the parsnips for **Winter Parsnip Puff** *(back left)* gives you the finest vegetable flavor plus fast cooking. Once the pie is assembled, conventional baking assures that the delicate egg, cream cheese, and cream mixture turns out light, fluffy, and irresistible.

For convenience and speed, prepare the saucy turkey-rutabaga filling for **Biscuit-Topped Turkey Pie** *(front left)* in the microwave oven; for golden color, pop the pie in your standard oven to bake the sage-garnished crust.

To shorten the time it takes to make such yeast breads as **Swirl Breakfast Loaf** *(front right)*, let the dough rise in your microwave oven. The 10 percent power setting (LOW) is required for proofing the dough in the microwave. Each tasty slice of the home-style loaf features spicy micro-plumped currants.

Piecrusts and pastries prepared in the microwave are tender and flaky, but lack the traditional golden color. In **Pear Meringue Tarts** *(back right)*, the ground pecans in the pastry add color and crunch. After you micro-cook the tart shells, pears, and orange sauce, assemble all the parts. A final piping of meringue and a few minutes under the broiler complete this party-special dessert.

ZESTY CHICKEN BITES

2 pounds chicken wings
¼ cup ground peanuts
¼ cup crushed plain croutons
1 tablespoon snipped parsley
1 tablespoon toasted sesame seed
¼ teaspoon paprika
Dash ground ginger
Dash ground red pepper
Milk *or* melted butter *or* margarine

Rinse the chicken wings; pat dry. Cut chicken wings at joints into three separate parts. Refrigerate tips and center portions for another use.*

In a mixing bowl stir together the ground peanuts, crushed plain croutons, parsley, sesame seed, paprika, ginger, and red pepper. Brush chicken with milk or butter or margarine; roll in crumb mixture.

Place chicken on a nonmetal rack in a 12x7½x2-inch nonmetal baking dish. Micro-cook, loosely covered with waxed paper, on 100% power (HIGH) for 5 to 6 minutes or till chicken is tender, giving the dish a half-turn once during cooking. Makes 8 to 10 servings.

Conventional method: Coat the chicken as directed. Place in a 13x9x2-inch baking pan, making sure pieces do not touch. Bake in a 375° oven about 30 minutes or till tender. *Do not turn.*

*Note: Use the chicken wing tips and center portions in recipes calling for chicken pieces.

PEA- AND CHEESE-STUFFED STEAK

2 slices bacon
1 cup frozen peas
1 slightly beaten egg yolk
2 tablespoons grated Parmesan cheese
¼ teaspoon dried basil, crushed
1 2-pound boneless beef top round steak, cut 1 inch thick
Italian parsley sprigs
1 recipe Basil Tomato Sauce

Arrange bacon slices on a nonmetal rack in a 12x7½x2-inch nonmetal baking dish. Cover with white paper toweling. Micro-cook on 100% power (HIGH) for 1½ to 2 minutes. Drain and crumble bacon; set aside. In a 1-quart nonmetal casserole combine peas and 1 tablespoon *water*. Micro-cook, covered, for 4 to 5 minutes, stirring occasionally. Mash peas. Stir in egg yolk, Parmesan, basil, and crumbled bacon; set aside.

Trim fat from meat. Cut a pocket in meat. Spoon pea mixture evenly into pocket. Close with wooden toothpicks. Place meat on rack in same baking dish. Micro-cook, covered, for 3 minutes; give dish a half-turn. Micro-cook, covered, on 50% power (MEDIUM) for 10 to 14 minutes, turning meat once. Let stand, covered with foil, while making sauce. Place steak on serving platter. Remove toothpicks. Spoon some of the sauce over steak; pass remainder. Garnish with parsley. Serves 8.

Basil Tomato Sauce: In a 2-cup glass measure combine *half* of a 10½-ounce can (½ cup) *tomato puree,* ⅓ cup *chicken broth,* 1 teaspoon *Worcestershire sauce,* ½ teaspoon *sugar,* and ½ teaspoon dried *basil,* crushed. Micro-cook, covered, on 100% power (HIGH) for 5 minutes. Mix 2 tablespoons *water* and 2 teaspoons *cornstarch;* stir into hot mixture. Micro-cook, uncovered, 2 minutes more, stirring every 30 seconds.

Conventional method: Cook bacon till crisp; drain and crumble. Prepare the stuffing as directed, *except* cook peas according to package directions. Prepare and stuff meat as directed. Place the stuffed meat on unheated rack of a broiler pan. Broil 3 inches from heat for 8 to 10 minutes or till done, turning once. Serve as directed.

Basil Tomato Sauce: Combine ingredients for sauce as directed above. Cook and stir over medium heat till mixture is thickened and bubbly. Cook and stir for 2 minutes more.

SHORTCUT GUMBO

½ pound fresh *or* frozen shelled shrimp with tails
2 teaspoons butter *or* margarine
1 cup quick-cooking rice
¼ cup all-purpose flour
¼ cup cooking oil
½ cup chopped onion
¼ cup chopped green pepper
2 tablespoons sliced celery
2 cloves garlic, minced
1 16-ounce can tomatoes, cut up
½ of a 10-ounce package frozen cut okra, thawed
1½ teaspoons lemon juice
1½ teaspoons Worcestershire sauce
1 teaspoon instant chicken bouillon granules
¼ teaspoon ground red pepper
¼ teaspoon ground allspice
1 bay leaf
3 ounces fully cooked ham, cut into ½-inch cubes (½ cup)

Thaw shrimp, if frozen. In a 1-quart nonmetal casserole combine butter or margarine, 1 cup *water,* and ¼ teaspoon *salt.* Micro-cook, uncovered, on 100% power (HIGH) for 3 to 4 minutes or till boiling. Stir in the uncooked rice; cover and set aside.

In a 3-quart glass casserole combine the flour and oil. Micro-cook, uncovered, for 20 minutes, stirring after the first 4 minutes, then after every minute. Add onion, green pepper, celery, and garlic. Micro-cook, covered, for 2 to 3 minutes. Stir in *undrained* tomatoes, okra, lemon juice, Worcestershire sauce, bouillon granules, red pepper, allspice, bay leaf, and ½ cup *water.*

Micro-cook, covered, 5 to 7 minutes; stir. Micro-cook, covered, on 50% power (MEDIUM) 5 to 8 minutes. Remove bay leaf. Stir in shrimp and ham. Micro-cook, covered, 5 to 7 minutes, stirring twice. Return the rice to oven. Micro-cook, covered, on 100% power (HIGH) 1 minute. Spoon rice into soup bowls. Ladle gumbo over rice. Serves 4.

Conventional method: Combine flour and oil. Cook over medium heat for 30 minutes, stirring often. Stir in onion, green pepper, celery, and garlic; cook till tender. Stir in remaining ingredients *except* the shrimp and ham. Bring to boiling; reduce heat. Cover; simmer 20 minutes. Remove bay leaf. Stir in shrimp and ham. Bring to boiling; reduce heat. Cover; simmer 5 minutes more. Cook rice. Serve as directed.

APPLE AND SPICE UPSIDE-DOWN CAKE

   2 tablespoons butter *or* margarine
   2 tablespoons sugar
   1 tablespoon lemon juice
   1 large baking apple, cored and
     very thinly sliced
   1 cup all-purpose flour
   ⅔ cup sugar
   1 teaspoon baking powder
   ½ teaspoon ground cinnamon
   ¼ teaspoon salt
   ⅛ teaspoon ground nutmeg
   ⅛ teaspoon ground cloves
   2 eggs
   ⅓ cup butter *or* margarine
   ⅓ cup milk
   ½ teaspoon vanilla

In an 8x1½-inch round nonmetal baking dish micro-cook the 2 tablespoons butter or margarine, uncovered, on 100% power (HIGH) for 30 to 45 seconds. Sprinkle the 2 tablespoons sugar and the lemon juice into pan. Overlap apple slices, spoke fashion, in the bottom of the pan. Press any additional apple slices onto sides of pan. Set aside.

In a mixer bowl combine flour, the ⅔ cup sugar, baking powder, cinnamon, salt, nutmeg, and cloves. Add eggs, the ⅓ cup butter or margarine, milk, and vanilla. Beat with an electric mixer on low speed till combined. Beat on medium speed for 2 minutes, scraping the sides of the bowl.

Spread the batter in the apple-lined dish. Micro-cook, uncovered, on 50% power (MEDIUM) for 8 to 10 minutes, rotating dish a quarter-turn after 5 minutes. Give dish another quarter-turn. Micro-cook, uncovered, on 100% power (HIGH) for 1½ to 2½ minutes more. Cool for 5 minutes; invert onto a serving platter (replace apple slices around sides). Serve warm. Serves 6.

Conventional method: Prepare as directed, *except* melt the 2 tablespoons butter or margarine in a saucepan. Bake in a 350° oven 30 to 35 minutes.

BISCUIT-TOPPED TURKEY PIE

   1½ cups all-purpose flour
   2 teaspoons sugar
   1½ teaspoons baking powder
   ½ teaspoon cream of tartar
   ⅓ cup shortening
   ⅓ cup buttermilk
   1 cup chopped rutabaga
   3 tablespoons butter *or* margarine
   1 cup chopped broccoli *or*
     ½ of a 10-ounce package frozen
     cut broccoli
   2½ cups diced cooked turkey *or*
     chicken
   2 tablespoons cornstarch
   2¼ teaspoons snipped fresh sage
     or thyme, *or* ¾ teaspoon dried
     sage *or* thyme, crushed
   1½ teaspoons instant chicken
     bouillon granules
   2 cups milk
   1 beaten egg

Stir together flour, sugar, baking powder, cream of tartar, and ¼ teaspoon *salt*. Cut in shortening. Make a well in the center; add buttermilk. Stir till the dough clings together. Knead on a lightly floured surface for 10 to 12 strokes. Roll *three-quarters* of the dough into a ¼-inch-thick oval or rectangle (should be ¼ *inch smaller* than baking dish). Cover; set aside. Roll remaining dough into a 7x3-inch rectangle. Using a pastry wheel, cut rectangle lengthwise into six ½-inch-wide strips. Cover with waxed paper; set aside.

In a 1½-quart oval nonmetal casserole or 10x6x2-inch nonmetal baking dish combine rutabaga and *1 tablespoon* butter. Micro-cook, covered, on 100% power (HIGH) for 2 minutes. Add broccoli; cover and micro-cook 3 to 4 minutes, stirring once. Stir in turkey; set aside. In a 4-cup glass measure micro-cook *2 tablespoons* butter on 100% power (HIGH) for 30 seconds. Stir in cornstarch, sage, and bouillon granules. Add milk. Micro-cook, uncovered, 3 to 5 minutes or till bubbly, stirring after every minute. Pour over turkey mixture; stir. Place dough oval or rectangle on top. Combine egg and 1 tablespoon *water;* brush onto pastry. Place pastry strips around edge; brush with egg mixture. If desired, garnish with sage leaves. Put on baking sheet. Bake in a 375° oven 30 minutes. Serves 6.

Conventional method: Make pastry as directed. Cook rutabaga and broccoli, covered, in *1 tablespoon* butter or margarine for 15 to 20 minutes, stirring frequently. Turn vegetable mixture into a 1½-quart oval casserole or 10x6x2-inch baking dish. Stir in turkey. In same saucepan melt the *2 tablespoons* butter or margarine. Stir in cornstarch, bouillon, and sage. Add milk all at once. Cook and stir till bubbly. Pour over turkey mixture; stir till combined. Continue as directed.

WINTER PARSNIP PUFF

   ¼ cup butter *or* margarine
   1¼ cups crushed stone-ground
     whole wheat crackers
   ¼ cup chopped walnuts
   3 slices bacon
   4 cups coarsely shredded parsnips
   1 3-ounce package cream cheese
   4 eggs
   ⅔ cup whipping cream
   2 tablespoons orange juice
Dash ground turmeric

Melt butter or margarine on 100% power (HIGH) for 35 to 40 seconds. Stir in crushed crackers. Stir walnuts into ¼ *cup* of the crumb mixture; set aside. Press the remaining crumb mixture into a well-greased 8-inch round nonmetal baking dish or an ovenproof 5½-cup ring mold. Arrange bacon slices in a 10x6x2-inch nonmetal baking dish. Micro-cook bacon, covered with white paper toweling, on 100% power (HIGH) for 3 minutes; drain. Crumble bacon, reserving 2 tablespoons. Sprinkle bacon over crumb mixture in baking dish.

Micro-cook parsnips in ⅓ cup *water,* covered, for 6 to 8 minutes; drain well. In a blender container combine cooked parsnips and cream cheese. Cover; blend till nearly smooth. Add eggs, cream, juice, turmeric, and ¼ teaspoon *salt*. Cover and blend till smooth. Spoon parsnip mixture atop bacon. Sprinkle with reserved crumb-walnut mixture. Bake in a 350° oven for 35 to 40 minutes. Let stand 10 minutes. Sprinkle with reserved bacon. Makes 6 servings.

Conventional method: Make the crumb crust as directed, *except* melt the butter or margarine in a saucepan. Cook bacon till crisp; drain. Crumble bacon; use as directed. Cook parsnips, covered, in water for 6 to 8 minutes. Drain well. Continue as directed.

SWIRL BREAKFAST LOAF

Test your microwave oven to determine if it can be used for raising bread dough. Place the 2 tablespoons butter or margarine called for below in a custard cup in the center of the oven. Micro-cook butter, uncovered, on 10% power (LOW) for 4 minutes. If butter is completely melted in less than 4 minutes, you will be unable to satisfactorily proof (raise) bread in your microwave oven.

3½ to 4 cups all-purpose flour
  1 package active dry yeast
  1 cup milk
 ¼ cup butter *or* margarine
  2 tablespoons sugar
  2 eggs
 ½ cup orange juice
  1 cup dried currants
 ⅓ cup packed brown sugar
 ½ teaspoon ground cinnamon
 ⅛ teaspoon ground cloves
  2 tablespoons butter *or* margarine, melted
Pearl sugar

In a mixer bowl combine *1½ cups* of the flour and yeast. Combine milk, the ¼ cup butter or margarine, sugar, and 1 teaspoon *salt*. Micro-cook, uncovered, on 100% power (HIGH) for 1 to 1½ minutes or till warm (115° to 120°). Add milk mixture to flour mixture; add eggs. Beat with an electric mixer on low speed for 30 seconds. Beat for 3 minutes on high speed. Stir in as much of the remaining flour as you can.

Turn dough out onto a lightly floured surface. Knead in enough remaining flour to make a moderately soft dough that is smooth and elastic (3 to 5 minutes). Shape into a ball. Place in a lightly greased nonmetal bowl; turn once to grease surface.

Measure 3 cups *water* into a 4-cup glass measure. Micro-cook, uncovered, for 4 to 6 minutes. Set to one side of microwave oven. Place the dough in bowl beside the water; cover dough with waxed paper. Micro-cook on 10% power (LOW) for 16 to 20 minutes. Punch dough down; divide in half. Cover; let rest for 10 minutes.

Micro-cook the juice, uncovered, on 100% power (HIGH) for 2 minutes. Stir in currants. Let stand for 5 minutes. Drain currants, reserving juice.

On a floured surface, roll one portion of dough into a 15x8-inch rectangle. Brush rectangle with *half* of the reserved juice. Combine the currants, brown sugar, cinnamon, and cloves. Sprinkle *half* of currant mixture atop. Roll up jelly-roll style, starting from one of the short sides; seal. Place in a greased 8x4x2-inch nonmetal loaf dish. Repeat to make second loaf.

Micro-cook the *same* 3 cups water, uncovered, on 100% power (HIGH) for 4 to 6 minutes. Set to side of oven. Place the loaves beside the water; cover with waxed paper. Micro-cook on 10% power (LOW) for 6 to 8 minutes. Spread the remaining 2 tablespoons butter atop. Sprinkle with pearl sugar. Slit top of loaf ½ inch deep. Bake in a 375° oven for 35 minutes. Cover with foil the last 10 minutes. Remove from dishes. Cool on wire racks. Makes 2 loaves.

Conventional method: Make the bread dough as directed; shape into a ball. Place in a greased bowl; turn once to grease surface. Cover; let rise till double (omit the microwave proofing step). Cover currants with juice. Bring to boiling. Remove from heat. Let stand 5 minutes; drain, reserving juice. Combine currants, brown sugar, cinnamon, and cloves; set aside. Punch dough down; divide in half. Cover; let rest for 10 minutes. Shape loaves as directed. Place, seam side down, in two greased 8x4x2-inch loaf pans. Cover; let rise till nearly double. Bake as directed.

PEAR MERINGUE TARTS

  1 cup all-purpose flour
 ⅓ cup ground pecans
Dash salt
 ⅓ cup butter *or* margarine
  3 to 4 tablespoons cold water
Nonstick vegetable spray coating
 ¼ cup sugar
  1 tablespoon cornstarch
 ½ teaspoon finely shredded orange peel
 ⅔ cup orange juice
 ½ teaspoon vanilla
  6 small pears
  2 egg whites
 ¼ teaspoon cream of tartar
 ¼ teaspoon vanilla
 ¼ cup sugar
Orange peel strips (optional)

For tart shells, stir together flour, pecans, and dash salt. Cut in butter or margarine. Sprinkle *1 tablespoon* of cold water over part of mixture; gently toss. Push to side of bowl. Repeat with remaining water till moistened. Form dough into a ball; divide into 6 portions.

On a floured surface roll each portion into a 4½-inch circle. Spray six 6-ounce inverted custard cups or the back of a microwave muffin pan with spray coating. Place the circles over inverted cups. Prick with a fork. Arrange inverted cups in a circle in microwave oven. Micro-cook, uncovered, on 100% power (HIGH) for 4½ to 5 minutes, rearranging or turning after 2 and 3 minutes. Cool 3 minutes. Remove; cool.

For sauce, in a 2-cup glass measuring cup combine ¼ cup sugar, cornstarch, and orange peel. Stir in juice. Micro-cook, uncovered, for 2 to 4 minutes, stirring after every minute. Stir in the ½ teaspoon vanilla. Cover surface with clear plastic wrap; cool slightly.

Peel and halve pears lengthwise. Remove cores and stems. Cut several lengthwise slashes in each pear half, cutting to, but not through, the other side of the pear. Place pears in a 12x7½x2-inch nonmetal baking dish with 2 tablespoons *water*. Micro-cook, covered, for 6 to 8 minutes, giving the dish a quarter-turn after every 2 minutes. Drain and cool.

Place tart shells on a baking sheet. Spoon *2 tablespoons* of the sauce into each shell. Stand two pear halves vertically in each shell; secure halves together with wooden toothpicks.

For meringue, beat egg whites, cream of tartar, and vanilla with an electric mixer on medium speed till soft peaks form (tips curl). Gradually add remaining sugar, about 1 tablespoon at a time, beating till stiff peaks form (tips stand straight). Pipe vertical rows of meringue to cover seam line between pear halves, bringing meringue up to a point at top. Broil 4 inches from heat for 3 to 4 minutes. Garnish with orange peel tied into knots, if desired. Serve warm. Makes 6 servings.

Conventional method: Make tart shells using custard cups as directed, *except* bake in a 450° oven for 10 to 12 minutes. Cool 10 to 15 minutes. Remove shells; cool. For sauce, combine ¼ cup sugar, cornstarch, and orange peel. Add juice. Cook and stir till bubbly. Cook and stir 2 minutes more. Remove from heat. Stir in vanilla. Cover surface with clear plastic wrap; cool slightly. Peel and halve pears as directed. Bring 1 cup *water* to boiling. Add pear halves. Reduce heat; simmer, covered, for 5 to 7 minutes. Remove the pears; drain well and cool. Continue as directed above.

MARCH

Better Homes and Gardens

March 1984 $1.50

Low-cost decorating:
High-style results

Fabulous
foods made
easy

Raised-bed
gardening—triple
the produce

The pleasures of
cross-stitching

Storage space
you never knew
you had

HOW YOU
CAN OWN
THIS HOUSE

The health problems of today's children

Fabulous Food Made Easy

You, too, can make those fabulous foods you thought only cooking buffs would attempt. Each of these five first-rate recipes is presented in steps that ensure success. For a special event or just for fun, help yourself to a new cooking adventure!

An extraordinary first course, for instance, can set the stage for a memorable party. Fried patties of cheese lend a unique temperature and texture contrast to crisp, chilled greens.

BY DIANA MCMILLEN
Photographs: William K. Sladcik, Inc.
Food stylist: Fran Paulson

Sizzling Cheese Salad

The slightly sweet flavor of each patty results from the blending of gjetost (YAY tohst) cheese and Neufchâtel. Hours in advance, you can prearrange the greens and vegetables on a platter, prepare the dressing, and shape patties. Then just fry the cheese before serving.

- 4 cups torn mixed greens
- ¼ cup pitted ripe olives
- 6 whole sun-dried tomatoes *or* 6 tomato wedges
- ¼ cup salad oil
- ¼ cup tarragon vinegar
- 2 teaspoons finely chopped green onion
- 1 teaspoon Dijon-style mustard
- 1 teaspoon walnut oil
- 1 egg
- 1 tablespoon water
- 2 tablespoons cornmeal
- 1 tablespoon fine dry bread crumbs
- 1 tablespoon toasted sesame seed
- 2 teaspoons grated Parmesan cheese
- 4 ounces Neufchâtel cheese, cut up
- 1 cup shredded gjetost cheese (4 ounces)
- 2 tablespoons butter *or* margarine, melted
- 6 pita bread rounds, split and toasted

A

B

1. On a serving platter arrange greens, olives, and tomatoes. Cover; chill.
2. In screw-top jar combine salad oil, vinegar, onion, mustard, and walnut oil. Cover. Shake; chill.
3. In small bowl combine egg and water. In shallow bowl combine cornmeal, crumbs, sesame, and Parmesan.
4. Beat the cheeses with an electric mixer till combined. Shape into 1-inch balls; flatten to form patties. Dip into egg mixture; coat with the cornmeal mixture *(photo A)*. Cover; chill.
5. To fry cheese: In a skillet heat butter or margarine. Add cheese; cook on medium-high heat 10 minutes or till golden, turning once *(photo B)*.
6. Shake dressing; drizzle atop salad. Arrange cheese and pita atop. Serves 6.

Seafood and Veal Spiral

Cod, green onion, and shrimp are centered in this exquisite roast, set off with stunning kohlrabi flowers.

1   3¼- to 3½-pound boneless veal loin roast
8   ounces fresh *or* frozen cod fillets
¾   cup butter *or* margarine, softened
Dash bottled hot pepper sauce
8   ounces fresh *or* frozen shelled shrimp
1   tablespoon sliced green onion
Kohlrabi Flowers
1   recipe Mushroom Sauce (see recipe, page 42)

1. Unroll roast. At V formed by butcher when boning, make two lengthwise cuts perpendicular to right and left of V; spread open. Cover with clear plastic wrap. Using meat mallet, flatten to a 14x10-inch rectangle.
2. Place cod in ½ cup *water*. Bring to boiling; reduce heat. Cover; simmer 6 to 8 minutes. Remove from heat. Drain; cool. Flake fish into a mixer bowl; add butter, pepper sauce, and ¼ teaspoon *salt*. Beat smooth.
3. Add shrimp to 1½ cups boiling *water*. Reduce heat; cook 1 to 3 minutes. Drain.
4. Spread cod-butter mixture on meat to within ½ inch of edges. Sprinkle with onion. Overlap shrimp atop meat in two rows 2 inches from short side of meat *(photo A)*. Roll up meat, jelly-roll style, starting from shrimp side. Tie securely with string.
5. Place on rack in roasting pan. Insert a meat thermometer in thickest portion. Roast in 325° oven 2 hours or till thermometer registers 160° to 170°.
6. Place on a platter; reserve juices for sauce. Garnish with flowers and carrot curls. Pass sauce. Serves 12.

Kohlrabi Flowers: Thinly slice 1 *kohlrabi.* Soak in salt water till softened. Drain. For each, overlap to form a row; loosely roll up *(photo B).* Secure with rubber band. Pull slices back to form petals; place in ice water. Remove band to serve.

Glazed-Fruit Almond Torte

This scrumptious cake holds even more enjoyment inside than you see. Ground nuts account for the unique texture and rich flavor.

- **13** ounces whole blanched almonds
- **6** egg yolks
- **1** tablespoon finely shredded lemon peel
- **1** cup sugar
- **6** egg whites
- **1** teaspoon cream of tartar
- **½** cup finely crushed vanilla wafers
- **1½** cups whipping cream
- **2** 11-ounce cans mandarin orange sections, drained
- **½** cup finely snipped dried golden figs
- **⅓** cup apricot preserves, sieved
- **1** cup seedless green grapes *and/or* sliced strawberries

Lemon and kiwi twist

1. Place almonds in a blender container or food processor bowl. Cover; blend till very finely ground (about 3 cups). Spread evenly in a shallow baking pan. Bake in a 350° oven till light brown, stirring twice. Set aside.

2. Grease three 8x8x2-inch baking pans or 8x1½-inch round baking pans. Line bottoms with waxed paper; grease. In a small mixer bowl beat yolks and peel with an electric mixer for 6 minutes. Gradually add ½ cup of sugar, 1 tablespoon at a time, beating till sugar is nearly dissolved.

3. Wash beaters. In a large mixer bowl beat egg whites and cream of tartar at high speed till soft peaks form. Gradually add the remaining sugar, 1 tablespoon at a time, beating till stiff peaks

form. Fold yolk mixture into beaten whites. Combine almonds and wafer crumbs. Sprinkle ¾ *cup* of the nut mixture over eggs; fold in lightly. Repeat with remaining nut mixture, ¾ cup at a time, folding in lightly. Turn into pans.

4. Bake in a 350° oven for 20 minutes (25 minutes for round pans). (Cakes will have a slight dip.) Cool 10 minutes. Using a narrow spatula, loosen from pans. Remove pans and waxed paper; cool on wire racks.

5. To assemble, beat cream to stiff peaks. Using pastry tube fitted with large star tip, pipe *1½ cups* whipped cream in lines over bottom layer *(photo A)*. Reserve *¼ cup* orange sections. Sprinkle *half* of the remaining oranges and *half* of the figs atop cream. Top with next layer. Repeat piping and arranging oranges and figs; top with final cake layer.

6. Melt preserves; spread some over cake. Arrange oranges, grapes, and/or strawberries atop *(photo B)*. Brush with preserves. Top with twist. Chill 1 hour. Serves 14.

Chocolate Lace Tray

Chocolate lovers' dreams are answered with this amazing sweet. And it's so easy to make! Just drizzle the melted German sweet chocolate over a chilled foil form, chill it again, and then remove the chocolate from the foil. Decorated spice cakes and assorted thrice-dipped fruits accompany the free-form tray.

2½ **4-ounce bars German sweet cooking chocolate (10 ounces)**
1 **recipe Petite Spice Cakes (see recipe, page 42)**
1 **recipe Dipped Fruit**

1. Press a large piece of heavy-duty foil on the bottom and up the sides of a shallow 1-quart au gratin dish. Chill in freezer.

2. In a heavy 1½-quart saucepan melt the German chocolate over low heat, stirring till smooth. *Do not add any liquid.* Using a small spoon, drizzle about *half* of the melted chocolate randomly over the bottom and up the sides

of the chilled foil inside the au gratin dish *(photo A)*. (Or, pipe melted chocolate through a pastry bag fitted with a writing tip.) Return to the freezer about 5 minutes or till firm. (Reheat chocolate if it becomes too thick.) Repeat drizzling with remaining melted chocolate over the bottom and up the sides of the foil-lined dish. Chill in the freezer for 15 minutes more.

3. To unmold chocolate tray, lift the chocolate-coated foil from dish. Carefully peel foil from chocolate. Using wide metal spatulas, transfer chocolate tray to a serving platter; chill up to 24 hours. Serve topped with cakes and fruit. Makes 6 to 8 servings.

Dipped Fruit: In separate small saucepans melt 2 ounces *white confectioners' coating*, 2 ounces *milk chocolate*, and 2 ounces *German sweet cooking chocolate*. (Or, place in small nonmetal bowls and melt in your microwave oven.) Using your choice of glacéed or nonjuicy fresh fruits, place one piece of fruit on end of a wooden skewer. Dip a portion of the fruit into each melted mixture, forming layers by dipping deeply into one, less deeply into the next, and just the tip into the last *(photo C)*. Place on a waxed-paper-lined pan; chill till firm or up to 2 hours.

POLLO EN PANE

Who'd ever guess that this blanket of yeast bread hides a whole roast chicken on a bed of wheat berry dressing?

2 cups water
¾ cup wheat berries
½ teaspoon instant chicken bouillon granules
4 slices bacon
½ cup chopped onion
½ cup shredded carrot
6 whole fresh mushrooms, quartered
1½ teaspoons dried thyme, crushed
1 2½- to 3-pound whole broiler-fryer chicken
Cooking oil
2 to 2½ cups all-purpose flour
1 package active dry yeast
½ cup milk
3 tablespoons sugar
3 tablespoons butter *or* margarine
½ teaspoon salt
1 egg
Milk
2 tablespoons all-purpose flour
1 cup light cream
2 tablespoons dry white wine
Fresh thyme (optional)

1. For dressing, in a saucepan combine the water, wheat berries, and chicken bouillon granules. Bring to boiling; reduce heat. Cover and simmer for 45 to 60 minutes or till tender. Drain.

2. In a skillet cook the bacon till crisp; drain, reserving the drippings. Crumble the bacon. In the same skillet cook the chopped onion and shredded carrot in drippings till tender; drain off fat.

3. Combine the cooked wheat berries, crumbled bacon, onion, carrot, quartered mushrooms, and *1 teaspoon* of the dried thyme. Cover and chill.

4. Rinse the chicken and pat dry with paper towels. Season the cavity of the chicken with salt and pepper. Tie the legs securely to the tail and twist the wing tips under back. Place chicken, breast side up, on a rack in a shallow roasting pan. Brush the skin with cooking oil. Insert a meat thermometer in the center of the inside thigh muscle, making sure bulb does not touch bone.

5. Roast chicken, uncovered, in a 375° oven for 1 to 1¼ hours or till the temperature reaches 185°. Brush chicken occasionally with pan drippings. Remove chicken, reserving pan drippings. Strain the drippings; reserve for sauce.

6. Meanwhile, for dough, in a large mixer bowl combine *1 cup* of the flour and the yeast. In a saucepan heat the ½ cup milk, sugar, butter or margarine, and salt just till warm (115° to 120°) and butter is almost melted, stirring constantly. Add to the flour mixture; add the egg. Beat with an electric mixer on low speed for 30 seconds, scraping the sides of the bowl constantly. Beat for 3 minutes on high speed. Using a spoon, stir in as much of the remaining flour as you can.

7. Turn the dough out onto a lightly floured surface; knead in enough of the remaining flour to make a moderately stiff dough that is smooth and elastic (6 to 8 minutes total). Shape the dough into a ball. Place in a lightly greased bowl; turn the dough once to grease the entire surface. Cover the dough with a cloth. Let rise in a warm place till nearly double (about 1 hour).

8. On a lightly floured surface roll out *two-thirds* of the dough into an oval or round shape, 2 inches larger than a shallow 1½- to 2-quart oval casserole or a shallow 2-quart round casserole.

9. Spoon the dressing into the bottom of the casserole. Place the roasted chicken, breast side up, atop dressing. Place the dough over the chicken; trim the dough to ½ inch beyond edge of the casserole. Seal dough to casserole edge.

10. Divide the remaining dough into 5 equal portions; roll each portion into an 18-inch-long rope. Twist *two* ropes together. Repeat with *two* more ropes. Brush ropes and dough with additional milk. Press the twisted ropes around the edge of the casserole (see photo, left); brush with milk. Pierce the top of the dough to allow for the escape of steam. Use the remaining rope to form decorations. Place the decorations atop dough; brush with milk.

11. Bake the dough-covered chicken in a 375° oven for 20 to 25 minutes or till golden. Cover the dough with foil the last 15 minutes of baking time to prevent overbrowning.

12. Meanwhile, for sauce, measure 2 *tablespoons* of the reserved drippings into a saucepan. Stir in the 2 tablespoons flour and the remaining thyme. Add light cream to saucepan all at once. Cook and stir till the mixture is thickened and bubbly. Cook and stir for 1 minute more. Stir in the dry white wine; heat through. Season the sauce with salt and pepper.

13. To serve, garnish the top of the baked bread-covered chicken with a sprig of fresh thyme, if desired. Serve the chicken, wheat berry dressing, and bread with the sauce. Makes 6 servings.

PETITE SPICE CAKES

Complete the Chocolate Lace Tray featured on pages 38 and 39 with these cardamom-flecked cakes. Or, top the edible tray with some purchased petits fours from your favorite bakery.

         1 **cup all-purpose flour**
         1 **teaspoon baking powder**
        ½ **teaspoon ground cardamom**
        ¼ **teaspoon salt**
         2 **eggs**
         1 **cup sugar**
        ½ **cup milk**
         2 **tablespoons butter *or***
            margarine
       1½ **cups sugar**
        ¾ **cup hot water**
         1 **teaspoon finely shredded lemon**
            peel
        ¼ **teaspoon cream of tartar**
         1 **teaspoon vanilla**
    Sifted powdered sugar
            (about 1¼ cups)
    Melted German sweet chocolate

Grease and lightly flour a 9x9x2-inch baking pan; set aside. In a mixing bowl stir together the flour, baking powder, cardamom, and salt; set bowl aside.

In a medium mixer bowl beat the eggs with an electric mixer on high speed about 4 minutes or till the eggs are thick and lemon colored. Gradually add the 1 cup sugar, beating on medium speed for 4 to 5 minutes or till the sugar is nearly dissolved. Add the dry ingredients to the beaten egg mixture; stir just till the mixture is combined.

In a small saucepan heat the milk and butter or margarine over low heat till the butter is melted; stir into the batter in the mixer bowl. Beat the batter on low speed till well mixed.

Turn the cake batter into the prepared baking pan. Bake in a 350° oven for 25 to 30 minutes or till the cake tests done. Place the cake on a wire rack; cool for 10 minutes. Remove the cake from the pan; cool thoroughly on the wire rack before icing.

For the vanilla icing, in a 1-quart saucepan stir together the 1½ cups sugar, the hot water, the finely shredded lemon peel, and the cream of tartar. Cook and stir over medium heat till sugar dissolves and mixture comes to boiling. Cover and cook for 30 to 45 seconds. Uncover and clip a candy thermometer to the saucepan. Cook the mixture over medium-low heat till the candy thermometer registers 226°. Remove the saucepan from heat.

Cool mixture, without stirring, to 110° (about 45 minutes). Stir in the vanilla. Stir in enough sifted powdered sugar to make an icing of pouring consistency. Beat the icing in the saucepan till smooth.

Using a knife or cookie cutter, cut the cooled cake into shapes such as squares, diamonds, and circles that are about 1½ inches wide. Place the cake pieces on a wire rack over waxed paper. Spoon the vanilla icing over the small cakes to coat evenly.

Drizzle the melted chocolate atop each iced cake to form a design. Chill the decorated cakes for a few minutes to firm the drizzled chocolate. Makes about 16 small cakes.

Note: For the best cooking results, check the accuracy of your candy thermometer before each use. To test, place the candy thermometer in a saucepan of boiling water. If the thermometer registers either above or below 212°, add or subtract the same difference of degrees from the recipe temperature and cook to that temperature.

For added accuracy, read the candy thermometer at eye level while it is clipped to the saucepan on the range top. When you clip the candy thermometer to the side of the saucepan, make sure the bulb of the thermometer is completely covered with the boiling liquid, not just foam, and that the bulb doesn't touch the bottom of the saucepan. This ensures a more exact reading.

MUSHROOM SAUCE

Serve this flavorful sauce over slices of Seafood and Veal Spiral, pictured on pages 34 and 35.

    Milk
         8 **ounces fresh mushrooms,**
            sliced
         2 **tablespoons sliced green onion**
         3 **tablespoons all-purpose flour**
        ⅛ **teaspoon salt**
    Dash pepper

Spoon off ¼ cup fat from the reserved pan juices from Seafood and Veal Spiral; set juices aside. Pour the remaining pan juices into a 2-cup glass measure. Add enough milk to the juices to measure 1¼ cups liquid; set mixture aside.

In a large skillet cook the sliced mushrooms and sliced green onion in the ¼ cup reserved fat over medium heat for 5 minutes. Stir in the flour, salt, and pepper. Add the 1¼ cups milk mixture all at once. Cook and stir till the mixture is thickened and bubbly. Cook and stir for 1 minute more. Pour the sauce into a serving container; pass with Seafood and Veal Spiral. Makes 2 cups sauce.

APRIL

Better Homes and Gardens.

April 1984 • $1.50

OMELET
PIZZA
BRING ON THE
BRUNCH !

**Petite treasures: Exquisite
crafts projects to make**

Style a home office

**Easy-care landscaping:
Vines and ground covers**

**Fabulous furniture
for today's home**

Solutions for problem kitchens

Welcome Spring With
FESTIVE BREADS

BY JOY TAYLOR

Although you can't live on bread alone, after sampling our fanciful rolls, coffee cakes, and loaves, you may want to try! These pages and the next show off an array of new-fashioned holiday breads and easier-than-ever international classics. Delight your loved ones with these delectables at spring celebrations—from Easter and Passover to informal gatherings.

Not all breads come warm from the oven. **Steamed Whole Grain Bread** *(far left),* enriched with whole wheat flour, millet, rolled oats, and sunflower nuts, cooks atop your range. Serve each sugar-dusted slice with brilliant **Strawberry Sauce.**

Mixed Nut Tea Ring *(top left)* embraces two splendid features: walnuts,

pistachios, macadamias, pecans, and hazelnuts speckle the top of this distinctive yeast bread; a velvety lemon butter graces the center.

Banana Sponge Coffee Cake *(center)* boasts a raspberry jam center and sesame seed border. This rendition of the traditional Passover sponge cake is ideal for breakfast.

Double-Good Crescent *(top right)* holds two fillings—rhubarb and coconut. This dough, made the night before, rises in the refrigerator; next morning, it's baked.

Kulich *(right)*, a dome-shaped loaf, highlights

Russian Easter feasts. Slices of this saffron-specked bread are spread with another Russian food: **Paskha** *(far right)*, an almondy cheese.

Photographs: Ernie Block
Food stylist: Vicki Johnson

45

*I*ndividual-size breads are just as impressive —and toothsome—as their larger counterparts. Here's proof:

Alfalfa sprouts, wheat germ, honey, and basil naturally accent the easy batter-type yeast dough for **Sprouted Herb Loaves** *(far left)*. Scaled-down pans are used to bake this healthful bread.

A drizzling of melted sugar becomes a crunchy coating on **Spun Caramel Fruit Gems** *(center)*. Dried apricots and dates dot the tender interiors of these teatime morsels.

In a snap, bake a batch of festive rolls with help from a purchased bread mix. Pineapple and cream cheese enrich **Glazed Springtime Rolls** *(top center)*. Icing adds a springlike touch to each delicately shaped portion.

Piping hot **Cheese-Filled Crumpets** *(top right)* glorify the classic griddle-fried cakes of Great Britain. This American interpretation, similar in texture to English muffins, features your choice of cheddar, Swiss, or Gouda cheese centers.

A pastel hard-cooked egg bedecks each braided **Lambropsomo Bun** *(above)*, a single-serving version of a classic Greek Easter bread.

47

STEAMED WHOLE GRAIN BREAD

¾ cup boiling water
3 tablespoons millet
2 beaten eggs
½ cup packed brown sugar
¼ cup milk
2 tablespoons cooking oil
1 cup whole wheat flour
¾ cup all-purpose flour
¼ cup quick-cooking rolled oats
1 teaspoon baking powder
½ teaspoon baking soda
¼ teaspoon salt
½ cup sunflower nuts
Powdered sugar
Fresh strawberries (optional)
1 recipe Strawberry Sauce
(see recipe, right)

In a mixing bowl combine the boiling water and millet; let stand 5 minutes. Stir in the eggs, sugar, milk, and oil. In a large mixing bowl stir together the whole wheat flour, all-purpose flour, rolled oats, baking powder, baking soda, and salt. Add the millet mixture to the dry ingredients; stir till moistened. Stir in the sunflower nuts. Turn the batter into a well-greased 6-cup heatproof mold or an 8-inch fluted tube pan. Cover tightly with foil.

   Place the mold or tube pan on a rack set in a large Dutch oven. Pour hot water into the Dutch oven to a depth of 1 inch. Bring the water to boiling; reduce heat. Cover and simmer for 1½ hours or till a wooden toothpick inserted near the center comes out clean, adding boiling water to the Dutch oven as needed. Remove the bread from the Dutch oven; let stand 10 minutes. Remove bread from mold or tube pan. Let stand just till warm. Sift powdered sugar over bread; garnish with fresh strawberries, if desired. Serve warm with Strawberry Sauce. Makes 1 loaf.

STRAWBERRY SAUCE

1 pint fresh strawberries
½ cup water
1 tablespoon honey
1 tablespoon cornstarch
1 tablespoon water
Few drops red food coloring

Slice enough of the strawberries to make ¾ cup; set aside. Mash the remaining strawberries. In a small saucepan combine the mashed strawberries and the ½ cup water. Bring to boiling; reduce heat. Cover and simmer for 2 to 3 minutes. Sieve the cooked strawberries. Return the sieved juices to the saucepan; stir in honey. Combine the cornstarch and the 1 tablespoon water; stir into the strawberry mixture in the saucepan. Cook and stir over medium heat till the mixture is thickened and bubbly; cook and stir 2 minutes more. Cool. Stir in the red food coloring and the ¾ cup reserved strawberries. Serve immediately. Makes 1½ cups sauce.

MIXED NUT TEA RING

Choose one, two, or all five of the nuts listed below for the crunchy topping.

2¾ to 3¼ cups all-purpose flour
1 package active dry yeast
⅔ cup milk
⅓ cup butter *or* margarine
3 tablespoons sugar
1 teaspoon ground ginger
½ teaspoon salt
1 egg
¼ cup butter *or* margarine
¼ cup sugar
1 teaspoon finely shredded lemon peel
1 tablespoon lemon juice
1 cup coarsely chopped nuts
(choose from:
pistachio, macadamia, pecans, walnuts, *and/or* hazelnuts)
1 teaspoon vanilla
1 recipe Fluffy Lemon Butter

In a large mixer bowl combine *1½ cups* of the flour and the yeast. In a saucepan heat the milk, ⅓ cup butter or margarine, the 3 tablespoons sugar, ginger, and salt just till warm (115° to 120°) and butter is almost melted, stirring constantly. Add to flour mixture; add egg. Beat on low speed of an electric mixer for ½ minute, scraping sides of bowl constantly. Beat on high speed for 3 minutes. Using a spoon, stir in as much of the remaining flour as you can. Turn the dough out onto a lightly floured surface. Knead in enough of the remaining flour to make a moderately soft dough that is smooth and elastic (3 to 5 minutes total). Shape into a ball. Place in a greased bowl; turn once. Cover; let rise in a warm place till double (about 1½ hours). Punch dough down. Cover; let rest 10 minutes.

   Meanwhile, in a small saucepan melt the ¼ cup butter or margarine. Stir in the ¼ cup sugar, lemon peel, and juice. Bring to boiling, stirring constantly. Remove from heat; stir in the nuts and vanilla; cool. Spoon nut mixture into a greased 6½-cup ring mold; set ring mold aside. Turn dough out onto a lightly floured surface. Shape dough into a 21-inch-long rope; place in mold atop nut mixture, gently patting dough to fit into pan. Seal ends of dough. Cover; let rise till almost double (about 1 hour).

   Bake in a 375° oven for 20 to 25 minutes or till done, covering bread with foil during the last 5 minutes to prevent overbrowning. Cool 5 minutes on wire rack; remove from pan. Spoon any nuts remaining in pan atop bread. Cool bread thoroughly on wire rack. Split the cooled bread in half horizontally. Spread Fluffy Lemon Butter over the bottom portion; top with the remaining bread half. Makes 12 servings.

   Fluffy Lemon Butter: In a small saucepan combine 3 tablespoons *sugar,* 2 teaspoons *cornstarch,* 1 teaspoon finely shredded *lemon peel,* and dash *salt.* Add ½ cup *milk.* Cook and stir till thickened and bubbly; cook and stir 2 minutes more. Gradually stir ⅓ *cup* of the mixture into 1 beaten *egg;* return to saucepan. Cook and stir 2 minutes more. Remove from heat. Stir in 2 teaspoons *lemon juice.* Cover surface with waxed paper; cool completely. In a small mixer bowl beat ½ cup softened *butter* or *margarine* till smooth. Gradually beat cooled lemon mixture into butter. Chill at least 30 minutes. Makes 1¼ cups filling.

BANANA SPONGE COFFEE CAKE

For a delicate texture and maximum volume, be sure to use an ungreased pan and cool the coffee cake inverted.

        6 egg yolks
        ½ cup sugar
        ½ cup mashed banana
             (1 large banana)
        ⅓ cup matzo meal
        ⅓ cup potato starch
             (potato flour)
        6 egg whites
        Sesame seed, toasted (about
             1 tablespoon)
        ⅓ cup raspberry jam

In a small mixer bowl beat the egg yolks on high speed of an electric mixer till light. Set aside *2 tablespoons* sugar. Gradually add the remaining sugar to the egg yolks and continue beating about 5 minutes or till thick and lemon colored. Beat in banana. Stir in the matzo meal and potato starch.

Wash the beaters thoroughly. In a large mixer bowl combine egg whites and reserved 2 tablespoons sugar; beat on high speed of an electric mixer till stiff peaks form (tips stand straight). Fold some of the beaten egg white mixture into the matzo mixture to lighten. Fold the matzo-egg white mixture into remaining beaten egg white mixture.

Turn the batter into an ungreased 9-inch springform pan. Sprinkle sesame seed around the edge of the batter. Bake in a 350° oven about 40 minutes or till done. Invert the pan on a rack to cool. When cake is cool, remove from pan. Split cooled cake in half horizontally. Spread jam over bottom portion; top with remaining cake half. Cut into wedges to serve. Makes 1 coffee cake.

KULICH

To decorate the top of the bread with a candied "flower," first cut pieces of candied pineapple and orange peel to resemble petals. Finish the flower with leaves made from candied green cherries.

        ½ cup light raisins
        ½ cup diced mixed candied fruits
             and peels, chopped
        1 tablespoon light rum
        ¼ teaspoon thread saffron,
             crushed *or* ⅛ teaspoon
             ground saffron
     2½ to 3 cups all-purpose flour
        1 package active dry yeast
        ⅔ cup milk
        ¼ cup butter *or* margarine
        3 tablespoons sugar
        ¼ teaspoon salt
        1 egg
        ½ cup chopped almonds
        1 recipe Powdered Sugar Icing
        Candied pineapple wedges, orange
             peel and green cherries
             (optional)
        1 recipe Paskha (see recipe, right)

In a small mixing bowl combine the raisins, the ½ cup candied fruits and peels, rum, and saffron; set bowl aside.

In a large mixer bowl combine *1 cup* of the flour and the yeast. In a small saucepan heat milk, butter or margarine, sugar, and salt till warm (115° to 120°) and butter is almost melted, stirring constantly. Stir into flour mixture; add egg. Beat on low speed of an electric mixer for ½ minute, scraping the sides of the bowl constantly. Beat on high speed of electric mixer for 3 minutes. Stir in raisin mixture and almonds. Using a spoon, stir in as much of the remaining flour as you can.

Turn the dough out onto a lightly floured surface. Knead in enough of the remaining flour to make a moderately stiff dough that is smooth and elastic (6 to 8 minutes total). Shape into a ball. Place the dough in a greased bowl; turn once. Cover; let rise in a warm place till double (about 1½ hours). Punch dough down. Cover; let rest 10 minutes. Shape dough into a smooth ball. Place in a greased 1½-quart soufflé dish. Cover;

let rise till almost double (about 45 minutes). Bake in a 350° oven for 40 to 45 minutes or till done. If necessary, cover bread with foil the last 10 minutes to prevent overbrowning. Cool for 10 minutes; remove from dish. Cool thoroughly on a wire rack. Drizzle Powdered Sugar Icing over the top of the loaf. Garnish with a candied fruit flower, if desired. Serve the bread with Paskha. Makes 1 round loaf.

Powdered Sugar Icing: Stir together 1 cup sifted *powdered sugar* and enough *milk* to make an icing of drizzling consistency.

PASKHA

Traditionally, this rich spread is shaped into a tower and decorated with Russian Easter symbols.

        1 cup packed dry cottage cheese
             (8 ounces)
        ⅓ cup sifted powdered sugar
        ¼ cup butter *or* margarine,
             softened
        1 egg yolk
        ¼ teaspoon vanilla
        ¼ cup whipping cream
        ¼ cup finely chopped almonds
        Fresh mint sprigs (optional)

Press the dry cottage cheese through a sieve. In a mixer bowl beat the sugar, butter or margarine, egg yolk, and vanilla on medium speed of an electric mixer till smooth. Add the sieved cottage cheese and whipping cream; beat on medium speed for 1 minute or till combined. Stir in the finely chopped almonds. Press the mixture into a cheesecloth-lined 2-cup mold. Cover and chill in the refrigerator till firm.

To unmold, invert the firm cheese mold onto a small serving plate. Remove the cheesecloth. Score the cheese mold into sections. Garnish with fresh mint, if desired. Makes 1¾ cups.

DOUBLE-GOOD CRESCENT

1⅓ to 1⅔ cups all-purpose
   flour
  1 package active dry yeast
  ⅓ cup milk
  ¼ cup butter *or* margarine
  ¼ cup packed brown sugar
  ¼ teaspoon salt
  ¼ teaspoon ground nutmeg
  2 eggs
  ¾ cup whole wheat flour
  1 recipe Rhubarb Filling
  1 recipe Coconut Filling
Milk
Coarsely chopped walnuts

In a small mixer bowl combine *1 cup* of the all-purpose flour and the yeast. In a saucepan heat the milk, butter or margarine, brown sugar, salt, and nutmeg just till warm (115° to 120°) and butter is almost melted, stirring constantly. Add to flour mixture; add eggs. Beat on low speed of an electric mixer for ½ minute, scraping the sides of the bowl constantly. Beat on high speed 3 minutes. Using a spoon, stir in the whole wheat flour and as much of the remaining all-purpose flour as you can.

Turn the dough out onto a lightly floured surface; knead in enough of the remaining flour to make a moderately stiff dough that is smooth and elastic (6 to 8 minutes total). Cover; let rise in a warm place till double (about 1 hour). Punch dough down. Cover with clear plastic wrap. Chill for 2 to 24 hours.

Punch dough down. Turn out onto a lightly floured surface; halve dough. Roll each half into a 10x7-inch rectangle. Spread the Rhubarb Filling on 1 rectangle; spread the Coconut Filling on the remaining dough rectangle. Roll up each dough portion from long side, jelly-roll style. Pinch ends to seal. (The two rolls should be equal in size and shape.) Shape each roll into a crescent.

Intertwine the two crescents by placing the end of one crescent in the curved center of the other dough portion (see photo, page 45). Place, seam side down, on a greased baking sheet. Cover; let rise till almost double (40 minutes). Brush the dough with milk. Sprinkle the nuts atop. Bake in a 350° oven for 20 minutes. Cover with foil to prevent overbrowning and bake for 15

to 20 minutes more or till done. Cool on a wire rack. Makes 1 large crescent.

Rhubarb Filling: In a 9-inch pie plate place ¾ cup finely chopped *fresh or frozen rhubarb*. Sprinkle ¼ cup *sugar* over fruit. Cover and bake in a 325° oven about 20 minutes or till thickened. Cool. Drain.

Coconut Filling: In a small saucepan melt ¼ cup *peach preserves*. Stir in ⅓ cup *toasted, shredded coconut* and ¼ cup *light raisins*. Cool.

SPROUTED HERB LOAVES

Alfalfa sprouts add moistness and a distinctive flavor to this wholesome bread. Wrap the bread in plastic bags and store in the refrigerator to keep fresh.

  2 cups all-purpose flour
  1 package active dry yeast
  ¾ cup milk
  2 tablespoons shortening
  1 tablespoon honey
  ½ teaspoon salt
  1 egg
  1 cup snipped alfalfa sprouts
  ½ cup toasted wheat germ
  ½ teaspoon dried basil, crushed
Whipped cream cheese (optional)

In a large mixer bowl combine *1 cup* of the flour and the yeast. In a small saucepan combine the milk, shortening, honey, and salt. Stir over low heat just till warm (115° to 120°). Add the milk mixture to yeast mixture. Add the egg. Beat on low speed of an electric mixer for ½ minute, scraping sides of bowl constantly. Beat on high speed for 3 minutes.

Using a wooden spoon, stir in the remaining flour, sprouts, wheat germ, and basil. Use the spoon to beat for 1 minute or till smooth. Cover; let rise in warm place till double (about 1 hour).

Beat down with wooden spoon. Cover; let rest 10 minutes. Spoon batter into four greased 4½x2½x1½-inch loaf pans or one greased 8x4x2-inch loaf pan. Cover; let rise in warm place till almost double (about 20 minutes).

Bake in a 375° oven till done; allow about 20 minutes for the small loaves and 40 minutes for the large loaf (cover with foil the last 20 minutes to prevent overbrowning). Remove the bread from pan(s). Cool on a wire rack. Serve with the whipped cream cheese, if desired. Makes 4 small loaves or 1 large loaf.

SPUN CARAMEL FRUIT GEMS

Work quickly while drizzling the filigree over the muffins. If the sugar syrup hardens, reheat it to remelt the sugar.

  ½ cup boiling water
  ¼ cup finely snipped dried apricots
  1 cup all-purpose flour
  1 teaspoon baking powder
  ¼ teaspoon salt
  ¼ teaspoon ground cinnamon
  ⅓ cup butter *or* margarine
  ½ cup sugar
  2 eggs
  2 tablespoons milk
  ¼ cup finely snipped pitted dates
  ½ cup sugar
  ¼ teaspoon hot water

Pour boiling water over apricots; set them aside. In a mixing bowl stir together the flour, baking powder, salt, and cinnamon. In a small mixer bowl beat butter or margarine on medium speed of electric mixer for 30 seconds. Add the ½ cup sugar; beat till fluffy. Add eggs, one at a time, beating well.

Add dry ingredients and milk alternately to beaten mixture, beating on low speed after each addition. Drain apricots. Stir in apricots and dates. Fill greased 2-inch tassie pans or muffin cups or 2½-inch muffin cups ⅔ full.

Bake in a 375° oven till done; allow 15 minutes for the smaller muffins and 20 minutes for the larger ones. Place waxed paper under a wire rack. Transfer the muffins to the wire rack.

For syrup, in a small heavy saucepan heat the remaining ½ cup sugar over medium-low heat. Do not stir till sugar starts to melt. Cook and stir about 10 minutes or till sugar turns a caramel color. Remove from heat. Carefully stir in the ¼ teaspoon water.

Immediately drizzle the syrup over the muffins with a spoon, using a back-and-forth motion. Serve warm. Makes sixteen 2-inch muffins or twelve 2½-inch muffins.

GLAZED SPRINGTIME ROLLS

Make sure the breads are completely cool before decorating, so the icings don't melt. Give each roll its own look by making different shapes and using combinations of colored icings.

    1 8-ounce can crushed pineapple
         (juice pack)
    1 13¾-ounce package hot roll mix
    1 3-ounce package cream cheese,
         cubed and softened
    1 beaten egg
    3 cups sifted powdered sugar
    1 teaspoon vanilla
    3 to 4 tablespoons milk
Few drops red, green,
         and yellow food coloring
Powdered sugar

Place the *undrained* pineapple in a blender container; cover and blend till smooth. Transfer to a saucepan. Heat pineapple till warm (110° to 115°). Remove from heat; stir in the yeast from the hot roll mix. Let stand 5 minutes to dissolve yeast. Add cream cheese and egg; stir till smooth. Transfer mixture to mixing bowl. Add flour from hot roll mix; stir till well combined. Cover and let rise in a warm place till double (about 1¼ to 1½ hours).

Punch dough down; turn out onto a lightly floured surface. Divide dough into 12 equal portions. Form portions into desired shapes. For a coiled bun, roll each dough portion into a 10-inch rope; coil each end toward the center. For a star, divide one portion of dough into six pieces; position five of the pieces around one center piece to resemble a star. For a tree, pat each dough portion into a 3½x3½x2-inch triangle. To form the branches, cut five lengthwise slashes; curl the branches away from the center. For Easter eggs, shape dough into 3½x2-inch ovals.

Place shaped rolls on a greased baking sheet. Cover; let rise in a warm place till almost double (30 to 40 minutes). Bake in a 350° oven for 15 to 18 minutes or till golden brown. Cool on a wire rack. To decorate, stir together powdered sugar, vanilla, and enough milk to make icing of drizzling consistency. Tint ¼ cup of the icing pink, tint ¼ cup light green, and tint ¼ cup light

yellow. Do not tint remaining icing. Spread tinted or white icing evenly over each roll. Stir additional powdered sugar into each colored icing to get a piping consistency. Pipe in decorative patterns atop rolls. Makes 12 rolls.

LAMBROPSOMO BUNS

Aniseed, frequently used in European baking, has a licoricelike flavor. Here, the spice marries with orange peel to give the tender rolls a delightful taste.

2½ to 3 cups all-purpose
         flour
    1 package active dry yeast
    ⅓ cup milk
    ⅓ cup water
    ¼ cup sugar
    2 tablespoons butter *or* margarine
    1 teaspoon finely shredded orange
         peel
    1 teaspoon aniseed, crushed
    ½ teaspoon salt
    1 egg
    1 slightly beaten egg white
    8 small eggs, hard-cooked and
         dyed in pastel colors

In a small mixer bowl combine *1 cup* of the flour and the yeast. In a small saucepan heat milk, water, sugar, butter or margarine, orange peel, aniseed, and salt just till warm (115° to 120°) and butter is almost melted, stirring constantly. Add to flour mixture; add the 1 egg. Beat on low speed of an electric mixer for ½ minute, scraping bowl. Beat on high speed for 3 minutes. Using a spoon, stir in as much of the remaining flour as you can.

Turn out onto a lightly floured surface. Knead in enough of the remaining flour to make a moderately stiff dough that is smooth and elastic (6 to 8 minutes total). Shape into a ball. Place in lightly greased bowl; turn once. Cover; let rise in warm place till double (about 1 hour). Punch down; divide in half. Cover; let rest 10 minutes.

Divide each half into four portions. Shape each dough portion into a braided ring or a twist roll to make eight rolls total. For a braided ring, divide one piece of dough into thirds. Roll each third into a 12-inch rope; braid and seal ends. Shape into a ring. Pull center of ring to form a hole. Place crumpled foil, the size of an egg, in hole. For twist rolls, roll each piece of dough into a 12-inch rope. Tie the rope into a loose knot

and twist ends together to seal. Pull center of ring to make a hole. Place crumpled foil, the size of an egg, in hole.

Place on greased baking sheets. Cover; let rise in warm place till nearly double (35 to 45 minutes). Brush with beaten egg white. Bake in a 375° oven about 15 minutes or till done. Cool on wire racks. Remove foil. To serve, set a hard-cooked dyed egg in the center of each roll. Makes 8 rolls.

CHEESE-FILLED CRUMPETS

Use 3-inch crumpet rings or clean 3-inch tin cans (with both ends removed) to shape each bread portion.

1½ cups all-purpose flour
    1 package active dry yeast
    ½ teaspoon salt
    1 cup milk
    1 tablespoon sugar
    1 egg
Cheddar, Gouda, *or* process Swiss
         cheese, cut into 1½-inch
         squares (¼ inch thick)
Chutney (optional)

In a large mixer bowl combine the flour, yeast, and salt. In a small saucepan heat milk and sugar just till warm (115° to 120°). Add to flour mixture; add egg. Beat on low speed of an electric mixer for ½ minute, scraping the sides of the bowl constantly. Beat on high speed for 3 minutes. Cover the dough and let rise in warm place till double (about 40 minutes).

Stir batter down. Lightly grease four 3-inch-wide metal rings. Place the rings on a hot, lightly greased griddle or in a heavy skillet. Spoon 1 tablespoon batter into each, spreading to cover bottom. Top with a cheese square. Spoon 1 tablespoon batter atop cheese.

Cook, uncovered, over medium-low heat for 3 to 4 minutes or till brown. Remove rings; turn crumpets. Cook for 3 to 4 minutes more or till done. Arrange crumpets on a baking sheet and place in a warm oven. Repeat with the remaining batter. Serve the crumpets warm with chutney, if desired. Makes 10 crumpets.

Bring On The BRUNCH!

By Joy Taylor

Photographs: Ernie Block
Food stylist: Vicki Johnson

Celebrate spring's arrival with a warmhearted weekend brunch for family and friends. This tasty buffet for 12 is sure to appeal to both hosts and guests, from Grandpa to the tiniest tot. The big bonus for the hosts lies in the brunch preparation—each recipe is partially made before the fun begins, letting you avoid any sunrise helter-skelter. The versatile menu adapts to smaller and larger affairs, too. So set the date now and create your first-of-the-season social.

Your party revolves around **Omelet Pizza** (front) and a trayful of toppings for diners to custom-flavor each wedge. Refreshing accompaniments, including **Cinnamon Fruit Cups** (back right), enhance the meal. Add hot water, plus coffee crystals or liqueur, to portions of **Spiced Cocoa Mix** (center). Let fruit aficionados pour carbonated water or wine into cupfuls of **Apple Slush** (top right). Complete the festivities with a rainbow assortment of **Sherbetwiches** (left).

OMELET PIZZA

To prevent the egg filling from spilling over in the oven, it's important to crimp the crust's edge high (about ¾ inch) in the pizza pan.

2½ to 3 cups all-purpose
 flour
 1 package active dry yeast
 1 tablespoon sugar
 1 teaspoon salt
 1 cup warm water (115° to 120°)
 2 tablespoons cooking oil
Cornmeal
 1 medium onion, chopped (½ cup)
 1 tablespoon cooking oil
14 beaten eggs
⅔ cup milk
½ teaspoon salt
⅛ teaspoon pepper
 1 recipe Two-Way Sauce (see
 recipe, right)
Topping options:
 fully cooked ham strips *and/or*
 sliced sausage;
 sliced pitted ripe olives,
 avocado, fresh mushrooms,
 radishes, *and/or* red onion;
 cooked carrot slices, artichoke
 heart quarters, asparagus
 spears, pea pods, *and/or*
 broccoli flowerets;
 quartered cherry tomatoes;
 cooked and shelled shrimp;
 shredded cheese;
 sunflower nuts; *or*
 chopped chives

In a large mixer bowl combine *1¼ cups* of the flour, the yeast, sugar, and 1 teaspoon salt. Stir in the warm water and the 2 tablespoons oil. Beat on low speed of an electric mixer for ½ minute, scraping sides of the bowl constantly. Beat on high speed for 3 minutes. Using a spoon, stir in as much of the remain-

ing flour as you can. Turn mixture out onto a lightly floured surface. Knead in enough of the remaining flour to make a moderately stiff dough that is smooth and elastic (6 to 8 minutes total). Cover; let rest 10 minutes.

Divide dough in half. On a lightly floured surface roll each half into a 14-inch circle. (If dough is too elastic during rolling, cover and let rest for 5 minutes more.) Grease two 12-inch pizza pans and sprinkle lightly with cornmeal. Transfer the circles of dough to pizza pans. Press the dough up the sides and crimp the edges at least as high as the sides of the pizza pans, about ¾ inch. Cover the pizza crusts with clear plastic wrap or moisture- and vapor-proof wrap. Refrigerate the crusts for 2 to 4 hours or freeze.

To serve, allow the frozen crusts to thaw at room temperature for 40 to 45 minutes. In a small saucepan cook chopped onion in the 1 tablespoon oil over medium heat till the onion is tender but not brown.

In a large mixing bowl combine the beaten eggs, milk, the ½ teaspoon salt, pepper, and cooked onion. Uncover the crusts; prick generously with the tines of a fork. Bake the crusts in a 425° oven about 15 minutes or till the edges are light brown. Reduce the oven temperature to 400°. With a wooden spoon, press down any high spots in the crusts. Leave the crusts on the oven rack; carefully pour *half* of the egg mixture into each crust.

Bake the pizzas in a 400° oven for 10 to 12 minutes or till the egg mixture is almost set. Remove from oven; cut each pizza into 12 to 14 wedges. Serve the pizza wedges with Two-Way Sauce and desired toppings. Cover one pizza with foil to keep it warm while serving the other. Makes 12 to 14 servings.

TWO-WAY SAUCE

To avoid early morning hassles, prepare this versatile sauce a day before the brunch and store it overnight in the refrigerator. At serving time, slowly reheat each sauce, adding milk as necessary to thin. Transfer to a serving bowl.

¼ cup sliced green onion
¼ cup butter *or* margarine
¼ cup all-purpose flour
 1 cup water
 1 cup milk
 1 teaspoon instant chicken
 bouillon granules
 1 8-ounce can whole kernel corn,
 drained
½ cup shredded carrot
¼ cup finely chopped green pepper
½ cup shredded process Swiss
 cheese
½ cup dairy sour cream
 1 tablespoon all-purpose flour
 8 ounces fully cooked smoked
 sausage links, halved lengthwise
 and sliced, *or* diced fully
 cooked ham
½ teaspoon dried basil, crushed

In a medium saucepan cook green onion in butter or margarine till tender but not brown. Stir in the ¼ cup flour. Add the water, milk, and bouillon granules. Cook and stir over medium heat till mixture is thickened and bubbly. Pour *half* of the sauce (about 1 cup) into another saucepan. Stir the corn, carrot, and green pepper into one of the sauce mixtures. Return to boiling. Cook and stir 1 minute more. Add the Swiss cheese, stirring till melted. Remove from heat; keep warm.

Stir together the sour cream and the 1 tablespoon flour; stir into the remaining saucepan along with the sausage or ham and the basil. Cook and stir till the mixture is thickened and bubbly. Cook and stir 1 minute more. Makes about 2½ cups of each sauce.

CINNAMON FRUIT CUPS

For a striking presentation, reserve the pineapple crown and use it as a centerpiece on the salad's serving platter; surround the crown with the salad cups.

  1 **17-ounce can unpeeled apricot**
     halves
  1 **tablespoon sugar**
  1 **tablespoon lemon juice**
  3 **inches stick cinnamon, broken**
  ¼ **teaspoon cardamom seed**
  1 **fresh pineapple**
  4 **oranges, peeled and sliced**
  2 **heads Bibb** *or* **Boston lettuce,**
     separated into cups *or*
     fresh spinach leaves
  1 **pint fresh strawberries, halved**
Fresh mint sprigs

Place *undrained* apricot halves in a blender container; cover and blend till smooth. Pour the apricot puree into a saucepan. Add sugar, lemon juice, cinnamon, and cardamom seed to the apricot puree. Bring to boiling, stirring to dissolve sugar. Cover and simmer 10 minutes. Strain to remove spices. Set the sauce aside.

Remove the crown from the pineapple. (Wrap the crown in clear plastic wrap and chill till serving time.) Cut off the peel from pineapple; remove eyes. Cut the pineapple into spears, removing the core. Place the pineapple spears and orange slices in a large bowl; pour the apricot mixture over all, stirring carefully to coat. Cover and chill several hours.

Arrange lettuce cups on a large tray. (Leave space in the center of the tray for the pineapple crown.) Arrange pineapple, orange slices, and berries in each lettuce cup. Drizzle some of the apricot mixture left in the bowl over the fruits. Cover and chill till serving time. Garnish each fruit cup with mint. (Place the reserved pineapple crown on the platter.) Makes 14 servings.

SPICED COCOA MIX

For easy serving, place the cocoa mix, a teakettle of hot water, stick cinnamon, coffee crystals, and liqueur on a serving table. Then, let guests create their own warm beverage. If you think guests will clamor for more, double the recipe.

  2 **cups nonfat dry milk powder**
  ½ **cup powdered non-dairy**
     creamer
  ⅓ **cup sifted powdered sugar**
  ¼ **cup unsweetened cocoa powder**
  ¾ **teaspoon ground cinnamon**
  ½ **teaspoon ground nutmeg**
Boiling water
Stick cinnamon (optional)
Instant coffee crystals (optional)
Coffee liqueur (optional)

For cocoa mix, in a mixing bowl combine the nonfat dry milk powder, non-dairy creamer, the powdered sugar, unsweetened cocoa powder, cinnamon, and nutmeg; mix thoroughly.

For each serving, combine ⅓ cup cocoa mix and ¾ cup boiling water in a heat-proof mug. Stir to dissolve the cocoa mix. If desired, use a cinnamon stick to stir 1 teaspoon coffee crystals or 1 to 2 tablespoons coffee liqueur into each serving. Makes about 2¾ cups mix (eight 6-ounce servings).

APPLE SLUSH

Children especially will like this refresher mixed with a lemon-lime carbonated beverage.

  2 **20-ounce cans sliced apples**
  1 **6-ounce can frozen apple juice**
     concentrate
  1 **6-ounce can frozen orange juice**
     concentrate
Apple slice (optional)
Lemon juice (optional)
Lemon-lime carbonated beverage,
     carbonated water, apple wine,
     or **dry white wine, chilled**

In a blender container combine *one can* of the *undrained* apples and *half* of each fruit juice concentrate. Cover and blend till smooth. Pour the mixture into a 1-quart freezer container. Repeat with the remaining apples and juice concentrates. Seal, label, and freeze.

To serve, let the frozen apple mixture stand at room temperature about 30 minutes or till slushy; transfer to a serving container. Garnish the mixture with an apple slice dipped in lemon juice, if desired.

For each serving, half-fill an 8-ounce glass with the slush. Slowly pour in carbonated beverage or wine; stir to blend. Makes 18 (8-ounce) servings.

SHERBETWICHES

Instead of pressing the sherbet into a can and refreezing, try this method: Spread softened sherbet (about ¼ inch deep) in a shallow foil-lined baking pan; cover and freeze. Use 3-inch cookie cutters to cut sherbet slices for sandwiches.

  2 **pints orange, lemon, lime,** *or*
     raspberry sherbet
  1 **recipe Sugar-Pecan Cookies**
     (see recipe, page 56)
  1 **recipe Fudge Circles**
     (see recipe, page 56)

Spoon sherbet into two 16-ounce cans. Cover with foil; freeze. Prepare cookies. To assemble, remove ends of sherbet-filled cans. Press on one end, forcing sherbet out the other side.

Cut each sherbet log into 12 slices (about ¼ inch thick), making 24 slices. Place each sherbet slice between two cookies. Arrange the filled cookies in a shallow pan. Freeze for 1 hour. Transfer to moisture- and vaporproof containers; freeze till serving time. Makes 24 filled cookies.

SUGAR-PECAN COOKIES

Eat these nutty cookies by themselves or use them for Sherbetwiches on page 55.

1¼ cups all-purpose flour
¼ teaspoon baking soda
Dash salt
¼ cup butter *or* margarine
¼ cup shortening
½ cup sugar
1 egg
¼ teaspoon vanilla
¼ cup finely chopped pecans

In a small mixing bowl stir together all-purpose flour, baking soda, and salt; set bowl aside. In a large mixer bowl beat the butter or margarine and shortening on medium speed of an electric mixer for ½ minute. Add the sugar and beat till mixture is fluffy. Add the egg and vanilla; beat well.

Gradually add the flour mixture to the beaten mixture, beating on low speed till well combined. Stir in the finely chopped pecans. Divide dough in half. Cover and chill the dough in the refrigerator for 1 hour.

On a lightly floured surface roll *half* of the dough to ⅛-inch thickness. Using 3-inch cookie cutters, cut the dough into ten circles, rerolling the dough as necessary. Transfer the dough circles to ungreased cookie sheets. Repeat rolling and cutting with the remaining dough. Bake in a 375° oven for 8 to 10 minutes or till done. Transfer the cookies to wire racks to cool. Makes 20 cookies.

FUDGE CIRCLES

Your chocolate-loving guests will go for Sherbetwiches made with these cookies. They're especially tasty with an orange sherbet filling.

1½ cups all-purpose flour
½ cup unsweetened cocoa powder
¼ teaspoon baking soda
¼ teaspoon baking powder
½ cup butter *or* margarine
1 cup sugar
1 egg
1 teaspoon vanilla

In a medium mixing bowl stir together the all-purpose flour, unsweetened cocoa powder, baking soda, and baking powder; set bowl aside.

In a large mixer bowl beat the butter or margarine on medium speed of an electric mixer for ½ minute. Add the sugar; beat on medium speed till the mixture is fluffy. Add the egg and vanilla; beat well.

Gradually add the flour mixture to the beaten mixture, beating on low speed of electric mixer till well combined. On a lightly floured surface roll the dough to ⅛-inch thickness.

Using 3-inch cutters, cut the dough into 3-inch circles, rerolling as necessary. Transfer the dough circles to ungreased cookie sheets. Bake in a 375° oven about 8 minutes or till cookies are done. Transfer the cookies to wire racks to cool. Makes 30 cookies.

SEAFOOD CHEESE ROUND

You can make this quick and easy brunch appetizer ahead, if you want to offer your guests something to nibble on before brunch.

2 8-ounce packages cream cheese, softened
¼ cup mayonnaise *or* salad dressing
2 tablespoons lemon juice
1 teaspoon Worcestershire sauce
Dash garlic powder
½ cup finely chopped celery
1 tablespoon snipped chives (optional)
¾ cup chili sauce
2 tablespoons sweet pickle relish
1 4½-ounce can small shrimp, drained
1 6-ounce can crabmeat, drained, flaked, and cartilage removed
2 tablespoons snipped parsley
Assorted crackers

In a large mixer bowl combine the cream cheese, the mayonnaise or salad dressing, lemon juice, Worcestershire sauce, and garlic powder. Beat on medium speed of an electric mixer till the mixture is smooth. Stir in the finely chopped celery and the snipped chives, if desired.

To serve, spread the cream cheese mixture into a 9-inch circle on a serving platter. Combine the chili sauce and sweet pickle relish; spread atop the cheese circle. Arrange the shrimp and crab atop the cheese mixture and sauce. Sprinkle the snipped parsley over all. Serve with crackers. Makes 18 to 20 appetizer servings.

MAY

Better Homes and Gardens

May 1984 • $1.50

SOUTHWEST STYLE YOU CAN ADD TO YOUR HOME

Getting the most for your home improvement dollars

New Orleans bound! Best vacations and super recipes

How you can remodel a has-been house

A family fitness program that works

7 bright flowers to grow in shade

NEW ORLEANS BOUND!

Great Recipes, Great Vacations

By Barbara Humeston, Nancy Byal, and Diana McMillen

The South is an enduring national treasure, worthy of a family vacation anytime. It's a land of living history and enormous variety, blessed with traditions of delicious dining and generous hospitality. This year, the six-month World's Fair in New Orleans is an extra incentive to head south. So we surveyed the best New Orleans-bound routes, plus how to make the most of a visit to New Orleans and the fair when you get there. People and places along the way provide a chance to sample three of the South's distinctive personalities. Each adventure is enhanced with recipes typical of the region to prepare and enjoy at home as remembrances of your tour.

Illustration: The Art Factory

RIVER COUNTRY

The past seems close at hand along the lower Mississippi River. From Vicksburg and Natchez to Baton Rouge and New Orleans, the relentless waterway rolls through country that gloried in the golden years of the South. Along the River Road (US-61) and well-chosen byways, the river's commanding presence remains and the Old South is remembered.

Country cuisine

Home cooking goes with country living here. Dinner-table classics include corn bread, biscuits, and Southern vegetables— okra, collards, black-eyed peas. Restaurant entrées like fried chicken, catfish, and country ham and red-eye gravy are memorable. Desserts are another indulgence. You won't find tastier cobblers, creamier custards, or richer pecan and sweet potato pies.

An oak archway leads to Oak Alley plantation home.
Bluegrass music echoes from the Old Court House.
Outdoor activities await at Grand Gulf Military Park.

*H*am-**Stuffed Bell Peppers** (front), *with a colorful filling, are a tasty accompaniment to fried chicken.*

Fritters, both sweet and savory, are popular throughout the South. Cooked winter squash and onion season these **Squash Fritters** *(left).*

Yes, there's ¼ cup hot pepper sauce in the marinade for **Natchez Fried Chicken** *(back right). But don't let that keep you from trying it. Much of the hotness tempers during the slow-fry cooking.*
Food stylist: Bonnie Rabert

Photographs: Hedrich-Blessing

Old South sister cities

The Civil War dealt different fates to Vicksburg and Natchez, premier river cities 65 miles apart. Devastated by a Union seige, Vicksburg remains shadowed in somber memories. The best-preserved Civil War battlefield presents a gripping look at the past, and the Old Court House Museum is a treasure trove of war memorabilia.

The elegance of the Old South lingers in Natchez, relatively untouched by the Union thrust. Scores of antebellum homes sparkle like gems. Some are open for tours all year. You can almost see wealthy planters and hoop-skirted ladies sipping mint juleps.

Rural byways

Make part of your adventure driving country byways and stopping at sleepy communities. Many, like Port Gibson, between Vicksburg and Natchez, have stories to tell. In Lorman, the general store stocks everything from sunbonnets to walking canes. Kudzu and pine drape the hills in green. Some routes lead to sunny river sandbars; others snake beside cotton fields.

Crossing the state line, you enter the serene hills of English Louisiana, settled by Tories fleeing Georgia and the Carolinas. Plantation homes bracket the river south from St. Francisville beyond Baton Rouge to New Orleans. At St. Francisville, Rosedown is the most lavish. Oak Alley near Vacherie has a lovely setting. You can crisscross between levees on car ferries.

The *Mississippi Queen* churns up the mighty river.

Sweet pralines are for sale around Natchez's Stanton Hall, which you can tour.

Civil War cannons still smoke at Vicksburg National Military Park.

The Old Country Store near Lorman is a friendly gathering spot for a stop.

Riverboat photograph: Danny Richardson/Natchez

Savory

Stuffed Ham (back) *is filled and capped with bread stuffing flecked with green pepper, celery, and onion. The delicate sweet-sour flavor of the stuffing contrasts with the unique country ham flavor.*

Skillet Okra and Vegetables (front right) *combines okra, onion, tomatoes, corn, and butter beans into a multicolored vegetable medley.*

Buttermilk Biscuits (front left) *will help your cooking reputation spread. They're quickly made and extra flaky, thanks to self-rising flour.*

ACADIANA

Ribbons of roads through the south Louisiana lowlands penetrate a bayou-blessed land that's been home to Acadians, called Cajuns, since the British banished them from Nova Scotia over two centuries ago. The Cajuns, originally French, borrowed the best from other ethnic groups, while remaining true to their heritage. That includes a remarkable zest for life. To appreciate the culture and spirit that make this area unique, plan to linger awhile. Rush through on the interstate and you'll miss everything.

Cajun cookery

Bring a good appetite to Acadiana, where Cajun cooking has become an art. It's an ingenious blend of local harvest from the land and sea. Rice fills out the dishes, and pepper, herbs, and spices heat them up. Asking locals is the secret to finding the best restaurants featuring Cajun specialties. Crawfish, gumbo, bread pudding, and seafood with a Cajun touch are a few dishes to try.

Browsing the bayous

The hub city of Acadiana is Lafayette, between Lake Charles, Louisiana, and New Orleans. The most interesting approach from the west follows the Gulf's curve south from Lake Charles along the Creole Nature Trail (State-27), then east on State-82. Acadian Village, near Lafayette, is a re-created bayou village that gives a glimpse at early Cajun life.

Villages that are the soul of Cajunland surround Lafayette. You travel bayou-side roads beside rice and sugarcane fields.

Cajun Redfish Roulades (front in picture opposite) *exemplify the elegant side of bayou cooking. Creole-style mustard accents the sauce.*

Oysters Rockefeller Soup (back) *is gaining as much fame today as its cousin, Oysters Rockefeller, first did in New Orleans 84 years ago. Serve it as an appetizer or first course.*

The bonus flavor in **Coconut Bread Pudding with High-Top Meringue** (picture right, back left) *is sherry-soaked raisins.*

Pastry leaves encircle **River-Bottom Pecan Pie** (back right). *This specialty flaunts a dark, rich filling.*

Taffy Tarts (front left) *are ideal for tea or a dinner finale. The filling forms a chewy topping as it bakes.*

Location: Shadows-on-the-Teche, New Iberia, La.

Fresh crawfish are a true Cajun country delicacy.

Feathered creatures cloak an island rookery at sunset.

Annie Miller, who guides swamp tours from near Houma, knows every niche of the Acadian wetlands.

Friendly people with twinkling eyes help "pass a good time" in Acadiana.

Crawfish photograph: Philip Gould

ACADIANA

In New Iberia, there are tours of an Acadian planter's home and the old Konriko rice mill. A stately courthouse and church frame twin town squares in Abbeville. Rosy lights wink outside bakeries, signaling that French bread is hot from the ovens. Crossroads groceries stock everything from headcheese to boudin (BOO-dan), a sausage that's spicy hot. Losing your way can be fun. You can get directions from quick-witted Cajuns, who speak with a French patois.

The good times roll

Cajuns always seem to be celebrating something with festivals that span the seasons. Friends and good times are dear to their hearts. Among the liveliest gatherings is Festivals Acadiens in Lafayette (September 15 and 16).

One way to get to know Acadiana is through its music. For Cajun music in a family setting, try Mulate's, near the town of Breaux Bridge. Groups that put forth include old-timers who've played together almost forever. You can't sit still when the fiddles and accordions get hot.

Wetland wonders

More Cajun mystique lies hidden in Acadiana's swamps and marshes. For a trip to remember, take a swamp-boat tour with Annie Miller from near Houma, southeast of Lafayette. This Cajun lady won't let you miss a thing—from camouflaged critters like nutria to herons. Best of all is gator-feeding time, when reptiles jump from the water for snacks.

Acadian Village, near Lafayette, salutes the life-style of the early Cajuns.

Gruesome gators cruise the swamps at snoot level.

At Cajun festivals, fast-stepping tunes entice dancers of all ages.

Cajun bands specialize in folk songs passed down through the generations.

Albert Lirette makes shrimp nets by hand along the bayous near Houma.

Cajun band photograph: Philip Gould

*S*auce **Piquante** (front left) *tops* **Peppered Pork Chops** *here. Cajun cooks also serve this sauce with many other meats, such as chicken, alligator, and frog legs.*

*   **Crawfish Étouffée** (AY-too-FAY) (front right) consists of shellfish smothered in vegetables and served over rice.*

*   A debate centers on whether to thicken gumbo with filé powder or okra.* **Chicken Andouille Gumbo** *(back) relies on filé, plus another Southern specialty: spicy-hot andouille (on-DOV-ee) sausage.*

*   Location: Acadian Village, Lafayette, La.*

THE GULF COAST

The Gulf Coast creates a glimmering panorama of beaches, islands, bays, and moody-blue waters through an amalgam of coastal towns from Mobile to New Orleans. Along this roughly 200 miles of Gulf shore, days pass leisurely in tune with the semitropical mood.

The sea's delicacies

A fond preoccupation is indulging in fresh catches. Shrimp, crabs, oysters, flounder, and snapper are fixed in delicious ways. Creole creations, sparked by the coast's French and Spanish beginnings, further titillate appetites. Folks who fix them usually share secrets of their specialties.

Coastal amblings

From the bayside city of Mobile, which reveals its rich past in four historical districts, loop south to Dauphin Island. West from the island through the shrimping village of Bayou La Batre, your route intersects with US-90.

Sounds of the ocean are never far away as US-90 leapfrogs via bridges and causeways between towns with seaworthy names. Sand seems to stretch forever around Biloxi and Gulfport, at the center of the coast. This sunny playground is fine-tuned with amenities for visitors. Communities farther east and west are more low key.

To get a sense of the ocean, travel to a sliver of sand offshore like Ship Island. Pack a picnic and make a day of it. Waves break across wide beaches as breezes rustle sea oats and shift the shapes of the dunes.

There's a farmers' market nearly every day along the Mississippi coast.

Skies glow with pink dawns and orange sunsets.

With a net and a chicken neck, you can try crabbing.

Structures like the Malaga Inn reflect the rich heritage of the city of Mobile.

Dauphin Island beaches are perfect for family fun.

Sailing and other water sports abound on the Gulf.

Gulf-Style **Gumbo** (back), jam-packed with a combination of shrimp, crab, and oysters, is a likely find down Mobile way. Two kinds of hot pepper sauce add fire to this seafood-based main dish that's served with hot cooked rice.

A mustard-horseradish marinade highlights the seafood in chilled **Shrimp Remoulade** (front right). Spoon the mixture over lettuce leaves for a colorful appetizer.

Complete your Gulf Coast-inspired meals with golden **Southern Corn Bread** (front left). The Southern rendition of this all-American favorite has no sugar added and includes flavorful bacon drippings. Be true to tradition and bake it in an iron skillet to get a crisp crust and serve it drizzled with sorghum.

NEW ORLEANS

Cradled in an easy curve of the Mississippi near the brink of the Gulf, New Orleans celebrates the moment, while nurturing the history of nearly three centuries. Inspired by its colorful past, great food, and music, this legendary city turns having a good time into an art. The secret to appreciating New Orleans' charm is opening your heart to the city.

Culinary pride

The city is a gourmand's delight. An array of fabled owner-operated eating establishments boasts quality dining. But don't miss treats served up at unpretentious po' boy shops, oyster bars, and outdoor cafés. They're also New Orleans institutions.

Culinary artistry ranges from simple to extravagant, with Creole cuisine the most distinctive. This zesty blend heralds the tastes of early French and Spanish residents, combined with touches of this and that, like sweet peppers and golden saffron. Distinctive fare to try includes shrimp creole, jambalaya, bananas foster, mile-high pie, and muffuletta sandwiches.

Old-quarter tapestry

A sense of the past surrounds the French Quarter, where you can sample most of the things New Orleans is famous for. Iron balconies cast shadows on quaint cottages. Old rowhouses with simple facades conceal fountains and courtyards.

Exploring should be a leisurely adventure. Along cobbled streets, galleries and shops lie tucked away in unlikely spots, and carriage horses clip-clop by.

Jazz played by old-timers at Preservation Hall ($1) is the city's best bargain.

Clowns add to the French Quarter's carnival mood.

Jackson Square artists do portraits of passersby.

St. Louis Cathedral towers above Jackson Square.

*P*o' boys
(front), *individual French bread loaves filled with fried Gulf oysters, must be included on your culinary tour of the South. Spread the bread with mayonnaise, sprinkle with hot pepper sauce, and serve with lemon wedges, as shown, or top generously with shredded lettuce, tomato slices, or some catsup.*

Red Beans and Rice
(right center) *is a stewlike meal that has been known to feed many hungry families at a slim price. It combines red beans, ham bone, smoked sausage, and red pepper.*

Grillades and Grits
(back) *traditionally graced the Old South's breakfast tables, but this dish fares well at suppertime, too. Slow-cooked tomatoes, onions, and garlic provide a self-made gravy for the veal round steak.*

Satisfy the biggest of appetites with a **Muffuletta** *(left center). The folklore indicates that this sandwich was created in New Orleans during the early 1900s. A round Italian loaf envelopes sliced salami, cheese, cappicola, and a juicy pickled vegetable mixture.*

Location: New Orleans waterfront.

Field editor: Bonnie Warren

NEW ORLEANS

Delicious aromas beckon from every direction.

A carnival mood engulfs Jackson Square, in the heart of the quarter. Bands entertain, kids work crowds with dance routines, magicians and mimes ply their trades, and quick-study artists fashion portraits while you wait. Steps away are the Moonwalk, a riverside promenade; The Jackson Brewery, a renovated complex of eateries and shops; famous arteries like Royal Street, the quarter's best shopping stretch; and the old French Market.

The city pulses with jazz, which was born in the streets of New Orleans. Low-down or red hot, music echoes from classy clubs, honky-tonks, and simple halls. Families can hear old-timers at Preservation Hall play jazz as it used to be played or celebrate Sunday with a jazz brunch.

The soft light at sunset shows off nostalgic French Quarter architecture.

Muffuletta sandwiches originated in New Orleans at the Central Grocery.

*D*oberge **Cake** *(DO-bash)* *(right) exemplifies the ingenuity of New Orleans' bakers. It's an adaptation of the famous European Dobos Torte.*

You won't be able to resist these light powdered-sugar-dusted **Beignets** *(ben-YAZE) (front left).*

Calas *(back left) appear to mirror Beignets, except the recipe starts with rice.*

Location: The Historic New Orleans Collection.

NATCHEZ FRIED CHICKEN

- 1 2½- to 3-pound broiler-fryer chicken, cut up
- 1 2-ounce bottle (¼ cup) hot pepper sauce
- 1½ cups water
- ¼ teaspoon salt
- Shortening *or* cooking oil for shallow frying
- ½ cup all-purpose flour
- 1 recipe Cream Gravy
- Ornamental peppers (optional)

Rinse chicken pieces; pat dry with paper towels. Set aside the neck and the back pieces of chicken. Season the remaining chicken pieces with salt and pepper; place in a large bowl. Sprinkle chicken with hot pepper sauce. Cover bowl and refrigerate about 3 hours, turning chicken every hour.

In a saucepan combine the reserved neck and back, water, and ¼ teaspoon salt. Cover and cook for 30 minutes. Skim off fat and remove neck and back; reserve broth for gravy.

In a heavy 12-inch skillet heat ½ inch shortening. Coat seasoned chicken with flour. Add the chicken to skillet with meaty portions toward center. (If necessary, use two skillets to cook the chicken in a single layer.) Cook chicken, uncovered, over medium heat for 10 to 15 minutes, turning to brown evenly. Reduce heat; cover tightly. Cook 30 minutes. Uncover; cook 10 to 15 minutes more or till chicken is done. Reserve *3 tablespoons* drippings in skillet for gravy.

Place the chicken, uncovered, in a warm oven to keep warm while preparing gravy. Serve the fried chicken with Cream Gravy. Garnish with peppers, if desired. Makes 6 servings.

Cream Gravy: In the same skillet stir 3 tablespoons *all-purpose flour* into the reserved 3 tablespoons drippings. Cook and stir over medium-low heat 30 minutes or till very brown. Add 1 small *onion*, chopped, to skillet; cook, uncovered, till tender. Add ¾ *cup* of reserved broth from neck and back pieces and enough *milk* to make of desired consistency (about 1 cup). Season to taste with salt and pepper. Heat through. Makes 1¼ cups.

HAM-STUFFED BELL PEPPERS

- ¼ cup butter *or* margarine
- ½ cup chopped onion
- ¼ cup chopped celery
- 1 clove garlic, minced
- 1 cup ground fully cooked ham
- 1 7½-ounce can tomatoes, cut up
- ½ cup tomato juice
- 1¼ cups coarsely crushed saltine crackers (27 crackers)
- 1 beaten egg
- ½ teaspoon sugar
- Several dashes bottled hot pepper sauce
- ⅛ teaspoon ground red pepper
- 4 green peppers, halved crosswise and seeded
- 1 tablespoon butter *or* margarine, melted

For stuffing, in a large skillet melt the ¼ cup butter or margarine. Add the onion, celery, and garlic; cook till tender. Add the ham, *undrained* tomatoes, and tomato juice. Bring to boiling, then reduce heat. Simmer, uncovered, about 10 minutes or till liquid is slightly reduced. Stir in *1 cup* of the crushed crackers, the beaten egg, sugar, hot pepper sauce, and ground red pepper.

Meanwhile, in a large saucepan cook the green pepper halves in boiling water for 3 to 4 minutes; invert to drain. Fill green pepper halves with the ham-vegetable mixture. Arrange peppers, filled side up, in a 13x9x2-inch baking pan. Cover with foil. Bake in a 350° oven for 10 minutes.

For topping, combine the remaining crushed crackers and the 1 tablespoon melted butter or margarine. Top green peppers with crumb mixture and return to oven. Bake, uncovered, for 15 minutes more. Transfer to a serving platter. Garnish with parsley. Makes 8 side-dish servings.

SQUASH FRITTERS

You can substitute 2 cups of leftover mashed white potatoes for the mashed, cooked squash.

- 1 medium butternut squash
- 2 eggs
- ¼ cup finely chopped onion
- ½ teaspoon salt
- ¼ teaspoon pepper
- 1½ cups self-rising flour
- Shortening *or* cooking oil for deep-fat frying

Halve squash lengthwise; scoop out seeds and membrane. Place the squash, cut side down, in a baking pan. Bake in a 350° oven about 1 hour or till tender. Scoop out squash; mash squash (should have about 2 cups).

In a large mixing bowl stir together the 2 cups mashed squash, eggs, onion, salt, and pepper. Gradually stir in the flour till mixture is well combined. Drop by heaping tablespoons into deep hot fat (365°) and fry for 1½ to 2 minutes or till golden. Drain on paper towels. Serve warm. Makes 24 fritters.

SKILLET OKRA AND VEGETABLES

If fresh okra is not available, substitute 2 cups frozen cut okra.

- 3 slices bacon
- 1 large onion, chopped
- 1 28-ounce can tomatoes, cut up
- 2 cups sliced okra
- 1 16-ounce can butter beans, drained
- 1 8-ounce can whole kernel corn, drained

In a heavy 12-inch skillet cook the bacon till crisp. Remove bacon; drain on paper towels. Reserve *2 tablespoons* bacon drippings in skillet. Add onion to the skillet. Cook, uncovered, just till onion is tender.

Add the *undrained* tomatoes, okra, butter beans, and corn. Season with salt and pepper. Simmer, uncovered, about 20 minutes or till liquid is almost evaporated. Transfer to a serving platter. Crumble the bacon; sprinkle atop. Makes 6 to 8 servings.

BUTTERMILK BISCUITS

2 cups self-rising flour
1 tablespoon sugar
½ cup shortening
¾ cup buttermilk or sour milk
Melted butter or margarine

In a medium mixing bowl stir together the flour and sugar. Cut in the shortening till the mixture resembles coarse crumbs. Make a well in the center; add the buttermilk or sour milk all at once. Stir the mixture just till the dough clings together.

On a lightly floured surface knead the biscuit dough gently for 10 to 12 strokes. Roll or pat the dough to ½-inch thickness. Cut with a 2½-inch biscuit cutter, dipping the cutter into flour between cuts. Transfer the biscuits to an ungreased baking sheet. Brush the tops with melted butter or margarine. Bake in a 400° oven about 15 minutes or till light brown. Makes about 10 biscuits.

SAVORY STUFFED HAM

Country ham, aged and cured, is a Southern specialty. It's necessary to soak the country ham to remove some of the salty flavor. You can also prepare this recipe using a sugar-cured ham slice.

1 8- to 10-pound bone-in country ham*
7 to 8 slices thin-sliced coarse-textured bread, cut into ¼-inch cubes (3 cups)
¾ cup chopped onion
¾ cup chopped celery
½ cup chopped green pepper
2 tablespoons butter or margarine
3 tablespoons brown sugar
2 tablespoons vinegar
1 teaspoon dried sage, crushed
¾ teaspoon dry mustard
¼ teaspoon ground red pepper
¼ teaspoon black pepper
2 beaten eggs

Thoroughly scrub and rinse the ham. Soak overnight in enough water to cover; drain. Place ham in a large kettle or Dutch oven; add enough water to cover. Bring to boiling; reduce heat. Simmer 20 minutes per pound. Remove ham from water. When ham is cool enough to handle, remove skin and excess fat. Cut out bone. Set ham aside.

For stuffing, place bread cubes in a shallow baking pan. Bake cubes in a 350° oven for 10 to 12 minutes or till toasted, stirring occasionally.

In a saucepan cook onion, celery, and green pepper in hot butter or margarine till tender. Stir in brown sugar and vinegar. In a large mixing bowl combine the bread cubes, sage, dry mustard, red pepper, and black pepper. Add the onion mixture; toss to mix. Add eggs; toss gently to moisten.

Stuff ham where bone was removed, using about *half* of the stuffing to fill the ham. Score top of ham, if desired. Place ham on a rack in a roasting pan; cover loosely with foil. Bake in a 350° oven for 1½ hours. Pat remaining stuffing on top of ham; return to oven and bake, uncovered, for 15 to 20 minutes more or till stuffing is light brown. Transfer ham to a serving platter; slice to serve. Garnish ham with fresh sage, if desired. Makes 16 to 20 servings.

*Note: You can substitute one 2½-pound fully cooked *ham slice,* cut 1 inch thick, for the country-style ham. Do not cook the ham slice in water; trim and slash edges. Prepare stuffing as directed. Place ham slice on a rack in a roasting pan. Bake, uncovered, in a 350° oven for 20 minutes. Pat a thin layer of the stuffing (about ¼ inch thick) over the top of the ham slice. (Any extra stuffing may be heated in a small covered casserole with the ham.) Return ham to oven. Bake, uncovered, 15 to 20 minutes more or till stuffing is light brown. Makes 6 to 8 servings.

CAJUN REDFISH ROULADES

4 6-ounce fresh or frozen redfish or red snapper fillets
8 ounces fresh or frozen shelled crawfish tails, shrimp, or crabmeat
Lemon juice
4 ounces fresh mushrooms, sliced
2 small shallots or 1 green onion, thinly sliced
1 clove garlic, minced
1 tablespoon butter or margarine
1 cup finely snipped fresh basil
¾ teaspoon Creole seasoning or Homemade Creole Seasoning (see recipe, opposite)
½ cup light cream or milk
½ cup chicken broth
¾ cup soft bread crumbs (1 slice)
Chicken broth
Butter or margarine
1 recipe Creole Mustard Sauce (see recipe, opposite)
1 lemon (optional)
Watercress (optional)

Thaw fish and seafood, if frozen. Place fillets between 2 pieces of clear plastic wrap. Pound lightly to flatten to ¼-inch thickness. Remove plastic wrap; sprinkle fillets with lemon juice.

For stuffing, in a saucepan cook the mushrooms, shallots or green onion, and garlic in 1 tablespoon hot butter or margarine till tender. Add the seafood, basil, and Creole seasoning. Stir in cream or milk and ½ cup broth. Heat till mixture almost boils; reduce heat. Cook and stir, uncovered, for 5 minutes. Stir in bread crumbs. Remove from heat.

Spread about ⅔ cup stuffing atop each fish portion. Roll up fish, jelly-roll style, starting from narrow end. Place the fish rolls, seam side down, in a 12x7½x2-inch baking dish. Drizzle fish with additional chicken broth; dot with additional butter. Cover and bake in a 350° oven for 20 to 25 minutes or till the fish flakes easily when tested with a fork. Using a slotted spatula, transfer cooked fish to platter. To serve, top with Creole Mustard Sauce. If desired, for garnish, use a sharp knife to halve lemon, cutting a scalloped edge. Garnish platter with lemon half and watercress, if desired. Makes 4 servings.

HOMEMADE CREOLE SEASONING

Try this seasoning to spice up hamburgers, too. Just mix in 1 teaspoon of the seasoning for each pound of uncooked ground beef.

2 tablespoons salt
1 tablespoon ground red pepper
1 tablespoon chili powder
1 teaspoon garlic powder
1 teaspoon black pepper

Combine salt, red pepper, chili powder, garlic powder, and black pepper. Store, tightly covered, at room temperature. Use to season such foods as meat, fish, vegetables, and soups. Makes about ¼ cup seasoning.

CREOLE MUSTARD SAUCE

Creole-style mustard is coarse-textured and flavorful. You'll find it in large supermarkets or specialty food shops. Or, substitute a German-style mustard.

4 egg yolks
½ cup butter *or* margarine, cut into thirds and at room temperature
4 teaspoons lemon juice
3 tablespoons Creole-style mustard
Few dashes bottled hot pepper sauce

In the top of a double boiler place the egg yolks and *one-third* of the butter. Cook mixture, stirring rapidly, over boiling water till butter is melted. Add one-third more of the butter; continue stirring rapidly. As butter melts and mixture thickens, add the remaining butter, stirring constantly.

When butter is melted, remove pan from water; stir rapidly for 2 more minutes. Gradually stir in lemon juice. Add the mustard and hot pepper sauce. Heat again over boiling water, stirring constantly, for 2 to 3 minutes or till thickened. Immediately remove from heat. Makes about 1 cup sauce.

COCONUT BREAD PUDDING WITH HIGH-TOP MERINGUE

½ loaf French bread (8 ounces)
2½ cups milk
½ cup light raisins
¼ cup cream sherry, warmed
4 slightly beaten egg yolks
¾ cup sugar
½ cup coconut
1 tablespoon vanilla
3 tablespoons butter *or* margarine
4 egg whites
¼ teaspoon cream of tartar
1 cup sifted powdered sugar

Into a large mixing bowl break or tear bread into small pieces to measure 8 cups. Pour milk over bread and let soak about 15 minutes or till the bread is completely softened, stirring often.

Soak raisins in the warm sherry for 15 minutes. Beat together the egg yolks, sugar, coconut, and vanilla. Stir in the raisins and sherry. Add the raisin-coconut mixture to bread mixture and stir till thoroughly blended.

Preheat oven to 350°; melt butter or margarine in an 8x8x2-inch baking pan or dish in the oven while it heats. Swirl melted butter around pan to coat bottom and sides. Pour excess butter from pan into bread mixture and stir. Turn bread mixture into the warm pan. Bake about 25 minutes or till a knife inserted halfway between center and edge comes out clean.

For meringue, in a small mixer bowl beat egg whites and cream of tartar on high speed of electric mixer till soft peaks form (tips curl). Slowly add the powdered sugar to the beaten egg whites and continue beating till stiff peaks form (tips stand straight).

Gently spread the meringue evenly over the hot baked pudding, making swirls and peaks. Return pan to oven and increase oven temperature to 375°. Bake for 10 to 15 minutes more or till golden. Serve warm. Makes 9 servings.

RIVER-BOTTOM PECAN PIE

1 recipe Pastry
¾ cup sugar
3 tablespoons butter *or* margarine
Dash salt
3 eggs
1 cup dark corn syrup
2 teaspoons vanilla
1 cup chopped pecans
¾ to 1 cup pecan halves
1 cup whipping cream
2 tablespoons praline liqueur *or* Amaretto
2 teaspoons powdered sugar

Prepare Pastry. For filling, in a mixer bowl combine the sugar, butter or margarine, and salt; beat on high speed of an electric mixer till well mixed. Add eggs, one at a time, beating 1 minute after each addition. Beat in corn syrup and vanilla. Stir in chopped pecans. Turn filling into the prepared pastry.

Arrange pecan halves in a pattern atop the filled pie. Garnish with reserved pastry leaves, if desired. Cover edge with foil to prevent overbrowning. Bake in a 350° oven for 25 minutes. Remove foil. Bake about 25 minutes more or till a knife inserted near center comes out clean. Cool on a wire rack.

Before serving, beat the whipping cream, liqueur, and powdered sugar till soft peaks form. Serve whipped cream mixture atop wedges of pie. Makes 8 servings.

Pastry: Stir together 1¼ cups *all-purpose flour* and dash *salt.* Cut in ⅓ cup *butter* or *margarine* till the pieces are the size of small peas. Sprinkle with 1 tablespoon *ice water;* gently toss with a fork. Push to side of bowl. Repeat with 2 to 3 tablespoons additional *ice water* till all is moistened. Form the dough into a ball.

On a lightly floured surface roll the dough into a 12-inch circle. Place in a 9-inch pie plate. Trim pastry to edge of pie plate. Roll out pastry scraps. Using a sharp knife, cut the rolled pastry into small leaf shapes. Brush the dough leaves with water and place around the edge of the pie. If desired, cut out a few large leaf shapes and set aside to garnish the top of the filled pie.

TAFFY TARTS

- ½ of an 8-ounce package cream cheese
- ¾ cup butter *or* margarine
- 1½ cups all-purpose flour
- 2 cups packed brown sugar
- 2 slightly beaten eggs
- 2 tablespoons all-purpose flour
- 1 tablespoon butter *or* margarine
- 1 tablespoon vanilla

For pastry, in a large mixer bowl beat cream cheese and the ¾ cup butter or margarine for 30 seconds. Add the 1½ cups flour; beat well. Form into a ball.

For filling, in a small mixer bowl combine the brown sugar, eggs, the 2 tablespoons flour, the 1 tablespoon butter or margarine, and the vanilla; beat till combined.

Shape the pastry dough into 36 balls; place each ball in an ungreased 1¾-inch muffin cup. Press dough onto bottom and up sides of cups. Spoon *1 tablespoon* filling into *each* cup.

Bake in a 325° oven about 35 minutes or till golden. Cool for 15 minutes on wire racks. Remove tarts from pans; cool on racks. Store the tarts, covered, in the refrigerator. Makes 36 tarts.

OYSTERS ROCKEFELLER SOUP

- 1½ cups chicken broth
- 1 small onion, finely chopped
- 1 stalk celery, finely chopped
- 2 cloves garlic, minced
- 1 cup finely chopped fresh spinach
- 1 pint shucked oysters
- ⅓ cup grated Romano *or* Parmesan cheese
- 2 cups light cream *or* milk
- 2 tablespoons cornstarch
- 1½ teaspoons aniseed
- ½ teaspoon salt
- ⅛ teaspoon ground red pepper
- ¼ cup Pernod *or* Anisette

In a large saucepan combine ½ *cup* of the chicken broth, the onion, celery, and garlic. Bring to boiling; reduce heat. Cover and cook for 5 minutes. Stir in the spinach; cover and simmer for 5 minutes more.

Drain the oysters, reserving the liquid. Add oyster liquid and remaining chicken broth to mixture in saucepan. Simmer, uncovered, for 10 minutes, stirring occasionally. Stir in the cheese.

Combine the cream, cornstarch, aniseed, salt, and red pepper; stir into the mixture in the saucepan. Cook and stir till thickened and bubbly. Cook and stir for 2 minutes more. Stir in the oysters and Pernod; heat through. Makes 8 appetizer servings.

PEPPERED PORK CHOPS

Louisiana and Cajun cooks often season foods with a mixture of ground black, white, and red peppers. The black pepper adds aroma; the white pepper, bite; and the red pepper, burn. In Cajun country, the meat markets and grocery stores even stock peppered meats.

- 2 teaspoons black pepper
- 2 teaspoons white pepper
- 2 teaspoons ground red pepper
- 6 pork loin chops, cut 1 inch thick
- Sauce Piquante (see recipe, right)

Combine the black pepper, white pepper, and red pepper. Rub *each* chop with about *1 teaspoon* of the pepper mixture, coating evenly. Place chops on the rack of an unheated broiler pan. Broil chops 3 to 4 inches from the heat for 20 to 25 minutes, turning once. Serve the pork chops warm with Sauce Piquante. Makes 6 servings.

SAUCE PIQUANTE

The first step in making this sauce, cooking the flour and oil, forms a roux. The roux is done when its color changes to that of a dull copper penny. Use a heavy saucepan to prevent scorching.

- ⅓ cup all-purpose flour
- ⅓ cup cooking oil
- 1½ cups sliced green onions
- 1 large onion, chopped (1 cup)
- 1 medium green pepper, chopped
- ⅓ cup chopped celery
- 2 tablespoons snipped parsley
- 2 cloves garlic, minced
- 1 7½-ounce can tomatoes, cut up
- ¼ cup water
- 2 tablespoons tomato paste
- 2 tablespoons dry red wine
- 1 bay leaf
- ½ teaspoon salt
- ½ teaspoon black pepper
- ¼ teaspoon ground red pepper
- ¼ teaspoon dried basil, crushed
- ¼ teaspoon chili powder
- ⅛ teaspoon dried thyme, crushed
- Dash ground cloves
- 1 recipe Peppered Pork Chops (see recipe, left)
- Hot cooked rice
- Celery leaves (optional)

In a 2-quart heavy saucepan combine flour and cooking oil. Cook and stir over medium heat till mixture starts to brown; reduce heat to medium-low. Cook, stirring constantly, about 30 minutes total or till a dark reddish-brown roux is formed. Stir in green onions, onion, green pepper, celery, parsley, and garlic; cook and stir for 5 to 10 minutes or till vegetables are tender.

Stir in the *undrained* tomatoes, water, tomato paste, wine, bay leaf, salt, black pepper, red pepper, basil, chili powder, thyme, and cloves. Simmer the mixture, uncovered, about 45 minutes or till it reaches the desired consistency. Remove the bay leaf. Serve the sauce over warm Peppered Pork Chops with rice. If desired, garnish with celery leaves. Makes 6 servings.

GULF-STYLE GUMBO

Buy the hot Worcestershire-like Pickapeppa Sauce in specialty food shops.

- 1 pound fresh *or* frozen shelled shrimp
- 1 6-ounce package frozen crabmeat
- ½ cup all-purpose flour
- ½ cup cooking oil
- ¾ cup chopped onion
- ½ cup chopped green pepper
- ½ cup chopped celery
- 1½ cups chicken broth
- 1 ham hock
- 1 8-ounce can tomato sauce
- 1 7½-ounce can tomatoes, cut up
- 2 tablespoons snipped parsley
- 2 tablespoons Worcestershire sauce
- 1 tablespoon Pickapeppa Sauce (optional)
- 2 bay leaves
- 2 teaspoons dried oregano, crushed
- 1 teaspoon paprika
- ½ teaspoon garlic powder
- Several dashes bottled hot pepper sauce
- 1 10-ounce package frozen cut okra, thawed
- 1 pint shucked oysters, drained
- 1½ teaspoons filé powder
- Hot cooked rice

Thaw shrimp and crabmeat, if frozen. In a large heavy saucepan combine flour and oil. Cook and stir over medium heat till mixture starts to brown; reduce heat to medium-low. Cook and stir about 30 minutes total or till a dark reddish-brown roux is formed. Add onion, green pepper, and celery; cook and stir about 10 minutes or till tender. Add broth. Stir in ham hock, tomato sauce, *undrained* tomatoes, parsley, Worcestershire sauce, the Pickapeppa Sauce (if desired), bay leaves, oregano, paprika, garlic powder, hot pepper sauce, ½ teaspoon *salt*, and ¼ teaspoon *pepper*. Bring to boiling; reduce heat. Cover and simmer 1 hour.

Remove ham hock. When cool, cut meat from bone; discard bone. Chop meat; return to pan. Skim fat from broth. Add okra; cook, uncovered, 5 minutes. Add shrimp, crab, and oysters. Cook, uncovered, 5 minutes. Remove from heat. Stir in filé powder; let stand 5 minutes. Remove bay leaves. Serve with rice. Makes 8 servings.

CRAWFISH ÉTOUFFÉE

Crawfish, also known as crayfish, crawdads, creek crabs, and yabbies, are freshwater crustaceans. You can substitute one pound fresh or frozen peeled shrimp for the crawfish.

- 1 pound fresh *or* frozen shelled crawfish tails
- ¼ cup butter *or* margarine
- ¼ cup all-purpose flour
- ¼ cup butter *or* margarine
- 1 medium onion, chopped (½ cup)
- 1 small green pepper, chopped
- ½ cup chopped celery
- 1 clove garlic, minced
- 2 tablespoons snipped parsley
- ½ teaspoon salt
- ¼ teaspoon black pepper
- ⅛ to ¼ teaspoon ground red pepper
- ½ cup water
- Hot cooked rice
- Boiled whole fresh crawfish (optional)

Thaw crawfish tails, if frozen. In a heavy saucepan melt the first ¼ cup butter or margarine. Stir in the flour. Cook and stir over medium heat till the mixture starts to brown; reduce heat to medium-low. Cook, stirring constantly, about 30 minutes total or till a dark reddish-brown roux is formed.

Add the remaining ¼ cup butter or margarine, stirring till melted. Add the onion, green pepper, celery, and garlic. Cook and stir about 15 minutes or till the vegetables are very tender.

Add the crawfish tails, parsley, salt, black pepper, and ground red pepper. Stir in the water. Bring to boiling; reduce heat. Simmer, uncovered, for 5 to 10 minutes or till the crawfish are tender. Serve over hot cooked rice. Garnish with boiled crawfish, if desired. Makes 4 servings.

CHICKEN ANDOUILLE GUMBO

Filé (fee-LAY) powder is made by finely grinding dried sassafras leaves.

- 1 4- to 6-pound stewing chicken, cut up
- 1 teaspoon salt
- ¼ teaspoon black pepper
- ⅛ teaspoon ground red pepper
- ½ cup cooking oil
- ½ cup all-purpose flour
- 1 large onion, chopped (1 cup)
- 1 large green pepper, chopped
- 1 cup sliced green onions
- 1 cup chopped celery
- 1 clove garlic, minced
- 3 quarts hot water
- 1 pound andouille *or* smoked sausage, cut into ½-inch slices
- 1 teaspoon salt
- 2 to 3 tablespoons filé powder
- Hot cooked rice

Rinse chicken; pat dry. Sprinkle chicken with 1 teaspoon salt, black pepper, and red pepper. In a Dutch oven brown chicken on all sides in hot oil. Remove chicken, reserving pan drippings; set chicken aside.

Add the flour to the reserved pan drippings, scraping the bottom of the Dutch oven to loosen any crusty bits. Cook and stir over medium heat till the mixture starts to turn brown; reduce heat to medium-low. Cook, stirring constantly, about 30 minutes total or till a dark reddish-brown roux is formed.

Add onion, green pepper, green onions, celery, and garlic; cook and stir over medium heat for 5 to 10 minutes or till tender. Slowly stir in the water. Add browned chicken. Bring to boiling; reduce heat. Cover and simmer for 2 to 2½ hours or till chicken is very tender, adding more water, if necessary.

Add sausage and 1 teaspoon salt; cover and simmer for 20 to 30 minutes more or till sausage is done. Remove from heat; skim off fat. Stir in the filé powder; let stand for 5 minutes. Serve with hot cooked rice. Makes 8 servings.

SHRIMP RÉMOULADE

```
  3 cups water
1½ teaspoons salt
  1 pound fresh or frozen peeled and
    deveined shrimp
¼ cup vinegar
  2 tablespoons prepared
    Creole-style mustard or
    German-style mustard
  2 teaspoons prepared horseradish
1½ teaspoons paprika
¼ teaspoon salt
⅛ teaspoon pepper
  2 tablespoons olive or salad oil
¼ cup sliced green onions
  2 tablespoons snipped parsley
Lettuce leaves
```

In a saucepan combine the water and the 1½ teaspoons salt. Bring to boiling. Add shrimp. Simmer 1 to 3 minutes or till shrimp turn pink. Drain; chill.

Meanwhile, in a small mixer bowl combine the vinegar, mustard, horseradish, paprika, the ¼ teaspoon salt, and the pepper. Slowly add oil, beating well with an electric mixer. Stir in green onions and parsley.

In a medium mixing bowl stir together the shrimp and the oil mixture. Cover and chill 4 to 24 hours, stirring occasionally. Using a slotted spoon, spoon mixture atop lettuce on a serving platter. Makes 4 appetizer servings.

SOUTHERN CORN BREAD

```
1½ cups yellow or white cornmeal
½ cup all-purpose flour
  4 teaspoons baking powder
½ teaspoon salt
1¼ cups milk
  2 eggs
⅓ cup bacon drippings or
    shortening
```

In a mixing bowl combine the cornmeal, flour, baking powder, and salt. Beat together the milk and eggs.

In a 10-inch ovenproof skillet or corn bread skillet melt bacon drippings or shortening. Pour drippings into egg mixture, leaving about 1 tablespoon drippings in hot skillet. Add egg mixture to dry ingredients; beat just till smooth (do not overbeat). Pour batter into hot skillet; bake in a 425° oven for 18 to 20 minutes or till done. Serve in wedges. Makes 8 or 9 wedges.

Corn Sticks: Prepare the Southern Corn Bread batter as directed, melting bacon drippings in a small skillet or saucepan and brushing corn stick pans with the remaining 1 tablespoon melted drippings. Heat the pans in a 425° oven for 5 minutes. Spoon batter into heated corn stick pans, filling two-thirds full. Bake in a 425° oven about 12 minutes. Makes about 20 corn sticks.

GRILLADES AND GRITS

This flavorful main dish is pronounced gree-ODDS and grits.

```
1½ pounds veal leg round steak
    or beef round steak, cut
    ¾ inch thick
¼ cup all-purpose flour
  2 tablespoons lard or shortening
  1 16-ounce can tomatoes, cut up
  2 medium onions, chopped
½ cup water
  1 clove garlic, minced
½ teaspoon instant chicken
    bouillon granules
⅛ teaspoon ground red pepper
Hot cooked grits
```

Trim excess fat from meat. Remove and discard bones. Cut meat into 3-inch strips. Using a meat mallet, pound meat to ¼-inch thickness. Coat meat with the flour. In a large skillet brown meat, half at a time, on both sides in hot lard. Remove from skillet; set aside.

In the skillet stir together the *undrained* tomatoes, onions, water, garlic, bouillon granules, and red pepper. Return meat to the skillet. Bring mixture to boiling; reduce heat. Cover and simmer over low heat for 20 minutes. Uncover; simmer for 10 minutes more. Serve meat atop grits with gravy from pan. Makes 6 servings.

PO' BOYS

Traditionally, you would purchase these sandwiches wrapped in heavy brown paper to keep them crisp and piping hot.

```
  1 pint shucked oysters
  2 eggs
  1 cup corn flour or all-purpose
    flour
½ teaspoon salt
¼ teaspoon pepper
Cooking oil or shortening for
    deep-fat frying
  2 7-inch-long loaves French
    bread, sliced horizontally
  2 tablespoons butter or
    margarine, softened
Mayonnaise or salad dressing
Bottled hot pepper sauce
Lemon wedges
```

Drain the oysters; pat dry with paper towels. In a small mixing bowl beat the eggs. In another mixing bowl combine the flour, salt, and pepper. Dip the oysters into the beaten eggs; coat with flour mixture.

In a saucepan or deep-fat fryer heat about 2 inches of oil to 365°. Fry oysters, a few at a time, in the hot oil for 2 to 3 minutes or till golden. Drain the fried oysters on paper towels. Keep warm in a 325° oven while frying the remaining oysters.

Meanwhile, spread the cut side of each roll bottom with the butter or margarine. Heat rolls in a 325° oven about 5 minutes or till warm. Spread the cut side of each roll top with mayonnaise. Heap the fried oysters onto the bottoms of the rolls. Sprinkle oysters with hot pepper sauce; add the tops of rolls. Serve sandwiches warm with lemon wedges. Makes 2 servings.

RED BEANS AND RICE

Any leftover bean mixture freezes well. To serve, just thaw the bean mixture and reheat in a saucepan, adding more water as necessary. It should be the consistency of thick chili.

  1 **pound dry red beans *or* dry red kidney beans**
  6 **cups cold water**
  6 **cups hot water**
  1 **pound meaty ham bone *or* smoked pork hocks**
  1 **large onion, chopped (1 cup)**
  2 **cloves garlic, minced**
  1 **bay leaf**
  ¼ **to ½ teaspoon ground red pepper**
  1 **pound smoked sausage, cut into bite-size pieces**
Hot cooked rice
Sliced green onion

Rinse the beans. In a large Dutch oven cover beans with the 6 cups cold water. Bring to boiling; reduce heat. Simmer for 2 minutes. Remove from heat. Cover; let stand for 1 hour. (Or, soak beans in water overnight in covered pan.) Drain and rinse the beans.

In the same Dutch oven combine the rinsed beans, 6 cups hot water, the ham bone, onion, garlic, bay leaf, and red pepper. Bring to boiling; reduce heat. Cover and simmer about 2½ hours or till the beans are tender, adding more water, if necessary, and stirring occasionally.

Remove ham bone or hocks. When ham bone is cool enough to handle, cut meat from bone; discard bone. Chop meat; return to pan. Stir in sausage. Cook gently, uncovered, for 15 to 20 minutes more or till a thick gravy forms, stirring the mixture occasionally. Serve over hot cooked rice. Sprinkle with green onion. Makes 8 servings.

MUFFULETTA

  ½ **cup chopped pimiento-stuffed olives**
  ½ **cup chopped ripe olives**
  ½ **cup chopped celery**
  ½ **cup chopped mixed pickled vegetables**
  ⅓ **cup olive *or* salad oil**
  ¼ **cup snipped parsley**
  3 **tablespoons lemon juice**
  1 **clove garlic, minced**
  1 **teaspoon dried oregano, crushed**
Several dashes freshly ground pepper
  1 **recipe Muffuletta Loaf (see recipe, right) *or* one 1½-pound loaf purchased Italian bread**
  4 **ounces thinly sliced Genoa salami**
  4 **ounces sliced provolone *or* mozzarella cheese**
  4 **ounces sliced cappicola *or* fully cooked ham**
Lettuce leaves (optional)

In a medium mixing bowl combine the pimiento-stuffed olives, ripe olives, celery, pickled vegetables, olive or salad oil, parsley, lemon juice, garlic, oregano, and pepper. Cover and chill in the refrigerator for 8 hours or overnight, tossing once or twice.

To assemble the sandwich, cut the loaf of bread in half horizontally. Cut a ½-inch-thick slice from the cut side of the bottom half of the bread. (Wrap slice and use another time.)

Drain the olive mixture, reserving the liquid. Brush the cut sides of bread with some of the reserved liquid. Layer bottom of bread loaf with the sliced salami, provolone or mozzarella cheese, cappicola or ham, and the olive mixture. Top with lettuce leaves, if desired. Cover with the top half of the bread. Cut the sandwich into six wedges to serve. Makes 6 servings.

MUFFULETTA LOAF

2½ **to 3 cups all-purpose flour**
  1 **package active dry yeast**
  ¾ **teaspoon salt**
  1 **cup warm water (115° to 120°)**
  1 **slightly beaten egg white**
  1 **tablespoon water**
Sesame seed

In a large mixer bowl combine *1 cup* of the flour, the yeast, and the salt. Add the 1 cup warm water to the flour mixture. Beat with an electric mixer on low speed for ½ minute, scraping sides of the bowl. Beat with the electric mixer on high speed for 3 minutes.

Using a spoon, stir in as much remaining flour as you can. Turn out onto a lightly floured surface. Knead in enough of the remaining flour to make a moderately stiff dough that is smooth and elastic (6 to 8 minutes total). Shape the dough into a ball; place in a lightly greased bowl, turning once to grease the surface. Cover and let rise in a warm place till double (about 1 hour).

Punch the dough down; turn out onto a lightly floured surface. Cover and let rest for 10 minutes. Shape the dough into a ball; place on a greased baking sheet. Using the palm of your hand, flatten the dough slightly to form a 6-inch circle.

Combine the egg white and the 1 tablespoon water. Brush the loaf with the egg white mixture and sprinkle with sesame seed. Cover and let rise in a warm place till nearly double (30 to 40 minutes). Bake in a 375° oven about 40 minutes or till done. Remove the bread from the baking sheet. Place on a wire rack to cool. Makes 1 loaf.

BEIGNETS

Beignet is the French word for fritter. This New Orleans favorite is especially good served with French roast coffee with chicory.

2¾ to 3¼ cups all-purpose flour
  1 package active dry yeast
  ½ teaspoon ground nutmeg
     (optional)
  1 cup milk
  ¼ cup sugar
  2 tablespoons shortening
  ½ teaspoon salt
  1 egg
Shortening *or* cooking oil for
     deep-fat frying
Powdered sugar

In a large mixer bowl stir together *1½ cups* of the flour, the yeast, and the nutmeg, if desired. In a saucepan heat the milk, sugar, shortening, and salt just till warm (115° to 120°) and the shortening is almost melted; stir constantly.

Add the heated mixture to the flour mixture. Add the egg. Beat with an electric mixer on low speed for ½ minute, scraping sides of bowl. Beat for 3 minutes on high speed. Using a spoon, stir in enough of the remaining flour to make a soft dough.

Place dough in a greased bowl; turn once to grease the surface. Cover bowl and refrigerate the dough till well chilled.

Turn the dough out onto a lightly floured surface. Cover; let rest for 10 minutes. Roll into an 18x12-inch rectangle; cut into 36 3x2-inch rectangles. Cover; let rest for 30 minutes (dough will not be doubled).

Fry the dough rectangles, 2 or 3 at a time, in deep hot fat (375°) about 1 minute or till golden, turning once. Drain on paper towels. Sift powdered sugar atop. Makes 36.

CALAS

Serve these sweet Creole rice fritters with maple syrup.

  ½ cup long grain rice
  1 package active dry yeast
  ¼ cup warm water (110° to 115°)
  3 beaten eggs
1¼ cups all-purpose flour
  ⅓ cup sugar
  ½ teaspoon salt
  ¼ teaspoon ground nutmeg
Shortening *or* cooking oil for
     deep-fat frying

Cook the rice according to package directions, *except* increase the cooking time to 25 minutes. Drain the liquid. In a large mixing bowl mash the hot cooked rice. Let rice cool to lukewarm.

Dissolve the yeast in the warm water; stir the yeast mixture into the rice. Cover and let the mixture stand in a warm place overnight.

At serving time, stir the beaten eggs into the yeast mixture. Combine flour, sugar, salt, and nutmeg; add to yeast mixture. Stir till well mixed. Cover and let rise in a warm place about 30 minutes or till light.

Drop the batter by rounded tablespoons into hot fat (365°). Fry fritters, a few at a time, for 2 to 3 minutes or till golden. Drain the fritters on paper towels. Serve immediately. Makes about 25 fritters.

DOBERGE CAKE

Bake two layers at a time if you are limited to two cake pans.

  1 recipe Lemon Filling
2¼ cups all-purpose flour
  2 teaspoons baking powder
  ⅛ teaspoon salt
  ½ cup butter *or* margarine,
     softened
  ¼ cup shortening
1½ cups sugar
  1 teaspoon vanilla
  3 egg yolks
  ¾ cup milk
  3 stiff-beaten egg whites
  1 recipe Lemon Icing
Finely shredded lemon peel (optional)
Lemon leaves (optional)

Prepare and cool the Lemon Filling. Grease and lightly flour three 8x1½-inch round baking pans; set aside. Stir together flour, baking powder, and salt.

In a large mixer bowl beat butter or margarine and shortening for 30 seconds. Add sugar and vanilla; beat till light and fluffy. Add egg yolks, one at a time, beating 1 minute after each addition. Add dry ingredients and milk alternately to beaten mixture, beating till blended. Fold in egg whites.

To make the six cake layers, pour a generous ¾ cup batter into *each* prepared pan, spreading evenly over the bottom of pan. Bake in a 375° oven for 10 to 12 minutes or till cakes test done. Cool 5 minutes in pans. Remove; cool on wire racks. Wash, grease, and flour pans. Spoon the remaining cake batter into the three pans. Bake and cool as directed above.

To assemble, place one cake layer on plate. Spread a scant ½ *cup* of the Lemon Filling evenly atop. Repeat with four more layers and filling. Top with final layer. Cover and chill thoroughly.

Spread Lemon Icing over top and sides of cake. Cover; chill several hours or overnight. Sprinkle top with shredded lemon peel and garnish with lemon leaves, if desired. Makes 16 servings.

Lemon Filling: In a saucepan combine 1¼ cups *sugar*, 3 tablespoons *cornstarch*, 3 tablespoons *all-purpose flour*, and dash *salt*. Stir in 1½ cups *cold water*; cook and stir till thickened and bubbly. Cook and stir 2 minutes more.

Stir *1 cup* of the hot mixture into 3 beaten *egg yolks*. Return mixture to saucepan. Bring mixture to a gentle boil. Cook and stir 2 minutes more. Remove from heat.

Stir in 2 tablespoons *butter* or *margarine* and ½ teaspoon finely shredded *lemon peel*. Gradually stir in ⅓ cup *lemon juice*; mix well. Cover surface with clear plastic wrap. Cool the mixture to room temperature without stirring. Makes 2¼ cups.

Lemon Icing: In a mixer bowl beat one 3-ounce package *cream cheese*, softened, and 1½ cups sifted *powdered sugar* till fluffy. Add 1 teaspoon finely shredded *lemon peel* and ¼ teaspoon *vanilla* and beat till smooth. Makes ⅔ cup icing.

JUNE

Outdoor living: 19 fabulous projects for your yard, deck, porch, patio

Better Homes
and Gardens.

June 1984 • $1.50

Restyling your kitchen: Great low-cost ideas

Step by step: How to build railings and fences

Parenting: Finding the best day care for your child

32 RECIPES
PERFECT SUMMER MEALS

TROPICAL FRUIT MEDLEY
RECIPE INSIDE

SUMMER EATING, TROPICAL STYLE

By Joy Taylor

*S*ummer is synonymous with carefree living and fun, and that's what your cooking should be, too. Cooks in such tropical regions as Southeast Asia, the South Pacific, and the Caribbean Islands parlay their native foods into refreshing meals with minimal effort. Now, you and your family can savor equatorial treats at home with our 20 tropically inspired recipes. The easy-to-do recipes for outdoor cooking, everyday main dishes and desserts, and a complete entertaining menu feature authentic ingredients available in specialty shops, along with their more common supermarket substitutes.

CAREFREE OUTDOOR COOKING

Twelve months a year, alfresco dining prevails in hot and humid locales. Although most of the cooking traditionally occurs over a pit, these recipes are simplified for the grill.

Satay is to Indonesians what hamburgers are to Americans. **Lamb Satay** *(front left)* served with **Peanut Sauce** pays homage to this nationally famous food. An orange marinade doubles as a basting sauce for Polynesian **Marinated Fish Steaks** *(back left)*. If you've visited Hawaii, you've probably sampled a rendition of **Grilled Laulau** *(back right)*. Here, each ti leaf holds bacon, fish, chicken, and spinach. For a fuss-free meal, a la the Caribbean, consider **Roast Pork Calypso** *(front right)* with plantains.

Photographs: William K. Sladcik, Inc.
Food stylist: Fran Paulson

LIGHT and EASY MAIN DISHES

Replace steamy meals in the summertime with refreshing culinary creations. Surprisingly—and deliciously—some of the most satisfying dishes from the tropics are spicy hot!

Made-ahead delicacies, such as **Red Snapper with Avocado Sauce** *(back left)*, can help you put the chill in summer eating. When time allows, poach the whole fish, blend the creamy sauce, and refrigerate both. For a meal in a snap, line a platter with cilantro and top with the cooked fish and lime-enlivened sauce.

Tropical Scallop Salad *(back right)* combines a variety of ingredients found throughout the Caribbean and South Pacific Islands. For dinnertime convenience, you season the seafood, chicken, and carrots in a pineapple-wine dressing several hours before serving. Adorn the salad with cream-cheese-stuffed litchis and guava slices.

Stuffed Edam Cheese *(center)* personifies Latin American dining that's festive and easy on the cook, too. The hollowed cheese round holds a peppery shrimp and tomato filling. Serve **Cassava Biscuits** *(right)*, a Caribbean favorite, with this impressive entrée.

Egg roll lovers in your family will clamor for **Lumpia** *(left front)*—the Philippine version of this Chinese concoction. To add fun to the occasion, make this a participation meal. Let each person fill a shallow-fat-fried skin with a spiced pork and vegetable mixture. Include plum sauce or sweet soy sauce at the table for dipping.

SPLENDID DESSERTS and SIPPERS

Dreams of faraway islands inevitably include tantalizing thoughts of fruit-based desserts and tall sippers. This lineup of first-rate treats will fulfill all of your sweet fantasies.

Exotic fruits are common in all tropical countries because of similar climates. Super-quick *Tropical Fruit Medley (front left)* demonstrates Jamaican-style use of the bountiful produce. Carambola (star fruit), kiwi, berries, orange sections, and figs are capped with strawberry or cactus pear puree and whipped cream.

Tahitians make first-class use of papayas in such desserts as *Cheese-Stuffed Papayas (back left)*. Serve this luscious fruit, filled with spiced ricotta cheese, warm from the oven.

When humid days hover, fend off the heat with *Pineappleade (in pitcher)* or *Tamarind Slush (center)*. It's easy when you stash these refreshers in the refrigerator. For a silky-smooth sipper in seconds, whirl together fruit and milk for *Mango Frappé (back right)*.

The island of Curaçao stakes claim to two-layer *Rum-Ginger Mousse (right)*. Blue orange-flavored Curaçao liqueur colors the bottom half of this whipped-cream creation; rum and ginger mellow the top portion. It's an ideal chill-before-serving dessert.

If you're a coconut connoisseur, *Haupia (front right)* is the dessert for you. These Hawaiian molds are based on just three ingredients—coconut milk, sugar, and cornstarch. Garnish each portion with sliced guava or peaches and toasted coconut; serve them with *Raisin Anise Pralines.*

A RIJSTTAFEL for a SUMMER PARTY

For a novel party scheme, adapt an Indonesian idea. The *Rijsttafel* (RYE-sta-ful), an elaborate food affair, is an ideal summer buffet. The menu provides a variety of contrasts: meat—seafood; spicy—bland; sweet—sour; crisp—soft; hot—cold. Follow custom and sample each specialty with hot rice. For a no-fuss parade of food, divvy up the recipes among friends to stage the potluck.

Aromatic dishes highlight the dinner. Cumin spikes **Skewered Meatballs with Banana** *(front right)*. **Sweet Beef Braise** *(middle right)* owes its exceptional flavor to sweet soy sauce and a mixed bag of spices. The provocative sauce for **Coconut Chicken** *(front left)* starts with fresh coconut milk plus garlic, coriander, turmeric, lemongrass, red pepper, and tamarind.

A trayful of accompaniments *(middle left)* rounds out the menu. Shape and chill **Fish and Crabmeat Fritters**, then fry them during the party. **Pickled Cucumber Slices** counter the spicy-hot foods. Fry **Crisp Shrimp Wafers** and store till needed.

Follow Rijsttafel tradition and shape **Festive Rice** *(back left)* into a cone. Temper palates with **Mixed Vegetable Salad** *(center back)*. Peanut Sauce accentuates the layers of vegetables and tofu. Two fiery side dishes—**Sambal Condiment** and **Coconut Condiment** *(far right)*—complement all of the foods.

TROPICAL FLAVORS

5. Salam leaf—This Far Eastern variety of the bay leaf is available fresh and dried. Use it to flavor saucy dishes; discard the leaf before serving.

6. Litchi—A fresh litchi (also spelled lychee) resembles a strawberry; when the hard covering is removed, a white, sweet-tasting fruit is revealed. Most litchis available in America are canned. When dried, litchis are used like nuts.

7. Mango—The best way to enjoy the brilliant, juicy mango fruit is raw. This avocado-size fruit tastes somewhat like an apricot. A ripe mango ranges from green to yellow and red, depending on the variety. Purchase firm fruit and allow it to ripen at room temperature till soft to the touch, then chill. To serve, carefully cut the fruit away from the pit as you would a cling peach.

8. Papaya—This pear-shaped fruit is thin skinned and buttery tasting. Edible black seeds with a peppery flavor fill the center cavity. The skin of the papaya is similar to that of a green mango, and the two fruits often are mistaken for each other. Small spots on the papaya skin are signs of ripeness. Select yellowish fruit that yields slightly when pressed. Store ripe papayas in the refrigerator. Ripen green papayas at room temperature.

9. Plantain—Also called the cooking banana, the green plantain is longer and thicker than a banana and unsuitable for eating raw. Plantains, a starchy fruit, are best baked, broiled, or fried.

10. Shrimp wafers—These seafood-seasoned dried chips swell into crisp and puffy wafers when deep fried. After opening a wafer package, securely wrap any remaining uncooked wafers to ensure puffing.

11. Tamarind—The tart-tasting pod from the tamarind tree is used to create distinctive beverages, candies, chutneys, and curries in Indonesian cooking. In addition to the pods, you'll find tamarind dried and in paste form. Soften tamarind in a small amount of water before using.

12. Lemongrass—Also called sereh, this Southeast Asian lemon-flavored grass is available fresh, as dried blades, or as a powder. Use it in meat, fish, poultry, and vegetable dishes. Remove the fresh or dried pieces from the dish before serving.

Photograph: Hedrich-Blessing

*S*ome of the ingredients used in the tropical dishes on the preceding pages may be uncommon to you. To locate these exotic items you'll probably need to browse a gourmet food shop, Oriental shop, or Latin American grocery store. But first, familiarize yourself with the specialties listed here.

1. Ti leaf—Use the shiny oblong leaf from the ti (pronounced "tee") plant to enclose or decorate food. (The leaf is too tough for eating.) You can purchase Pacific Island-grown ti leaves through most florists. Wrap leaves in plastic wrap and chill to keep them fresh for several weeks.

2. Carambola—Also called star fruit, this wonderful treat has a mild flavor and may be sweet or sour, depending on the variety. The juicy flesh, protected by a waxy, edible skin, is best eaten raw.

3. Laos—This Southeast Asian seasoning, available ground and sliced, is related to the ginger family. You should use small amounts of laos (pronounced "LAH-ohs") to flavor meat, poultry, and vegetable dishes.

4. Annatto seeds—Mexicans call these seeds achiote. Used for subtle flavoring, annatto seeds also impart a reddish color to foods. To use annatto, crush the seeds to a fine powder with a mortar and pestle.

LAMB SATAY

Traditionally, vegetables are not a component of Indonesian satay (sah-TAY), but for a colorful accent you may want to add green pepper squares to each kabob before cooking.

- ½ of a small onion, finely chopped
- 2 cloves garlic, chopped
- 2 tablespoons Sweet Soy Sauce (see recipe, right)
- 1 tablespoon cooking oil
- 1 teaspoon sugar
- 1 teaspoon ground cumin
- 1 teaspoon finely snipped dried tamarind pulp *or* tamarind paste
- ¼ teaspoon salt
- 1½ pounds boneless lean lamb, cut into 1-inch pieces
- Coconut Milk (see recipe, right) *or* milk
- 1 recipe Peanut Sauce (see recipe, right)
- Red Pepper Flower (optional)
- Hot cooked rice (optional)

Using a mortar and pestle, crush together the onion, garlic, Sweet Soy Sauce, oil, sugar, cumin, tamarind, and salt. (Or, combine the ingredients in a blender container. Cover and blend till smooth.) Place meat pieces in a large bowl; add the soy mixture and stir to coat. Cover and marinate for 2 hours at room temperature or for 4 to 6 hours in the refrigerator.

Thread lamb onto 6 long skewers or 12 short skewers. Grill kabobs over *hot* coals for 12 to 15 minutes, turning once and brushing occasionally with the Coconut Milk. While grilling, place Peanut Sauce in a small saucepan atop grill to heat through. Garnish kabobs with Red Pepper Flower, if desired. Pass the warm sauce to serve with the kabobs and rice. Makes 6 servings.

Red Pepper Flower: Using a small paring knife, cut one whole *red chili pepper* into thin strips, keeping stem end intact. Immerse in ice water for several hours to curl ends; drain.

SWEET SOY SAUCE

You can substitute purchased sweet soy sauce from Oriental food shops for this homemade version.

- 1½ cups sugar
- ¾ cup water
- ¾ cup soy sauce
- 1 star anise, finely crushed

In a heavy 10-inch skillet heat the sugar over medium heat till it begins to melt, without stirring. Once the sugar begins to melt, cook and stir for 2 to 3 minutes or till golden.

Remove skillet from heat; slowly and *carefully* stir in the water, soy sauce, and anise. (Adding liquid to hot sugar may cause spattering.) Return the skillet to heat. Bring to boiling; reduce heat. Simmer about 15 minutes or till the mixture is slightly thickened and the caramelized sugar is dissolved, stirring constantly. Cool.

Skim off foam and any anise pieces that float to the top. Using a small sieve, strain to remove any additional crushed anise. To store, place in a tightly covered container and chill. Makes about 1⅔ cups.

PEANUT SAUCE

For a spicier version of this versatile sauce, stir in ¼ teaspoon ground red pepper or 1 teaspoon grated gingerroot.

- ½ cup finely chopped onion
- 1 clove garlic, minced
- 1 tablespoon butter *or* margarine
- 1 4-ounce can green chili peppers, rinsed, seeded, and chopped
- 2 tablespoons lemon juice
- 1 teaspoon brown sugar
- ½ teaspoon anchovy paste (optional)
- 1½ cups Coconut Milk (see recipe, right) *or* water
- 1 cup peanut butter

In a saucepan cook onion and garlic in butter or margarine till tender. Stir in chili peppers, lemon juice, sugar, and anchovy paste, if desired. Mix well.

Combine Coconut Milk and peanut butter; add to onion mixture. Cook and stir till mixture is smooth and heated through (do not boil). Cover surface with plastic wrap; cool. Makes 3 cups.

COCONUT MILK

When this Coconut Milk is chilled, a thin layer may form on the top. In this case, warm the milk over low heat till the fat in this layer dissolves. Canned coconut milk is a handy alternative to this tropical staple. If you purchase canned coconut milk, be sure to select the type that has no sugar added.

- 1 fresh coconut
- Water

Pierce coconut eyes with an ice pick; drain and reserve liquid. Crack the shell with a hammer and remove. Peel off brown skin from coconut meat. Rinse and coarsely chop the coconut meat; set aside. Add water to the coconut liquid to measure 2 cups. Heat liquid almost to boiling.

Place about *half* of the coconut pieces in a blender container. (Do not use a food processor; mixture may overflow bowl.) Add *1 cup* of the warm coconut liquid. Cover tightly and blend for 45 to 60 seconds or till finely ground. Transfer the mixture to a cheesecloth-lined sieve. Repeat with the remaining chopped coconut and liquid.

Press the coconut mixture through the sieve, squeezing as much liquid out of coconut as possible. Store the coconut milk in a tightly covered container in refrigerator. Use the pressed coconut in Coconut Condiment (see recipe, page 96). Makes about 2 cups milk.

Easy Coconut Milk: Stir together 1½ cups *packaged grated unsweetened coconut* and 2 cups *boiling water.* Let stand for 5 minutes.

Place mixture in a blender container. Cover and blend for 1 minute. Transfer mixture to cheesecloth-lined sieve. Press mixture through the sieve, squeezing out as much liquid as possible. Store as directed above. Makes about 1½ cups milk.

GRILLED LAULAU

Instead of using the ti, cabbage, or romaine leaves, you can spoon the filling onto eight 12x6-inch foil rectangles. Close bundles and cook as directed.

- 8 **ounces bacon, cut up**
- 1 **whole large chicken breast, skinned, boned, and cut into thin strips**
- 1 **cup sliced green onion**
- 10 **ounces torn fresh spinach** *or* **chopped bok choy (about 6 cups)**
- 8 **ounces fresh** *or* **frozen fish fillets, thawed and cubed**
- ½ **cup water**
- ¼ **cup Coconut Milk (see recipe, page 89), (optional)**
- 16 **ti leaves,** *or* **8 large cabbage** *or* **romaine leaves**

For filling, in a 10- or 12-inch skillet cook the bacon till crisp. Drain bacon pieces on paper towels, reserving *2 tablespoons* drippings in skillet. Cook the chicken strips and green onion in hot drippings for 4 to 5 minutes or till chicken is tender. Add the spinach or bok choy; cook and stir for 1 to 2 minutes or till slightly wilted. Transfer the mixture to a mixing bowl.

Add the fish and water to skillet. Bring to boiling; reduce heat. Cover and simmer about 5 minutes or till fish flakes easily when tested with a fork; drain. Add fish and bacon to the chicken mixture. If necessary, stir Coconut Milk into mixture to moisten.

Remove the stiff center rib from the underside of each ti leaf by running a sharp knife along the rib, continuing through the stem to remove an 8- to 10-inch strip. Soften the strip by pressing with a rolling pin. Remove and discard any remaining stems from leaves. (Or, immerse the cabbage or romaine leaves in boiling water for 2 to 3 minutes or till leaves are limp; drain. Remove and discard the center rib from each leaf.)

For *each* serving, place ½ *cup* of the filling near one end of a ti leaf. Tuck the tip of the ti leaf under the filling; roll up the leaf around filling. Roll a second ti leaf around the bundle to enclose filling, as shown. Secure bundle with a reserved midrib or string. (Or, wrap one cabbage or romaine leaf around ½ *cup* filling; tie with string.)

Arrange the bundles on a steamer rack set in a shallow baking pan. Add boiling water to the pan to a depth of 1 inch. Place the baking pan on a grill over *hot* coals. Cover the grill. Cook for 15 to 20 minutes, adding more water to pan if necessary. (Or, place bundles on rack over hot water in a Dutch oven. Cover and simmer over medium-low heat for 15 to 20 minutes.) To serve, transfer the bundles to a serving platter; slit open with a sharp knife. Makes 8 side-dish servings.

MARINATED FISH STEAKS

- 4 **fresh** *or* **frozen salmon steaks (about 1 inch thick)**
- ⅓ **cup orange juice**
- ⅓ **cup soy sauce**
- 2 **tablespoons snipped parsley**
- 2 **tablespoons cooking oil**
- 1 **clove garlic, crushed**
- ½ **teaspoon dried basil, crushed**

Thaw fish, if frozen. Place fish in a shallow dish. For marinade, combine the orange juice, soy sauce, parsley, oil, garlic, and basil; pour over fish. Let stand at room temperature for 2 hours or in the refrigerator for 4 to 6 hours, turning the steaks occasionally.

Drain the fish, reserving the marinade. Place fish in a well-greased wire grill basket or directly on the grill. Grill over *medium-hot* coals about 8 minutes or till fish is light brown. Baste with marinade and turn. Grill for 8 to 10 minutes more or till fish flakes easily when tested with a fork.

Meanwhile, heat the remaining marinade to boiling. Transfer the fish to a serving platter. Drizzle marinade over each serving. Makes 4 servings.

ROAST PORK CALYPSO

Have your butcher loosen the backbone of the roast.

- 3 **cups hickory chips**
- 1 **5-pound pork loin center loin roast**
- ½ **cup packed brown sugar**
- 2 **tablespoons rum**
- 2 **cloves garlic, minced**
- 1 **teaspoon finely shredded lime peel**
- 1 **teaspoon ground ginger**
- ¼ **teaspoon ground cloves**
- 1 **bay leaf, crumbled**
- ¼ **teaspoon salt**
- **Dash pepper**
- 4 *or* 5 **large ripe plantains**
- ¼ **cup butter** *or* **margarine, melted**
- **Lime slices, halved**
- **Lemon balm (optional)**
- **Bok choy blossom (optional)**

About an hour before cooking, soak hickory chips in enough water to cover; drain chips. Using a sharp knife, make a 1-inch-deep slash between each rib on the fat side of the roast, about eight slashes in all.

In a small mixing bowl stir together the brown sugar, rum, garlic, lime peel, ginger, cloves, bay leaf, salt, and pepper. Spoon about *½ teaspoon* of the spice mixture into *each* slash in meat.

Insert a meat thermometer in the center of the roast, without touching bone or fat. Arrange *medium-slow* coals around drip pan. Add hickory chips to coals. Place roast on grill rack over drip pan. Grill, covered, about 2 hours or till meat thermometer registers 160°.

Meanwhile, cut off ends of plantains. Peel and cut in half crosswise, then lengthwise. Brush plantains with melted butter or margarine; wrap in foil. Place plantains on grill over coals when the meat thermometer registers 160°. Spread the remaining spice mixture over top of roast.

Grill meat and plantains for 10 to 15 minutes more or till thermometer registers 170°. To serve, insert lime slices into slashes in roast. Garnish with lemon balm and a bok choy blossom, if desired. Makes 10 servings.

RED SNAPPER WITH AVOCADO SAUCE

- 1 3- to 4-pound fresh *or* frozen dressed red snapper *or* other fish (with tail)
- 4 cups water
- ½ of a lime, sliced
- 1 large onion, sliced and separated into rings
- ¼ cup snipped parsley
- 2 large cloves garlic, crushed
- 6 whole black peppers, crushed
- 1 teaspoon dried thyme, crushed
- 1 teaspoon dried oregano, crushed
- 1 recipe Avocado Sauce (see recipe, right)

Cilantro (optional)
Lemon and lime slices, quartered (optional)
Pitted ripe olives (optional)
Cherry tomatoes (optional)
- 1 avocado, halved lengthwise and seeded

Thaw fish, if frozen. In a fish poacher combine the water, lime, onion, parsley, garlic, pepper, thyme, and oregano. Bring to boiling; reduce heat. Cover and simmer for 5 minutes.

Lightly sprinkle fish cavity with salt. Place fish on a large piece of cheesecloth; fold cloth over fish. Place on rack in poaching pan. Immerse in boiling poaching liquid. (If necessary, add another ½ to 1 cup boiling water to nearly cover fish.) Cover and poach fish for 25 to 30 minutes or till fish flakes easily when tested with a fork. Remove from pan. Cool. Wrap fish in foil. Chill fish thoroughly. Meanwhile, prepare Avocado Sauce.

At serving time, unwrap and arrange fish on cilantro-lined platter. If desired, garnish with lemon and lime slices, olives, and tomatoes. Spoon some Avocado Sauce atop fish. Spoon remaining sauce into avocado halves and place on platter to serve with fish. To serve, cut fish crosswise into serving-size portions and remove bones. Makes 6 to 8 servings.

Note: If you like, you can substitute 2 pounds *fresh* or *frozen red snapper fillets* for the whole fish. In a 12-inch skillet combine enough water to cover fillets, plus the lime, onion, parsley, garlic, pepper, thyme, and oregano. Poach fillets for 5 to 10 minutes or till fish flakes easily when tested with a fork. Serve as directed.

AVOCADO SAUCE

Chill any leftover sauce, covered, to serve as a dip with tortilla chips.

- 2 ripe avocados, seeded, peeled, and cut into chunks
- ½ cup chicken broth
- ¼ cup lime juice
- 1 tablespoon grated onion
- ⅛ teaspoon salt
- ⅛ teaspoon pepper
- ½ cup milk

In a blender container or food processor bowl combine avocado chunks, chicken broth, lime juice, onion, salt, and pepper. Cover; blend just till smooth. Turn into a bowl. Stir in milk. Cover and chill till needed. Makes 2 cups.

TROPICAL SCALLOP SALAD

Pineapple chunks and orange slices can easily replace the guava and mango slices.

- 1 recipe Tropical Dressing
- 3 cups water
- ¼ cup lime juice
- 1 whole large chicken breast, skinned and boned
- 8 ounces fresh *or* frozen bay scallops
- 1 cup carrot cut into julienne strips
- ½ of a 3-ounce package cream cheese, softened
- ¼ teaspoon ground ginger
- 5 litchis

Chinese cabbage leaves
- 2 green onions, cut lengthwise into strips
- 1 guava, sliced
- 1 mango, sliced
- ¼ cup macadamia nuts (optional)

Prepare Tropical Dressing; chill. In a 3-quart saucepan bring the water and lime juice to boiling. Add the chicken breast. Simmer, uncovered, for 25 to 30 minutes or till chicken is tender. Remove chicken and cool. Add scallops to the hot liquid. Simmer for 1 to 3 minutes or till opaque. Remove and cool. Cut chicken into strips.

Toss together ¼ *cup* of the chilled dressing with chicken; ¼ *cup* dressing with scallops; and ¼ *cup* dressing with carrots. Cover; chill foods separately. Cover; chill any remaining dressing.

Stir together the cream cheese and ground ginger. Using a pastry bag fitted with a star tip, pipe cream cheese mixture into litchis. Cover and chill.

At serving time, line a platter with Chinese cabbage leaves. In a blender container combine remaining dressing and reserved pineapple from Tropical Dressing. Cover; blend till smooth.

Arrange the chicken, scallops, and carrots on the platter; spoon the pineapple dressing over each. Place the stuffed litchis, green onion, guava, and mango on the platter. If desired, sprinkle nuts over all. Makes 4 servings.

Tropical Dressing: Drain and reserve the juice from one 8-ounce can *crushed pineapple* (juice pack). Cover pineapple and chill. Measure juice; add water to equal ½ cup liquid. In a saucepan combine the pineapple juice mixture, ¼ cup *white wine vinegar,* 3 tablespoons *salad oil,* ½ teaspoon finely shredded *lime peel,* 1 tablespoon *lime juice,* ¼ cup ground *nutmeg,* and ¼ teaspoon *paprika.* Blend in 2 teaspoons *cornstarch.* Cook and stir till thickened and bubbly. Cook and stir for 2 minutes more. Stir in ¼ cup *dry white wine.* Remove from heat. Cover and chill. Makes 1 cup.

CASSAVA BISCUITS

The grain used for these crunchy biscuits also may be called tapioca flour.

- 1 cup all-purpose flour
- 1 cup cassava meal, cassava flour, *or* farina
- 1 tablespoon baking powder
- 2 teaspoons sugar
- ½ teaspoon cream of tartar
- ½ teaspoon salt
- ½ cup lard
- 1 5⅓-ounce can evaporated milk

In a mixing bowl stir together flour, cassava meal, baking powder, sugar, cream of tartar, and salt. Cut in lard till the mixture resembles coarse crumbs. Make a well in center. Add milk. Stir just till dough clings together.

Knead gently on well-floured surface for 10 to 12 strokes. Roll or pat to ½-inch thickness. Cut dough with a 2½-inch biscuit cutter, dipping cutter into flour between cuts. Transfer dough to an ungreased baking sheet. Bake in a 350° oven about 15 minutes or till golden. Serve warm. Makes about 12.

STUFFED EDAM CHEESE

Bake the stuffed cheese only 10 minutes because longer baking will make the cheese stringy and difficult to serve.

- 1 4-pound round *or* two 2-pound rounds Edam cheese
- 1½ pounds fresh *or* frozen shrimp in shells
- 6 cups water
- 1 large onion, finely chopped
- 2 tablespoons Annatto Oil (see recipe, right) *or* cooking oil
- 2 medium tomatoes, peeled, seeded, and chopped
- 2 whole sweet pickles, finely chopped (3 tablespoons)
- ¼ teaspoon ground red pepper
- ½ cup soft bread crumbs
- 1 recipe Cassava Biscuits (see recipe, page 91)

Using a vegetable peeler, remove all the red skin from the cheese. Cut a thin slice from the top. Using a grapefruit knife and spoon, hollow out the cheese, leaving ½-inch-thick shell(s). Soak the cheese shell(s) in lukewarm water for 1 hour. Finely shred enough scooped-out cheese to make *1 cup*. (Reserve remaining scooped-out cheese for another use.)

For filling, thaw shrimp, if frozen. Peel and devein shrimp; remove tails except for three shrimp to use as garnish. Meanwhile, heat the 6 cups water to boiling. Add shrimp; simmer for 1 to 3 minutes or till shrimp turn pink. Drain and chop shrimp.

In a skillet cook the onion in hot oil till tender but not brown. Add the tomatoes, pickles, and red pepper. Simmer, uncovered, about 5 minutes or till thickened. Stir in the chopped shrimp, bread crumbs, and the 1 cup finely shredded cheese; heat for 1 minute.

Drain the cheese shell(s) and pat dry with paper towels. Place the 4-pound cheese shell in a 3-inch-deep casserole; or, place each 2-pound cheese shell in a 1-quart casserole. (Casserole(s) should be just large enough to hold the cheese.)

Spoon the warm filling into center of cheese shell(s). Bake, uncovered, in a 350° oven about 10 minutes or till sides of cheese just begin to melt. Remove cheese from oven. Garnish with reserved shrimp with tails. Serve immediately. To serve, cut into serving-size wedges. Serve with Cassava Biscuits. Makes 8 to 10 servings.

ANNATTO OIL

This oil adds a golden-red color to food.

- ½ cup cooking oil
- 2 tablespoons annatto seeds

In a small saucepan heat the oil over medium heat for 3 minutes. Stir in annatto seeds. Heat 1 minute more. Cool. Strain oil into a jar; cover. Store in refrigerator. Makes ½ cup.

LUMPIA

For a crisper taste, place a romaine leaf atop each egg roll skin before filling.

- 2 tablespoons cooking oil
- 1 medium onion, chopped
- 2 cloves garlic, minced
- 1 pound lean boneless pork, cut into ¼-inch cubes
- 8 ounces fresh green beans *or* one 9-ounce package frozen cut green beans (thawed), finely chopped
- ½ cup finely chopped celery
- 1 16-ounce can hearts of palm *or* two 8-ounce cans water chestnuts, finely chopped
- 1 cup finely shredded cabbage
- 1 cup fresh bean sprouts
- 3 tablespoons soy sauce
- Cooking oil
- 12 egg roll skins
- 1 recipe Sweet Soy Sauce (see recipe, page 89) *or* plum sauce

Preheat a wok or large skillet over high heat; add oil. Stir-fry onion and garlic in hot oil for 2 minutes. Add pork; stir-fry for 4 minutes more. Remove. Add beans and celery to wok; stir-fry for 3 minutes. Add the hearts of palm, cabbage, and bean sprouts; stir-fry for 2 minutes more. Remove from wok. Combine the meat and vegetables; stir in the soy sauce.

Brush a little oil onto a large skillet. Cook one egg roll skin, on one side only, about 1 minute or till light brown. Turn out onto paper towels. Repeat with remaining skins. (Add more oil to skillet, as needed.) To assemble, place *each* egg roll skin unbrowned side up. Using a slotted spoon, spoon about ⅓ *cup* filling onto *each* skin. Roll up egg roll skins around filling. Serve with sauce. Makes 6 servings.

TROPICAL FRUIT MEDLEY

Serve this fresh dessert in an Ice Bowl, as featured on page 79.

- 2 cactus pears, peeled, *or* 1½ cups fresh strawberries
- 6 cups assorted fresh fruit (sliced kiwi*, sliced carambola*, whole *or* sliced strawberries, orange sections, banana chunks*, quartered figs, cubed mango, sliced guava, *and/or* sliced papaya)
- ½ cup whipping cream
- 1 tablespoon sugar

If using cactus pears, use a sharp knife to trim ends. Trim off the skin in lengthwise strips. Cut up cactus pears or the 1½ cups strawberries. Press cactus pears through a sieve; discard seeds. (Or, place berries in blender container or food processor bowl. Cover and blend till smooth.) Cover and chill the fruit puree for at least 2 hours.

At serving time, place the 6 cups fruit in a large glass bowl or in an Ice Bowl. Beat whipping cream and sugar till soft peaks form. Spoon fruit puree over cut fruit; pipe whipped cream atop. (Or, gently spoon fruit puree into whipped cream; spoon over cut fruit.) Serve immediately. Makes 10 servings.
* Brush with lemon juice after slicing.

Note: For Ice Bowl: Select one 3½- or 4-quart bowl or casserole and one 1½-quart bowl or mold. Add 1½ inches of water to the large bowl. Freeze overnight or till firm. Center the small bowl on the ice inside the larger bowl. (If surface freezes unevenly, break up surface with an ice pick to center small bowl on ice.) Fill small bowl with rocks or dry beans to weigh down. Pour water into large bowl around small bowl. Freeze just till surface starts to harden. Stir and break up top layer of ice every 15 to 20 minutes for 1 to 1½ hours or till top layer is slushy. Arrange nontoxic flowers or leaves (pineapple ginger, freesia, tea roses, baby carnations, lilies) or fresh fruit slices in slush, pressing decorations against the outer side of large bowl. Alternate small flowers and leaves, allowing tips of leaves to stick up above surface. Freeze several hours or till firm. To unmold, remove rocks or dry beans. Pour warm water into small bowl; remove. Press a warm, damp cloth around outside of large bowl; remove. Freeze till needed.

CHEESE-STUFFED PAPAYAS

- 2 **large papayas, halved and seeded**
- 2 **3-ounce packages cream cheese, softened**
- ½ **cup ricotta cheese**
- ⅓ **cup raisins**
- 3 **tablespoons sugar**
- 2 **tablespoons butter** *or* **margarine, melted**
- 2 **tablespoons sugar**
- ½ **teaspoon ground cinnamon**

Lime slices (optional)

Trim the bottom of each papaya half so that it sits level. For filling, in a mixer bowl beat together cream cheese, ricotta cheese, raisins, and the 3 tablespoons sugar. Spoon some of the mixture into each papaya half.

Place the papaya halves in a shallow baking pan. Stir together butter or margarine, the 2 tablespoons sugar, and cinnamon; spoon over filling.

Place pan in a 400° oven. Pour boiling water into the pan around papayas to a depth of ¾ inch. Bake about 20 minutes or till heated through. Garnish with lime slices, if desired. Serve warm. To serve, halve each papaya half. Makes 8 servings.

HAUPIA

The cornstarch sufficiently thickens this pudding for small molds only; the pudding will not hold its shape in a large mold.

- 2 **cups Coconut Milk (see recipe, page 89)**
- ¼ **cup sugar**
- 2 **tablespoons cornstarch**

Sliced guava, peaches, *or* **strawberries**

Shredded coconut, toasted

In the top of a double boiler combine the Coconut Milk, sugar, and cornstarch. Place over, but not touching, boiling water. Cook and stir about 15 minutes or till thickened. Pour into six ½-cup oiled molds. Cover and chill till firm. To serve, unmold pudding; serve with fruit. Sprinkle coconut atop each serving. Makes 6 servings.

RUM-GINGER MOUSSE

Any orange-flavored liqueur can be used in place of the blue curaçao liqueur.

- ½ **cup sugar**
- 1 **envelope unflavored gelatin**
- 1¼ **cups milk**
- 3 **slightly beaten egg yolks**
- 3 **egg whites**
- 1 **cup whipping cream**
- 3 **tablespoons blue curaçao liqueur**
- 3 **tablespoons finely chopped crystallized ginger**
- 3 **tablespoons light rum**

Crystallized ginger (optional)

In a small saucepan stir together sugar and gelatin. Combine milk and egg yolks. Stir into saucepan; cook and stir till gelatin and sugar are dissolved. Remove from heat. Cover surface with clear plastic wrap. Chill about 2 hours or till mixture is the consistency of corn syrup, stirring several times.

Remove gelatin mixture from refrigerator (mixture will continue to set). Immediately begin beating egg whites till stiff peaks form (tips stand straight). Beat whipping cream till soft peaks form. When gelatin mixture is partially set (the consistency of unbeaten egg whites), fold in the beaten egg whites and whipped cream.

Divide the mixture in half. Stir the curaçao into half of the mixture; spoon into a glass bowl or six goblets. Chill till nearly set (15 to 20 minutes).

Stir the chopped ginger and rum into the remaining mixture. Leave at room temperature till curaçao mixture is set. Spoon the rum mixture atop the curaçao mixture. Cover; chill till firm. Garnish with ginger, if desired. Makes 6 servings.

TAMARIND SLUSH

Look in Oriental markets to find jars of pure tamarind paste and other products that have the tamarind diluted with water. Carefully read the product label to see if you're purchasing pure paste or a thinned version, then use the ingredient level suggested here.

- 1½ **cups boiling water**
- ¼ **cup finely snipped tamarind pulp, 2 tablespoons tamarind paste,** *or* **½ cup tamarind-water concentrate**
- ½ **cup sugar**

Carbonated water

Lemon balm (optional)

In a small mixing bowl pour the boiling water over the tamarind. Using the back of a wooden spoon, press the tamarind against the side of the bowl. Let stand, covered, at room temperature for 30 minutes. Add the sugar; stir till dissolved. Pour mixture into a 9x5x3-inch loaf pan. Cover and freeze till firm.

For *each* serving, use a spoon to scrape *¼ cup* of the tamarind mixture and put into a glass. Pour *¼ cup* carbonated water into glass. Stir to form a slush. If desired, garnish with lemon balm. Makes 1⅔ cups tamarind mixture or about 7 (4-ounce) servings.

MANGO FRAPPÉ

- 1½ **cups chopped mango** *or* **banana**
- ½ **cup milk**
- 2 **tablespoons sugar**
- 1 **tablespoon lime juice**
- ¼ **teaspoon vanilla**
- 4 to 6 **ice cubes**

Freeze chopped fruit for 30 minutes. In a blender container combine the fruit, milk, sugar, lime juice, and vanilla. Cover; blend till smooth. With blender running, add ice cubes through lid. Blend till thick and slushy. Pour into chilled glasses. Makes 2 servings.

PINEAPPLEADE

Reserve the cooked pineapple to serve over ice cream or cake.

  1 medium fresh pineapple
  2 cups water
  ¾ cup sugar
  ¼ cup lightly packed fresh mint leaves *or* 4 teaspoons dried mint, crushed
  2 tablespoons lime juice
Pineapple chunks (optional)

Remove crown from pineapple. Cut off the peel. Halve pineapple; cut out core. Finely chop pineapple (should have about 3 cups). Place chopped pineapple in a 2-quart saucepan. Add water and sugar. Bring to boiling; reduce heat. Cover and simmer for 15 minutes. Stir in mint. Let stand, covered, about 1½ hours or till cool. Strain; discard mint. Reserve pineapple for another use. Stir lime juice into pineapple liquid. Pour into jars. Cover and chill. To serve, pour liquid into a pitcher with ice cubes. If desired, garnish with a skewer of pineapple chunks. Makes about 3½ cups.

RAISIN ANISE PRALINES

This interesting candy may remind you more of penuche than of Southern-style pecan pralines.

  1½ cups granulated sugar
  1½ cups packed brown sugar
  1 cup whipping cream
  1½ cups light raisins
  3 tablespoons Anisette

Butter the sides of a heavy 3-quart saucepan. Stir together sugar, brown sugar, and cream in the saucepan. Bring to boiling over medium heat, stirring frequently. Cook to 234° (soft-ball stage), about 2 to 5 minutes, stirring only as necessary to prevent sticking. Remove from heat; do not stir. Let stand about 30 minutes or till mixture cools to 150°.

Meanwhile, combine raisins and liqueur; set aside. When candy mixture reaches 150°, stir in raisin mixture. Beat about 5 minutes or till thick and glossy. Drop candy from a tablespoon onto a baking sheet lined with waxed paper. If candy becomes too stiff, stir in a few drops hot water. Makes about 30.

SKEWERED MEATBALLS WITH BANANA

Combined with rice, these kabobs could serve five or six as an entrée.

  2 eggs
  1½ cups soft bread crumbs (2 slices)
  1 large onion, chopped (1 cup)
  ⅓ cup Coconut Milk (see recipe, page 89) *or* milk
  ¾ teaspoon salt
  ¾ teaspoon ground cumin
  ½ teaspoon ground nutmeg
  ¼ teaspoon ground cloves
  ¼ teaspoon pepper
  2 pounds ground beef
Chutney
  2 bananas, sliced into 2½-inch pieces and quartered

In a mixing bowl combine the eggs, bread crumbs, onion, Coconut Milk or milk, salt, cumin, nutmeg, cloves, and pepper. Add beef; mix well. Shape mixture into 20 mini-loaves, 2½ inches long and 1 inch wide. Cover and chill.

At serving time, thread two 6-inch bamboo skewers through the widths of two mini-loaves so that skewers connect the mini-loaves. Repeat with the remaining mini-loaves and additional skewers to make 10 kabobs.

Place kabobs on unheated rack of broiler pan. Broil 5 inches from heat for 10 minutes; brush with chutney (if necessary, chop chutney). Turn kabobs. Broil for 8 minutes more. Add a banana slice to one end of each double skewer. Brush meat and banana with chutney. Broil for 2 minutes more. Serve kabobs with additional chutney. Makes 10 appetizer servings.

SWEET BEEF BRAISE

You'll find long Chinese beans in Oriental food shops or some large supermarkets. Steam them whole or halved.

  1½ pounds boneless beef chuck, cut into 1-inch pieces
  2 tablespoons cooking oil
  1½ cups water
  3 tablespoons Sweet Soy Sauce (see recipe, page 89)
  2 teaspoons grated gingerroot
  1 teaspoon wine vinegar
  ¼ teaspoon ground nutmeg
  ¼ teaspoon ground cloves
  ⅛ teaspoon pepper
  2 salam *or* bay leaves
  2 medium onions, cut into wedges
  12 ounces Chinese beans *or* pea pods
  2 tablespoons cold water
  1 tablespoon cornstarch

In a Dutch oven brown meat, *half* at a time, in hot oil. Drain off fat. Add water, Sweet Soy Sauce, gingerroot, vinegar, nutmeg, cloves, pepper, and salam or bay leaves. Bring to boiling; reduce heat. Cover; simmer for 40 minutes. Add onion wedges. Simmer, uncovered, about 20 minutes or till tender.

Meanwhile, place beans or pea pods in a steamer basket. Place over boiling water. Cover and steam for 20 to 30 minutes or till crisp-tender.

Remove the salam leaves. Combine cold water and cornstarch; stir into mixture. Cook and stir till bubbly. Cook and stir 2 minutes more. To serve, transfer to a platter; surround with beans. Garnish with hot peppers, if desired. Serve immediately. Serves 6 to 8.

Microwave directions: In a 3-quart nonmetal casserole combine the meat, *½ cup* water, Sweet Soy Sauce, gingerroot, vinegar, nutmeg, cloves, pepper, and salam leaves. Micro-cook, covered, on 50% power (MEDIUM) for 30 minutes, stirring once. Add onion.

Micro-cook about 10 minutes more or till meat and onion are tender. Remove leaves. Combine cold water and cornstarch; stir into meat mixture. Micro-cook on 100% power (HIGH) for 2 to 3 minutes or till thickened and bubbly, stirring after every minute. Keep warm. Arrange beans or pea pods in a 1-quart casserole. Add 2 tablespoons *water*. Micro-cook, covered, on 100% power (HIGH) for 2 to 3 minutes or till tender. Drain. Serve as directed.

COCONUT CHICKEN

This Southeast Asian dish also is called Opor Ajam.

  3 **pounds chicken legs and wings** *or* **one 2½- to 3-pound broiler-fryer chicken, cut up**
  2 **tablespoons cooking oil**
  ¼ **cup macadamia nuts**
  1 **large onion, chopped**
  2 **cloves garlic, minced**
  1 **teaspoon ground coriander**
  1 **teaspoon ground laos** *or* **grated gingerroot**
  ½ **teaspoon ground cumin**
  ¼ **teaspoon ground turmeric**
  ¼ **teaspoon finely snipped dried lemongrass** *or* **1 teaspoon finely shredded lemon peel**
  2 **cups Coconut Milk (see recipe, page 89)**
  1 **teaspoon sugar**
  ½ **teaspoon salt**
  ¼ **to ½ teaspoon ground red pepper**
  1 **tablespoon water**
  1 **teaspoon finely snipped tamarind pulp** *or* **tamarind paste**
  Cilantro (optional)
  Hot cooked rice

In a large skillet brown chicken pieces on both sides in hot oil for 15 minutes; remove from skillet. Set chicken aside, reserving 1 tablespoon drippings.

Meanwhile, place nuts in a blender container or food processor bowl. Cover and blend till finely ground.

For sauce, in reserved drippings cook the onion, garlic, coriander, laos or gingerroot, cumin, turmeric, and lemongrass or lemon peel till onion is tender but not brown. Stir in the ground nuts, Coconut Milk, sugar, salt, and red pepper. Return chicken to the skillet. Cover and simmer about 20 minutes or till chicken is tender.

Transfer chicken to a serving platter and keep warm. Stir water into tamarind. Stir tamarind into sauce. Gently boil the sauce, uncovered, till thickened and reduced (should measure about 1⅓ cups). Strain sauce, if desired. Spoon sauce over chicken. If desired, garnish with cilantro. Serve with hot cooked rice. Makes 6 servings.

FISH AND CRABMEAT FRITTERS

Serve these unique patties as an entrée or appetizer.

  12 **ounces fresh** *or* **frozen cod** *or* **flounder fillets**
  1 **6-ounce package frozen crab meat, thawed and drained**
  2 **beaten eggs**
  ⅓ **cup rice flour** *or* **all-purpose flour**
  1 **green onion, finely chopped**
  ½ **teaspoon finely shredded lemon peel**
  1 **teaspoon lemon juice**
  1 *or* **2 cloves garlic, minced**
  ¼ **teaspoon salt**
  ⅛ **teaspoon pepper**
  Cooking oil

Thaw fish fillets, if frozen. Using a fork, flake the raw fish. In a blender container or food processor bowl combine the flaked fish, crab, eggs, rice flour or all-purpose flour, chopped green onion, shredded lemon peel, lemon juice, garlic, salt, and pepper. Cover and blend till the mixture is smooth.

For *each* patty, spoon about *¼ cup* batter onto a hot, lightly greased large skillet, allowing space between each scoop; spread to 3-inch-wide patties. (Or, shape the patties several hours ahead. Cover and chill in the refrigerator till ready to cook.)

Cook the patties about 3 minutes on each side or till golden. Repeat with the remaining batter or patties. Keep the fritters warm in a 325° oven while frying remainder. Arrange on a serving platter. Makes 10 appetizer servings or 6 main-dish servings.

PICKLED CUCUMBER SLICES

Small servings of this spicy, yet refreshing, dish are sufficient.

  2 **medium cucumbers**
  ¼ **cup rice vinegar** *or* **white vinegar**
  3 **tablespoons lime juice**
  1 **tablespoon sugar**
  ¼ **teaspoon salt**
  1 **red chili pepper, seeded and sliced,** *or* **¼ teaspoon crushed red pepper**
  ¼ **cup finely chopped red onion (optional)**
  Lettuce leaves

Score cucumbers lengthwise; cut crosswise into ⅛-inch-thick slices. In a small saucepan combine the vinegar, lime juice, sugar, salt, and red pepper. Bring to boiling; reduce heat. Simmer for 2 minutes. Remove from heat. Pour over cucumber slices and toss to coat. Cover and chill till serving time.

Before serving, stir in red onion, if desired. Using a slotted spoon, transfer the cucumber mixture to a lettuce-lined plate. Makes about 3 cups.

CRISP SHRIMP WAFERS

You may find packages of this unique snack labeled krupuk. Purchase your choice of multicolored wafers or plain white ones. When cooked, the wafers should rise to the surface and puff within 5 seconds; older wafers may require more cooking time.

  Cooking oil for deep-fat frying
  8 **ounces dry shrimp wafers**

In a large saucepan or deep-fat fryer heat 2 to 3 inches cooking oil to 375°. Fry shrimp wafers, a few at a time, about 5 seconds or just till they puff and rise to top. Remove with a slotted spoon; drain on paper towels. Serve immediately or store in an airtight container for up to two days.

FESTIVE RICE

Indonesians call this cone-shape dish Nasi Kuning.

1½ cups long grain rice
1½ teaspoons ground turmeric
¼ teaspoon finely snipped dried lemongrass *or* 1 teaspoon finely shredded lemon peel
1 tablespoon cooking oil
3 cups Coconut Milk (see recipe, page 89)
2 salam leaves *or* bay leaves
¾ teaspoon salt
3 beaten eggs
1 tablespoon cooking oil
Fresh salam leaves (optional)
1 red *or* green sweet pepper, seeded and cut into strips

In a 3-quart saucepan cook and stir the uncooked rice, turmeric, and lemongrass or peel in the first 1 tablespoon oil for 2 minutes. Add the Coconut Milk, the salam or bay leaves, and salt. Bring to boiling; reduce heat. Cover and simmer over low heat about 15 minutes or till liquid is absorbed and rice is tender.

Meanwhile, in a 10-inch skillet cook the eggs in the remaining 1 tablespoon oil, without stirring, till set. Invert skillet over a baking sheet to remove cooked eggs; cut the eggs into short, narrow strips.

Remove and discard salam or bay leaves from rice. Press hot rice into an oiled 5-cup cone-shape mold. Place a serving plate upside down over the mold; invert to remove rice. Garnish top of rice with salam leaves, if desired. Arrange egg strips, red pepper strips, and salam leaves (if desired) around base of rice. Serve immediately. Makes 10 servings.

SAMBAL CONDIMENT

This meal accompaniment is especially good with fish dishes.

2 fresh hot red peppers
2 fresh hot green peppers
2 medium tomatoes, peeled, seeded, and finely chopped
¼ cup finely chopped shallots *or* green onions
1 teaspoon finely shredded lime peel
¼ cup lime juice

Cut peppers open. Discard stems and seeds. Finely chop peppers. In a small bowl combine the red and green hot peppers, tomatoes, shallots or green onions, lime peel, and juice. Cover; chill till serving time. Makes about 1¼ cups.

COCONUT CONDIMENT

If you haven't made Coconut Milk, substitute sweetened flaked coconut for the fresh. Bake only 10 to 15 minutes or till the coconut is dry.

2 cups grated fresh coconut from Coconut Milk (see recipe, page 89)
1 tablespoon brown sugar
1 tablespoon ground coriander
1 teaspoon finely snipped tamarind pulp (optional)
1 teaspoon ground cumin
½ teaspoon ground cardamom
¼ teaspoon salt
½ cup dry roasted cashews *or* peanuts, chopped

In a medium mixing bowl stir together grated coconut, brown sugar, coriander, tamarind (if desired), cumin, cardamom, and salt. Spread the mixture in a 15x10x1-inch baking pan. Bake in a 300° oven for 40 to 50 minutes or till the coconut is toasted and dry, stirring the mixture occasionally.

Add the cashews or peanuts. Cool completely. Store the condiment in an airtight container. Serve as a meal accompaniment with hot cooked rice. Makes about 2 cups.

MIXED VEGETABLE SALAD

Throughout Indonesia there are many variations of vegetables used in this salad, known as Gado-Gado.

1 recipe Peanut Sauce (see recipe, page 89)
8 ounces fresh bean curd (tofu)
1 tablespoon cooking oil
1 large onion, thinly sliced and separated into rings (optional)
8 ounces pea pods *or* green beans
2 cups cauliflower flowerets
3 carrots, cut into julienne strips
Lettuce leaves
3 hard-cooked eggs, chilled and sliced
2 cups fresh bean sprouts, snipped

Prepare Peanut Sauce; set aside. Place tofu in double thickness of cheesecloth or paper towels. Press gently to extract as much moisture as possible. Cut tofu into cubes; set aside.

If using onion, preheat a wok or medium skillet over medium-high heat; add cooking oil. Stir-fry the onion over medium-high heat for 4 to 5 minutes or till golden brown. Drain onion on paper towels.

In a covered saucepan cook pea pods or beans, cauliflower flowerets, and carrot strips in a small amount of boiling salted water about 5 minutes or till just crisp-tender; drain well.

Line a large serving platter with lettuce leaves. Arrange tofu cubes, carrots, cauliflower, pea pods or beans, egg slices, and bean sprouts in layers atop lettuce leaves. Top the vegetables with the cooked onion. Serve at room temperature or cover and chill. Pass Peanut Sauce to drizzle atop each serving. Makes 10 servings.

STEP-BY-STEP TO RE-SIDING YOUR HOUSE

Better Homes
and Gardens.

July 1984 • $1.50

Fabulous gardeners share their secrets

Start a successful business at home

New discoveries to help you lose weight

Recipes that make your parties perfect

A do-it-yourself dream house

Create country style in the suburbs

AMERICANS AT HOME

With great ideas you can use!
Projects you can do!

Great Party Fare

Our homes are the centers of our lives—havens of family love and comfort, places to enjoy and places to share. Here you'll meet three families who exemplify the sharing spirit. For them, entertaining is an expression of their personal styles—whether it means an elegant dinner with host and hostess acting as waiters, a re-creation of the artistic serenity of dining Japanese style, or a casual spur-of-the-moment outdoor buffet.

Like many two-career families, Bryan McCay and Ann Levine of Des Moines, Iowa, wish they could spend more time enjoying their home. So their philosophy is to make up in quality what they can't have in quantity.

They carefully furnished their architect-designed contemporary house with cozy warmth in mind. Their goal? To create an inviting haven, not only for themselves, but also for their frequent gatherings of family and friends. Ann is emphatic: "We are proud of our home, and whenever we can, we enjoy sharing it with the people we love."

It was this pride that inspired the couple to stage a festive at-home dinner party to honor Ann's father on his birthday. Four close friends of the Levines were asked to share the memorable evening. And to lend a special touch to the occasion, Bryan and Ann dressed up as waiters and served the elegant dinner in classic style.

To make sure that they themselves enjoyed the party as much as their guests, Ann and Bryan carefully planned the menu to include not only the guest-of-honor's favorite foods, but dishes that they could prepare ahead and have fun serving.

The splendid array of courses they provided is displayed on the opposite page. A colorful Four-Layer Party Hors d'Oeuvre started dinner on a festive note. In this elegant concoction, layers of sour cream, avocado, and hard-cooked eggs are crowned by caviar laced with lemon and a sprinkling of sliced green onions.

The Marinated Celery Hearts get their tang from chopped capers in the wine-and-chicken-broth marinade.

As a palate refresher before the main course, Ann and Bryan served icy Grapefruit Sorbet that's sweetened with honey and garnished with delicate shreds of grapefruit peel.

The scrumptiousness of Seafood Linguine develops out of the recipe's special ingredients—shrimp and fresh mushrooms in a rich sauce of whipping cream and egg yolk.

For Ann and Bryan's Fruit Crostada, assorted fruits top a pastry shell that's spread with sweetened cream cheese.

Photographs: Hedrich-Blessing.

Top left, Bryan and Ann; above left, their contemporary home; above, scene of the happy party.

*Opposite, **Seafood Linguine** (front), **Fruit Crostada** (center left), **Four-Layer Party Hors d'Oeuvre** (center right), **Grapefruit Sorbet** (back left), and **Marinated Celery Hearts** (back right).*

Recipes From Japan Your Family Will Love

Like many new Americans at home in our country today, the Jindo family brought with them an array of homeland traditions they are proud to share. The pleasures of preparing and serving their native foods are perhaps the most important.

For Hiro and Nobuko, recently settled in New York City, re-creating the artistic serenity of the Japanese dishes they grew up with is what home cooking is all about.

They like to prepare their weekend meals together, and their sons, Koki and Hideki, help—thus perpetuating the age-old culinary arts. The Jindos' meals usually consist of six to eight small courses that embody a variety of delicate flavors. One such course is *Fried Bean Curd Appetizers (above back)*. Each crisp-coated morsel contains tofu, a Japanese staple, and ground beef, an American favorite. *Salmon-Vegetable Soup (in dark bowls)* combines taro root, a tropical root with a potatolike flavor, and daikon, a large white Japanese radish. A marinade of gingerroot, soy sauce, and mirin, a light-tasting Japanese wine, flavors the chilled *Rolled Ginger Chicken (front)*.

Two other traditional Jindo delicacies *(opposite)* exemplify artful Japanese cooking. Bite-size bundles of beef sirloin and green onions are cooked in a soy-mirin sauce for *Green Onion and Beef Rolls (front)*. *Curry Fried Mackerel (back)* gets its flavor from the curried coating mixture.

Photographs: Maris/Semel

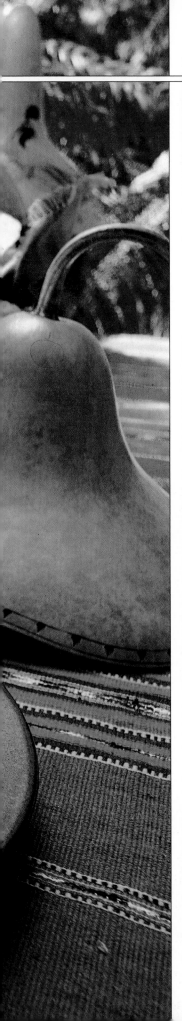

Foods For Family-Style Entertaining

Ridge and Leena Kunzel's San Diego home is on a cul-de-sac, which makes for a closely knit neighborhood where folks often drop in on one another. That suits the Kunzels just fine. Together with their sons Brent, 6, and Brook, 4, they like nothing better than to family-host spur-of-the-moment buffets. As Ridge points out, "We try to live our lives so that everything includes the boys *if* they want: Choice is vital." Of course, the kids—and their friends—are usually eager to join the fun.

Ridge, who describes his family as "seat-of-the-pants cooks," devises recipes on the spot with whatever Southwestern ingredients happen to be at hand. This goes for the guests, too. At a Kunzel buffet, everyone gets the chance to create a personalized meal by mixing and matching ingredients.

Build-Your-Own-Tacos or burritos *(opposite front)* are served from heat-holding gourds. ***Calabacita Filling*** and ***Chili Colorado*** are ladled onto tortillas to combine flavors of zucchini, corn, and two kinds of cheese with a beef chili.

Pollo Adobo *(left center)* combines grilled chicken with a chili-seasoned coating mixture. The coating is just as tasty served on beefsteaks.

The golden beverage, ***Aztec Tequila Punch*** *(back left),* has a tequila base enlivened with grapefruit juice and ginger ale. For a surprising chocolate dessert, turn to the next page.

Photographs: de Gennero Studios

Festive Finale

For dessert, Ridge often assembles **Tortilla Torte** *(above)*, which combines two favorite Mexican ingredients—flour tortillas and chocolate—and is easy to make. He simply stirs together melted semisweet chocolate with sour cream and spreads it between tortilla layers. Then he combines some sour cream and powdered sugar to top this delectable dessert. (Sometimes, for dessert he just serves **Sopaipillas**, a fried biscuitlike puff *(back right)*.

"My recipes are easily combined in bits and pieces," Ridge says. "It's a way of eating that lets you add guests at the drop of a hat. Your guests can come late or bring other guests, and children can come and go as they like. It reflects what I think of as the best aspect of the Southwestern life-style: freedom with togetherness."

To Ridge and Leena, home is central to this togetherness; so much so, in fact, that both Kunzels operate businesses out of their home. Ridge sells his handcrafted hard-shell gourds, and—when she is not working at a local accessories store—Leena designs table linens.

Not surprisingly, Brent and Brook are partners here, too. They help Dad with the gourds, and even made their own place mats for the dinner table.

The McCay-Levines

SEAFOOD LINGUINE

Linguine are long and thin flat noodles. You can substitute spaghetti noodles if you like.

    2 cups sliced fresh mushrooms
      (about 6 ounces)
    4 shallots *or* green onions, finely
      chopped
    ½ cup butter *or* margarine
    1½ cups Madeira wine
    1 tablespoon tomato paste
    1 tablespoon snipped fresh
      tarragon *or* 1 teaspoon dried
      tarragon, crushed
    ¼ teaspoon salt
Dash freshly ground black pepper
    10 ounces linguine, spaghetti,
      or other pasta
    1½ pounds fresh *or* frozen shelled
      shrimp
    4 beaten egg yolks
    1½ cups whipping cream
Fresh tarragon sprigs (optional)

In a 10-inch skillet cook mushrooms and shallots or green onions in the butter or margarine, uncovered, over medium-high heat for 4 to 5 minutes or till vegetables are tender but not brown. Remove with slotted spoon. Set aside.

Stir wine, tomato paste, tarragon, salt, and pepper into butter in the skillet. Bring to boiling; boil vigorously about 10 minutes or till mixture is reduced to ½ cup.

Meanwhile, cook pasta according to package directions. Drain and keep warm. Add fresh or frozen shrimp to boiling water; return to boiling. Reduce heat and simmer for 1 to 3 minutes or till shrimp turn pink. Drain shrimp and keep warm.

In a small mixing bowl stir together the egg yolks and whipping cream. Stir in the wine mixture. Return to skillet. Cook and stir till thickened. Stir in the shrimp and the mushroom mixture; heat through. Season to taste with salt and pepper. Toss with the cooked pasta. Transfer to a serving platter. Garnish with fresh tarragon sprigs, if desired. Makes 6 servings.

FRUIT CROSTADA

    1 cup all-purpose flour
    1 tablespoon sugar
    ¼ cup butter *or* margarine
    1 tablespoon shortening
    1 egg yolk
    1 8-ounce package cream cheese,
      softened
    1 3-ounce package cream cheese,
      softened
    ¼ cup sugar
    2 teaspoons finely shredded
      lemon peel
    1 tablespoon lemon juice
    1½ pounds bananas *and/or* peeled
      fresh peaches, thinly sliced
      (3 cups)
    1 to 1¼ cups fresh strawberries,
      sliced, *and/or* seedless green
      grapes, halved
    1 kiwi, peeled and thinly sliced
    ⅓ cup orange marmalade

In a mixing bowl combine flour, the 1 tablespoon sugar, and ⅛ teaspoon *salt*. Cut in butter and shortening till pieces are the size of small peas. Make a well in the center. Combine the egg yolk and 2 tablespoons cold *water*. Add to flour mixture. Using a fork, stir just till dough forms a ball. If necessary, add additional water, *1 tablespoon* at a time, till dough forms a ball.

Turn out onto a lightly floured surface. Knead three or four times. Roll dough from center to edge, forming a circle 14 inches in diameter. Fit the dough into an 11-inch flan pan, pressing gently to remove air bubbles. Trim edges, reserving trimmings for garnish.

Cover the bottom and sides of pastry with heavy foil; fill with dry beans. Bake in a 400° oven for 10 minutes. Remove the foil and beans. Bake for 5 to 10 minutes more or till golden. Set pastry aside to cool.

If desired, reroll trimmings. Cut out three leaves. Use dull side of knife to press veins into pastry leaves; shape leaves over small pieces of foil. Place on baking sheet. Bake in a 400° oven about 12 minutes or till golden.

Meanwhile, in a mixer bowl combine cream cheese, the ¼ cup sugar, lemon peel, and juice; beat till smooth. Spread onto bottom of baked pastry. Arrange the fruit atop cheese mixture. Melt marmalade; brush or spoon atop fruit. Chill several hours or overnight. Garnish with pastry leaves, if desired. Cut into wedges. Makes 12 servings.

THREE-LAYER PARTY HORS D'OEUVRE

Here's a lavish treat. You can afford to serve caviar when you use it as the star ingredient in this fancy hors d'oeuvre. The recipe calls for red caviar, but black or golden caviar works equally well.

    1 envelope unflavored gelatin
    ⅓ cup cold water
    1 8-ounce carton dairy sour cream
    2 medium avocados, seeded,
      peeled, and mashed
    2 tablespoons mayonnaise *or*
      salad dressing
    2 tablespoons lemon juice
    ¼ teaspoon salt
Dash bottled hot pepper sauce
    6 hard-cooked eggs, finely
      chopped
    ¼ cup mayonnaise *or* salad
      dressing
    2 tablespoons snipped parsley
    1 tablespoon chopped green onion
    ¼ teaspoon salt
    2 tablespoons red caviar, rinsed
      and drained
    1 teaspoon lemon juice
    2 tablespoons bias-sliced green
      onion
Assorted crackers

Lightly oil the bottom and sides of a 1-quart bowl. Soften gelatin in the water for 5 minutes. Cook and stir over medium heat till gelatin is dissolved.

For the first layer, stir together the sour cream and *2 tablespoons* of the gelatin mixture. Spread evenly in the bottom of prepared bowl. Chill about 20 minutes or till almost firm.

Meanwhile, for the second layer, combine the avocado, the 2 tablespoons mayonnaise or salad dressing, the 2 tablespoons lemon juice, ¼ teaspoon salt, hot pepper sauce, and *2 tablespoons* of the gelatin mixture. Spread avocado mixture evenly atop first layer. Chill about 20 minutes or till almost set.

For the third layer, in a bowl combine hard-cooked eggs, the ¼ cup mayonnaise, parsley, chopped green onion, ¼ teaspoon salt, and remaining gelatin mixture. Spread evenly over avocado layer. Cover and chill overnight.

To serve, carefully invert the mold onto a platter. Sprinkle the 1 teaspoon lemon juice over the caviar; spoon atop the mold. Sprinkle with the bias-sliced green onion. Serve with assorted crackers. Makes 6 to 10 servings.

GRAPEFRUIT SORBET

To prepare sugar-edged glasses as shown on pages 97 and 99, rub the rim of each glass with a little water. Invert glasses in a shallow dish filled with a mixture of sugar and ground nutmeg just to coat the rim.

  1½ **cups water**
  ½ **cup honey**
  2 **teaspoons finely shredded grapefruit peel**
  1 **cup unsweetened pink grapefruit juice**
  2 **teaspoons finely shredded lemon peel**
  ¼ **cup lemon juice**
  1 **or 2 drops red food coloring (optional)**
Finely shredded grapefruit peel

In a medium saucepan combine the water and honey. Bring to boiling; reduce heat. Simmer, uncovered, for 5 minutes. Cool. Add the 2 teaspoons finely shredded grapefruit peel, the grapefruit juice, finely shredded lemon peel, lemon juice, and food coloring, if desired. Stir till combined. Turn the mixture into a 9x9x2-inch baking pan. Cover; freeze several hours or till firm.

Break frozen mixture into chunks; turn into a chilled mixer bowl. Use an electric mixer to beat till smooth. Return mixture to the cold pan; cover and freeze till firm.

Several hours before serving, let sorbet stand at room temperature for 5 minutes. Use a melon baller to scoop sorbet into individual sherbet dishes or glasses. Return to freezer till serving time. Garnish with additional shredded grapefruit peel. Makes 6 to 8 servings.

MARINATED CELERY HEARTS

The heart or center of the celery stalk is the prized portion. Store the branched parts of the stalk as well as the leaves of the hearts in the refrigerator for another use. Celery hearts can be purchased separately occasionally.

  3 **celery hearts**
  1 **cup chicken broth**
  ¾ **cup dry white wine**
  2 **tablespoons lemon juice**
  1 **tablespoon chopped capers**
  1 **tablespoon olive or salad oil**
10 **whole black peppers**
  1 **bay leaf**
  1 **teaspoon dried thyme, crushed**
Bibb lettuce
Snipped parsley (optional)
Chopped capers (optional)

Cut celery hearts in half lengthwise, then into 4-inch pieces. In a large saucepan combine the celery hearts, chicken broth, wine, lemon juice, the 1 tablespoon capers, oil, peppers, bay leaf, and thyme. Bring the mixture to boiling; reduce heat. Cover and simmer about 10 minutes or till tender. Cool celery in broth to room temperature.

Transfer celery mixture to a large bowl. Cover and chill in refrigerator for several hours or overnight. Drain celery hearts. Serve celery hearts on individual salad plates lined with Bibb lettuce. If desired, sprinkle with the snipped parsley and additional chopped capers. Makes 6 servings.

The Jindos

FRIED BEAN CURD APPETIZERS

20 **ounces fresh bean curd (tofu), drained**
  ½ **pound ground beef**
  1 **teaspoon soy sauce**
  1 **teaspoon mirin**
  ½ **of a 12-ounce package (about 1 cup) tempura mix**
Shortening or cooking oil for deep-fat frying
  1 **recipe Dashi Sauce**
Thinly sliced green onion

Cut the fresh bean curd into twelve 1½x1½x¾-inch pieces. Combine the ground beef, soy sauce, and the mirin.

Mound *1 tablespoon* of the beef mixture atop *each* tofu piece, pressing firmly.

Carefully roll each appetizer in dry tempura mix. Carefully place the tofu pieces in hot oil; fry, a few at a time, in deep hot fat (365°) about 4 minutes or till golden. Drain on paper towels. Keep warm. To serve, arrange a few fried appetizers in individual serving bowls. Top with some of the Dashi Sauce. Sprinkle thinly sliced green onion atop. Makes 4 appetizer servings.

Dashi Sauce: Combine 1 cup *dashi broth* or *beef broth*, 2 tablespoons *soy sauce*, 1 tablespoon *mirin*, 2 teaspoons *cornstarch*, and one ½-inch square *gingerroot*. Cook and stir till bubbly. Cook and stir for 2 minutes more. Remove the gingerroot. Makes 1½ cups sauce.

SALMON-VEGETABLE SOUP

You'll find these special ingredients in Oriental food markets.

  ½ **pound boneless fresh or frozen salmon steaks**
  ¼ **pound taro root, peeled and thinly sliced (about ⅔ cup)**
  4 **cups dashi broth or chicken broth**
  1 **1½-ounce package (about 1½ cups) fried bean curd (tofu)**
  ¼ **pound daikon, peeled, sliced, and cut into ½-inch pieces**
  6 **green onions, sliced into 1-inch pieces**
  1 **carrot, thinly sliced**
  ¼ **cup white miso (fermented soybean paste)**
Salt
  ¼ **pound sake lees (optional)**
Parsley sprigs

Thaw salmon, if frozen. Cut salmon into ½-inch cubes. In a small saucepan combine the taro root and enough water to cover. Bring to boiling; reduce heat. Simmer, uncovered, about 4 minutes or till tender. Drain. Rinse with cold water.

In large saucepan combine the broth, bean curd, daikon, green onions, carrot, and taro root. Bring to boiling. Add the salmon, miso, and salt to taste. Add sake lees, if desired. Simmer, uncovered, for 5 minutes. Ladle into soup bowls; serve at once topped with parsley. Makes 4 to 6 main-dish servings.

ROLLED GINGER CHICKEN

Shiso leaves, a popular Japanese garnish, come from the beefsteak plant. Look for shiso leaves in your Oriental food store.

**2 whole large chicken breasts
(about 2 pounds), skinned,
halved lengthwise, and boned**
1 1-inch piece gingerroot
½ cup soy sauce
⅓ cup mirin, sake, *or* dry sherry
½ cup water
Sliced pickled daikon (optional)
Shiso leaves (optional)

Place one chicken breast half between two pieces of clear plastic wrap. Working from center to edges, pound lightly with the flat side of a meat mallet to form a rectangle about ¼ inch thick. Repeat with remaining chicken. Place chicken in a shallow dish.

Cut gingerroot into julienne strips. In a small bowl combine gingerroot, soy sauce, and mirin. Pour over chicken in dish. Cover and let stand 40 minutes at room temperature, turning once.

Remove chicken. Starting from a short side, roll up each rectangle, jelly-roll style. Secure with string. In a large saucepan combine chicken and water. Simmer, covered, for 15 to 20 minutes or till chicken is tender; drain. Cover and chill for at least 3 hours.

To serve, cut each chicken roll into ½-inch-thick slices. Arrange on a serving plate. If desired, garnish with pickled daikon and shiso leaves. Makes 14 to 16 appetizers.

GREEN ONION AND BEEF ROLLS

You can order the ti leaves shown on page 100 from a florist shop. Or, you can substitute spinach leaves for a colorful presentation.

**1 pound boneless beef sirloin
steak**
12 green onions
2 tablespoons soy sauce
2 tablespoons mirin
1 tablespoon cooking oil
1 teaspoon sugar
2 tablespoons cold water
½ teaspoon cornstarch
**Ti leaves *or* spinach leaves
(optional)**
Shredded cucumber (optional)
Shredded carrot (optional)

Partially freeze meat. Slice *horizontally* into four thin, large rectangular pieces. Pound meat with a meat mallet, if necessary, to make ¼ inch thick. (Or, have butcher slice meat into ¼-inch-thick slices.) Roll one slice of meat, jelly-roll style, around three green onions, securing with string or wooden toothpicks. Trim onions even with edges of meat. Repeat with remaining meat and green onions.

In a 10-inch skillet combine soy sauce, mirin, oil, and sugar. Add beef rolls to skillet; turn to coat. Bring mixture to boiling; reduce heat. Cover and simmer about 10 minutes or till beef is done, turning occasionally. Remove the rolls from skillet, reserving juices.

For sauce, strain juices. Skim off fat. Measure juices and add water, if necessary, to make ½ cup. In a small saucepan combine the cold water and cornstarch. Stir in juices. Cook and stir till thickened and bubbly. Cook and stir for 2 minutes more.

Slice beef rolls into 1-inch-thick slices. To serve, arrange slices, cut side down, on platter lined with ti leaves or spinach leaves, if desired. Drizzle sauce atop slices. If desired, serve with finely shredded cucumber and carrot. Makes 4 or 5 main-dish servings.

CURRY FRIED MACKEREL

Mackerel is a rich-flavored fish that has firm and usually red flesh.

**1 3-pound fresh *or* frozen
dressed mackerel *or* frozen
perch fillets**
Lemon juice
⅓ cup all-purpose flour
1 tablespoon curry powder
1 teaspoon salt
**3 tablespoons butter *or*
margarine**
1 recipe Fried Onion and Potatoes

Thaw fish, if frozen. For the dressed fish, bone and halve lengthwise along backbone. Cut *each* half crosswise into *three* portions. Sprinkle with lemon juice. Combine flour, curry powder, and salt. Roll the fish in the curry mixture, coating evenly.

In a large skillet heat butter. Place fish, skin side down, in a single layer. Fry 3 to 4 minutes on each side or till golden and crisp, and fish flakes easily when tested with a fork.

To serve, arrange fish on platter with Fried Onion and Potatoes and cooked carrots, if desired. Garnish with sprig of parsley, if desired. Serves 6.

Fried Onion and Potatoes: Cook 3 large *potatoes,* covered, in boiling water about 30 minutes or till tender. Drain. Cool slightly. Peel and coarsely chop.

In a skillet cook potatoes and 1 medium *onion,* thinly sliced, in 2 tablespoons *butter* or *margarine* till light brown and onion is tender. Season to taste with *salt* and *pepper.* Sprinkle snipped parsley atop, if desired.

The Kunzels

CALABACITA FILLING

Serve on a tortilla shell in a taco or burrito as shown on page 102.

**3½ cups chopped zucchini
(3 medium)**
**2 cups cut fresh corn *or* one
10-ounce package frozen whole
kernel corn**
1 cup sliced green onions
2 cloves garlic, minced
1 tablespoon cooking oil
**2 medium tomatoes, peeled,
seeded, and chopped**
**½ teaspoon dried oregano,
crushed**
½ teaspoon dried thyme, crushed
**1 cup shredded Monterey Jack
cheese (4 ounces)**
**1 cup shredded cheddar cheese
(4 ounces)**

Place zucchini and corn in a steamer basket; place over, but not touching, boiling water. Cover and reduce heat. Steam for 15 minutes.

Meanwhile, in a small saucepan cook the green onions and garlic in hot oil till tender but not brown. In a 2-quart casserole combine cooked vegetables, tomatoes, oregano, and thyme. Bake, covered, in a 350° oven about 15 minutes or till heated through, stirring once. Stir in the cheeses just before serving. Serve with Chili Colorado (see recipe, page 108) as a filling for tacos or burritos. Makes 6½ cups.

POLLO ADOBO

½ of a small onion, cut into wedges
2 tablespoons chili powder
2 tablespoons cooking oil
2 tablespoons water
2 tablespoons vinegar
2 cloves garlic
1½ teaspoons dried oregano, crushed
½ teaspoon salt
¼ teaspoon pepper
1 2½- to 3-pound broiler-fryer chicken, split lengthwise
Lettuce leaves (optional)
Lemon slices (optional)

In a blender container or food processor bowl combine the onion, chili powder, cooking oil, water, vinegar, garlic, oregano, salt, and pepper. Cover and blend to form a paste. Break wing, hip, and drumstick joints of chicken; twist wing tips under back. Place chicken halves in a shallow container; spread chili mixture over chicken halves. Cover and chill overnight.

In a covered grill place *medium-hot* coals on both sides of drip pan. Place chicken, bone side down, on grill over drip pan. Lower grill hood. Grill for 25 to 30 minutes. Turn chicken. Grill, covered, for 25 to 30 minutes more or till chicken is tender. If desired, arrange on a lettuce-lined serving platter. Garnish with lemon slices, if desired. Makes 6 servings.

AZTEC TEQUILA PUNCH

4 cups tequila
1 cup lemon juice
2 46-ounce cans unsweetened grapefruit juice, chilled
1 28-ounce bottle ginger ale, chilled
Ice cubes

In a large bowl combine tequila and lemon juice. Slowly pour in chilled grapefruit juice and the ginger ale. Pour over ice in a large pitcher. Makes 25 to 30 (6-ounce) servings.

CHILI COLORADO

1 3½- to 4-pound fresh beef brisket
2 tablespoons all-purpose flour
1 teaspoon salt
¼ teaspoon pepper
2 tablespoons cooking oil
2 cups water
½ cup chopped onion
2 cloves garlic, minced
1 teaspoon dried oregano, crushed
6 to 8 large dried red chili peppers

Trim excess fat from meat. Combine flour, salt, and pepper; coat meat. In a Dutch oven brown meat on all sides in hot oil. Remove from heat; add water. Add onion, garlic, and oregano. Return to heat; cover and simmer about 3 hours or till meat is very tender.

Transfer meat to a serving platter, reserving cooking liquid. Cool meat completely. When meat is cool enough to handle, coarsely chop. Skim fat from the reserved cooking liquid. Set aside.

Under running water, remove the stems, seeds, and inner membranes from chili peppers. Place the peppers in a small saucepan; cover with water. Bring to boiling; reduce heat. Cover and simmer about 15 minutes or till tender.

Transfer peppers to a blender container or food processor bowl. Add ¼ cup of the reserved cooking liquid. Cover and blend or process till smooth. Stir pepper mixture and meat into remaining cooking liquid in Dutch oven; heat through. Makes 5 cups filling.

Build-Your-Own Tacos: Prepare *Chili Colorado* and *Calabacita Filling* (see recipe, page 107); spoon onto warm *flour tortillas* for tacos or burritos. If desired, garnish with fresh *cilantro sprigs* and *green* and *red chili peppers.*

TORTILLA TORTE

Chill this unique dessert overnight to soften the tortillas and make it easy to slice and serve.

1 12-ounce package (2 cups) semisweet chocolate pieces
3 cups dairy sour cream
10 7- *or* 8-inch flour tortillas
¼ cup sifted powdered sugar
Chocolate curls (optional)
Fresh strawberries (optional)

In a medium heavy saucepan melt the chocolate pieces over low heat, stirring often. Stir in *2 cups* of the sour cream. Remove from heat. Cool.

Place *one* tortilla on a serving plate. Spread about ⅓ *cup* of the chocolate mixture atop. Repeat with *eight* tortillas and the remaining chocolate mixture. Top with remaining tortilla.

In a small bowl stir together the remaining sour cream and the powdered sugar. Spread sour cream mixture on top of torte. Cover and chill overnight. If desired, garnish with chocolate curls and strawberries just before serving. Makes 6 to 8 servings.

SOPAIPILLAS

2 cups all-purpose flour
1 tablespoon baking powder
½ teaspoon salt
1 tablespoon shortening
⅔ cup lukewarm water (110° to 115°)
Cooking oil for deep-fat frying
Honey *or* sifted powdered sugar
Ground cinnamon

Stir together flour, baking powder, and salt. Cut in shortening till mixture resembles cornmeal. Slowly add water; stir with a fork (dough will be crumbly).

Turn onto a floured surface; knead into a smooth ball. Divide dough in half; cover and let stand 10 minutes. Roll each half into a 12½x10-inch rectangle. Using a knife or cookie cutter, cut eighteen 2½-inch squares or circles (do not reroll or patch dough).

Fry squares or circles, a few at a time, in deep hot oil (425°) about 30 seconds per side or till golden. Drain on paper towels. Serve sopaipillas with honey or powdered sugar, and ground cinnamon. Makes 18.

AUGUST

Installing your own phone system: now it's easy as pie!

Better Homes
and Gardens.

August 1984 • $1.50

GARDEN FRESH:
**New vegetables to try
15 fabulous recipes**

**Glorious peonies
and daylilies: for
a bonanza of color**

CHILDHOOD STRESS
The danger signals
and what you can do

**Kitchen
overstuffed?
Try our savvy
storage solutions**

The newest and best in
lamps and lighting ideas

**America's finest
crafts from the past
to make today**

Fresh Vegetables
VARIETY UNLIMITED

By Diana McMillen

New Ways To Use Classic Vegetables

Americans opt to serve fresh vegetables more and more in everyday meals. It's no wonder—selection, availability, and taste are better than ever. As garden enthusiasts and supermarkets explore the varieties of summer produce, the selection grows.

On these pages you'll find some new ways to use your vegetable favorites and some classic ways to cook with the vegetable newcomers.

It's often the everyday vegetables that present the greatest challenge in creating new recipes. But even the most ordinary produce, if used imaginatively, guarantees pleasant surprises.

Boost your recipe collection with **Eggplant Bread Wheel** *(left)*. This vegetable-flecked yeast bread will rival zucchini bread as a family favorite. Or, try tomatoes as the base for **Savory Tomato Ice** *(center)*. Raisins and shredded cabbage fill the unusual appetizer **Cabbage Patch Turnovers** *(front right)*. You'd never guess that shredded radishes are the secret to this moist **Surprise Marbled Cake** *(back right)*.

Photographs: de Gennaro Studios
Food stylist: Mable Hoffman

New Ways To Use Classic Vegetables

Don't forget vegetables as the start of fresh-tasting and satisfying main dishes as well as side dishes.

Spinach enhances the crust and filling of **Spinach Chicken Pie** *(back left)*. We've gone four steps beyond the potato pancake by adding squash, carrots, onion, and green pepper to **Chowchow Pancakes** *(front)*. Show off lettuce filled with savory rice in **Baked Lettuce Bundles** *(right)*.

Classic Ways To Use New Vegetables

The extensive vegetable variety at produce counters means exciting tastes for family meals. The easiest way to get to know the new vegetables is to try them in your favorite vegetable recipes.

Acquaint yourself with celeriac, a mild root vegetable that we've tossed with pasta for *Celeriac Alfredo (front left)*. *Filled Dumpling Squash (back left)* features this sweet vegetable prepared whole and filled with a savory cream cheese custard. For a conversation-piece condiment, serve *Mexican-Style Pickled Peppers and Jicama (back center)*. Banana peppers and crunchy jicama make zippy-flavored nibbles. Southern favorites, turnip and mustard greens, add their robust flavor to *Scalloped Greens and Knackwurst (front right)*.

In case the produce department of your supermarket doesn't stock these unique vegetable varieties, each recipe includes a more common vegetable option.

Classic Ways To Use New Vegetables

The large selection of new vegetables opens up many recipe possibilities. Sorrel leaves look a lot like spinach, and their flavor adds a distinctive tang to dishes like this appetizer: **Hot-Sour Sorrel and Rice Soup** *(left)*.

Choose any type of chili pepper—hot or mild—to spike **Peppy Avocado and Chili Dip** *(center)* that's served with crisp flour tortilla chips. For a sampler, mix and match an assortment of unforgettable produce to create colorful

Cabbage and More Slaw *(back right)*.

To learn how to buy and cook with novel vegetables, turn the page.

Vegetable Newcomers: How To Use Them

5. *Turnip Greens:* These greens are turnip tops. Wash to remove dirt and sand particles. Cut off any roots and remove damaged portions and large veins. Tear or cut up large leaves.

6. *Banana Pepper:* A mild pepper in comparison to other chili peppers. Fresh hot peppers should be handled carefully because the oil from the peppers can burn your skin and eyes. In fact, it's a good idea to wear rubber gloves during preparation or to hold peppers under cold running water while removing the stems, seeds, and inner membranes (these are very hot).

7. *Mustard Greens:* The pungent leaves should be thoroughly washed to remove dirt and sand particles. Cut off roots and remove damaged portions and large veins. Tear or cut up large leaves.

8. *Anaheim Chili:* A hot pepper, less fiery than the Serrano chili pepper identified here. Handle like the banana pepper.

9. *Sorrel:* A green that cooks like spinach, but has a definite tart flavor. Thoroughly wash. Cut off stems and remove damaged portions. Tear or cut up large leaves.

10. *Globe Zucchini:* Usually the tender, thin rind of this soft-shelled summer squash is not removed. To serve, cut off the ends; slice or cube.

11. *Jicama:* A juicy, slightly sweet, mild root that also is known as the Mexican potato. Peel and cut up to eat fresh or cook.

12. *Serrano Chili:* A very hot chili that should be used sparingly. Handle like the banana pepper.

Photograph: Terri Sandison/Lightra, Inc.

I ntegrating these tasty vegetables into your everyday cooking begins with knowing what they look like and how to prepare them. Use this information as a guide.

1. *Daikon:* A radish-flavored vegetable; grate for a condiment, slice for stir-frys, or cube for stews.

2. *Celeriac:* Tastes and smells like celery. Choose small celeriac because the large ones tend to be woody and hollow. To serve, trim off the greens and peel off the rough skin. Cut the celeriac into bite-size pieces, sticks, or cubes to eat fresh or to cook.

3. *Bok Choy:* An Oriental vegetable with a mild sweet taste. To use bok choy, cut off the root end and pull off the stalks. Discard tough leaves; remove the remaining leafy portions and cut them into strips. Slice the stems.

4. *Dumpling Squash:* A squash that also can be purchased at a more mature golden color. Its shell is hard, like that of an acorn squash. Its sweet taste becomes sweeter with age. You can peel this squash before cooking, but it's easier to cook it and then remove the peel. Serve whole; or cut it into serving-size pieces.

Note: To obtain the nutrition analysis of each recipe, the following guidelines were used:
- When ingredient options appear in a recipe, the analysis was calculated using the first ingredient choice.
- Optional ingredients were omitted in the analyses.
- The nutrition analyses for recipes calling for fresh ingredients were calculated using the measurements for raw fruits, vegetables, and meats.
- If a recipe gives two serving sizes (such as "Makes 6 to 8 servings"), the nutrition analysis was calculated using the first choice.

EGGPLANT BREAD WHEEL

The vegetable adds moistness to this savory seasoned dinner bread.

- 2 cups peeled and chopped eggplant *or* 1½ cups shredded zucchini
- 5½ to 6 cups all-purpose flour
- 2 packages active dry yeast
- ¾ cup milk
- ⅓ cup butter *or* margarine
- 2 tablespoons sugar
- 1 teaspoon salt
- ¼ teaspoon dried oregano, crushed
- ¼ teaspoon ground cinnamon
- 2 eggs
- 1 teaspoon water

In a medium saucepan cook chopped eggplant or shredded zucchini, covered, in a small amount of boiling salted water about 5 minutes or just till tender. Drain well and cool.

Meanwhile, for dough, in a large mixer bowl combine *1½ cups* of the flour and the yeast. In a saucepan heat the milk, butter or margarine, sugar, salt, oregano, and cinnamon just till warm (115° to 120°) and butter is almost melted, stirring constantly. Add to the flour mixture.

Separate *one* egg. Add the eggplant or zucchini, *one* egg, and *one* egg yolk (reserve the egg white) to the dough. Beat with an electric mixer on low speed for 30 seconds, scraping bowl. Beat for 3 minutes on high speed. Using a spoon, stir in as much of the remaining flour as you can.

Turn dough out onto a lightly floured surface. Knead in enough of the remaining flour to make a moderately stiff dough that is smooth and elastic (6 to 8 minutes). Shape into a ball. Place in a lightly greased bowl; turn once to grease surface. Cover and let rise till double (about 1 hour).

Punch dough down; divide in half. Cover; let rest 10 minutes. Grease two baking sheets. Shape the dough into two balls. On a lightly floured surface roll each portion of dough to form a ½-inch-thick oval.

Place each oval on a prepared baking sheet. Make six spokelike cuts, starting from the center of the dough and cutting to, but not through, the outside edge of each dough oval. Pull cuts apart to open.

Place small pieces of crumpled foil in cuts to keep cuts open during baking. Combine the reserved egg white and water; brush tops of ovals. Cover; let rise till nearly double (30 to 45 minutes). Bake in a 350° oven about 20 minutes or till done. Makes 2 loaves.

Per serving: 146 calories, 4 g protein, 24 g carbohydrate, 4 g fat, and 130 mg sodium.

SAVORY TOMATO ICE

Serve scoops of this icy refresher between courses of a meal or with a salad as featured on page 109.

- 1 tablespoon unflavored gelatin
- ¼ cup cold water
- 6 medium tomatoes, peeled, seeded, and chopped (3 cups)
- 2 tablespoons sugar
- 2 tablespoons lemon juice
- 1 tablespoon finely snipped fresh basil *or* 1 teaspoon dried basil, crushed
- Dash salt
- 2 egg whites
- Lettuce leaves

In a small saucepan soften the gelatin in the cold water for 5 minutes. Heat and stir over low heat till gelatin is dissolved; set aside.

Meanwhile, place the chopped tomatoes in a blender container. Cover and blend till pureed. (You should have 2 cups.) Pour into a mixing bowl.

Stir the gelatin mixture, sugar, lemon juice, basil, and salt into tomatoes. Beat egg whites till stiff peaks form (tips stand straight); fold into the tomato mixture. Pour the mixture into a 9x9x2-inch pan. Freeze for 3 to 4 hours or till almost firm.

Transfer the mixture to a chilled mixer bowl. Beat with an electric mixer till thoroughly mixed. Return to pan. Freeze till firm.

Let stand at room temperature for 15 minutes before scooping. To serve, scoop onto individual lettuce-lined salad plates. Store any remaining ice in a covered container in the freezer. Makes 8 (½-cup) servings.

Per serving: 37 calories, 2 g protein, 8 g carbohydrate, .2 g fat, 45 mg sodium.

CABBAGE PATCH TURNOVERS

Use this recipe to make either the small appetizer-size turnovers, or large side-dish turnovers.

- 2 slices bacon
- 1¼ cups all-purpose flour
- ½ teaspoon salt
- ⅓ cup shortening
- 3 to 4 tablespoons cold water
- ¼ cup water
- 2 tablespoons vinegar
- 1 tablespoon brown sugar
- ½ teaspoon caraway seed
- 4 cups finely shredded red or green cabbage
- ¼ cup raisins
- 1 tablespoon water
- 2 teaspoons cornstarch
- 1 beaten egg
- 1 tablespoon water
- Dairy sour cream

In a 10-inch skillet cook the bacon till crisp. Drain bacon on paper towels; crumble finely and set pieces aside for the pastry. Reserve *2 tablespoons* of the bacon drippings in the skillet for the cabbage filling.

For pastry, in a medium mixing bowl stir together the flour and salt. Cut in the shortening till pieces are the size of small peas. Stir in the crumbled bacon. Sprinkle *1 tablespoon* of the cold water over part of the mixture; gently toss with a fork. Push to the side of the mixing bowl. Repeat with remaining cold water till all is moistened. Form the dough into a ball; set aside.

For filling, to the reserved bacon drippings in the skillet, stir in the ¼ cup water, vinegar, brown sugar, and caraway seed. Add the shredded red or green cabbage and the raisins; stir to coat. Cover and cook the mixture over low heat about 10 minutes or till the cabbage is tender, stirring occasionally.

Combine 1 tablespoon water and the cornstarch; stir into the skillet mixture. Cook and stir till the cabbage is well-coated. Remove from heat.

For appetizer servings, divide the pastry into 24 portions. On a lightly floured surface flatten each portion; roll to form a 3-inch circle. Spoon *1 rounded tablespoon* of the cabbage filling in the center of *each* pastry oval. (For side-dish servings, divide pastry into six portions. On a lightly floured surface flatten each portion; roll to form an 8x4½-inch oval. Spoon about *½ cup* filling atop *each* dough oval.)

Fold the pastry ovals in half, enclosing the filling. Seal edges with the tines of a fork. Place the turnovers on ungreased baking sheets. Combine the egg and 1 tablespoon water; brush the tops of pastry. Use a sharp knife or a fork to slit or prick the tops to allow steam to escape.

Bake appetizer turnovers in a 400° oven about 15 minutes or till golden. (Bake side-dish turnovers for 20 to 25 minutes or till golden.) Serve turnovers warm with sour cream. Makes 24 appetizer or 6 side-dish turnovers.

Per serving: 108 calories, 2 g protein, 11 g carbohydrate, 6 g fat, and 105 mg sodium.

SURPRISE MARBLED CAKE

To thoroughly drain shredded radishes, place in a colander and press out the excess liquid.

- 3 cups all-purpose flour
- 2 teaspoons baking powder
- ½ teaspoon salt
- ¼ teaspoon baking soda
- ¾ cup butter or margarine
- 1½ cups sugar
- 1 teaspoon vanilla
- 4 eggs
- 1 cup shredded radishes, well drained
- ⅓ cup dairy sour cream
- 3 tablespoons milk
- 1 teaspoon finely shredded orange peel
- ½ cup instant cocoa mix
- 1 recipe Powdered Sugar Icing

Grease and lightly flour a 10-inch fluted tube pan; set aside. Stir together the flour, baking powder, salt, and baking soda. In a large mixer bowl beat the butter or margarine with an electric mixer on medium speed for 30 seconds. Add the sugar and vanilla; beat till fluffy. Add eggs, one at a time, beating for 1 minute after each.

In a small bowl stir together the drained radishes, sour cream, milk, and orange peel. Add dry ingredients and sour cream mixture alternately to butter mixture, beating on low speed after each addition just till combined.

Transfer *1 cup* of the cake batter to a small mixing bowl; gently fold in the cocoa mix. Spoon the plain cake batter into the prepared pan. Spoon the cocoa batter on top in a ring; do not spread the cocoa batter to the edges.

Bake in a 350° oven for 50 to 55 minutes or till cake tests done. Cool cake in pan on a wire rack for 10 minutes. Remove from pan; cool thoroughly on rack. Prepare Powdered Sugar Icing; drizzle atop. Makes 12 servings.

Powdered Sugar Icing: Combine 1 cup sifted *powdered sugar*, ¼ teaspoon *vanilla*, and enough *milk* (about 3 to 4 teaspoons) to make a mixture of drizzling consistency.

Per serving: 439 calories, 7 g protein, 71 g carbohydrate, 16 g fat, and 377 mg sodium.

SPINACH CHICKEN PIE

  2 **medium potatoes**
  5 **ounces fresh spinach**
  2 **tablespoons butter** *or* **margarine**
  ½ **teaspoon salt**
  1 **egg yolk**
2¼ **to 2½ cups all-purpose flour**
Olive *or* **cooking oil**
  1 **10½-ounce can tomato puree**
  1 **medium onion, chopped**
    (½ cup)
  2 **tablespoons dry white wine** *or*
    water
  1 **teaspoon dried tarragon**
    or **marjoram, crushed**
  1 **clove garlic, minced**
1½ **cups coarsely chopped cooked**
    chicken *or* **turkey**
  2 **cups shredded Swiss** *or*
    mozzarella cheese (8 ounces)
Fresh tarragon (optional)

In a covered saucepan cook the potatoes in enough boiling water to cover for 25 to 30 minutes or till tender; drain. Cool potatoes slightly; peel.

Meanwhile, finely chop the spinach leaves. Set aside ¼ cup of the chopped spinach for filling.

For the crust, in a medium saucepan cook the remaining chopped spinach, covered, in a small amount of boiling salted water for 4 to 5 minutes or till tender. Drain well, pressing to remove excess liquid.

In a large mixer bowl combine the warm potatoes, butter or margarine, and salt; beat till smooth. Beat in the cooked spinach. Add the egg yolk and about ⅓ cup of the flour; beat till smooth. Using a spoon, stir in enough of the remaining flour to make a moderately stiff dough.

Turn the dough out onto a lightly floured surface. Knead for 4 to 5 minutes. Roll or pat the dough to form a circle 12 inches in diameter. Place in a greased 11-inch flan or quiche pan. Flute edges. Do not prick crust. Brush the crust with olive or cooking oil.

Bake the crust in a 375° oven about 20 minutes or till brown. (Check crust while baking. If crust puffs up, use a fork to carefully lift the edge of the crust to allow steam to escape. Flatten crust carefully with the back of a wooden spoon.)

Meanwhile, for the filling, in a large saucepan combine the reserved chopped spinach, the tomato puree, chopped onion, white wine or water, the 1 teaspoon dried tarragon, and the minced garlic. Bring to boiling; reduce heat. Simmer, uncovered, for 10 minutes. Stir in the cooked chicken or turkey. Remove from heat.

To assemble pie, sprinkle *1½ cups* of the shredded Swiss or mozzarella cheese over the baked crust. Spoon on the chicken-tomato mixture. Cover the edges of the crust with foil to prevent overbrowning. Bake, uncovered, in a 375° oven about 15 minutes or till heated through.

Remove foil. Sprinkle the remaining shredded cheese around the edge of the filling. Return to oven; bake for 3 to 4 minutes more or till cheese is melted. Let stand for 5 minutes before serving. If desired, garnish the top of the pie with a fresh tarragon sprig. Makes 8 main-dish servings.

Per serving: 420 calories, 23 g protein, 44 g carbohydrate, 17 g fat, and 695 mg sodium.

CHOWCHOW PANCAKES

These vegetable-filled pancakes are named after the colorful relish, Chowchow, also made with a variety of garden produce. Serve them as you would hash browns, with broiled or roasted meats and poultry.

  2 **beaten eggs**
  1 **cup finely shredded potatoes**
  1 **cup finely shredded zucchini** *or*
    crookneck squash
  ½ **cup finely shredded carrots**
  ¼ **cup finely chopped onion**
  ¼ **cup finely chopped red** *or*
    green sweet pepper
  3 **tablespoons all-purpose flour**
  1 **teaspoon salt**
  ½ **teaspoon poultry seasoning**
Dash ground red pepper
Few drops Worcestershire sauce
  1 **recipe Applesauce Topping** *or*
    Sour Cream Topping
Lettuce leaves (optional)

In a large mixing bowl combine eggs, potatoes, zucchini or squash, carrots, onion, red or green pepper, flour, salt, poultry seasoning, ground red pepper, and Worcestershire sauce. Mix well.

For *each* pancake, spoon a scant ¼ cup of the mixture onto a hot, oiled griddle; flatten with spatula or back of spoon to ¼-inch thickness. Cook over medium heat for 3 minutes on each side or till golden.

Remove pancakes and arrange in a single layer on a baking sheet. Keep warm in a 250° oven. Repeat with remaining batter, cooking a few pancakes at a time. Meanwhile, prepare Applesauce or Sour Cream Topping. Arrange the pancakes on a platter. If desired, garnish with lettuce. Serve with topping. Makes 8 to 10 pancakes.

Applesauce Topping: In a small saucepan stir together one 8½-ounce can *applesauce* and 2 teaspoons *prepared horseradish;* heat through. If desired, garnish with a *fresh carrot top.*

Sour Cream Topping: Stir together one 8-ounce carton *dairy sour cream* and 2 teaspoons *Dijon-style mustard.*

Per serving (with Applesauce Topping): 125 calories, 3 g protein, 18 g carbohydrate, 5 g fat, and 337 mg sodium.

CELERIAC ALFREDO

The starches from the pasta thicken the cream sauce.

- **2 tablespoons butter *or* margarine**
- **⅓ cup sliced green onions**
- **1 clove garlic, minced**
- **1 tablespoon snipped fresh basil *or* 1 teaspoon dried basil, crushed**
- **¼ teaspoon pepper**
- **1 pound celeriac, peeled and cut into julienne strips (about 3 cups)**
- **2 medium carrots, thinly bias sliced (about ⅔ cup)**
- **⅓ cup dry white wine**
- **⅓ cup water**
- **½ teaspoon instant chicken bouillon granules**
- **2 tablespoons snipped parsley**
- **6 ounces linguine *or* spaghetti**
- **⅔ cup light cream**
- **Grated Parmesan cheese**
- **Fresh basil (optional)**

In a large saucepan melt the butter or margarine; stir in the green onions, garlic, fresh or dried basil, and pepper. Cook till onion is tender. Add celeriac, carrots, wine, water, and bouillon granules. Bring to boiling; reduce heat. Cover and cook about 10 minutes or till the vegetables are tender, stirring occasionally. Stir in the parsley.

Meanwhile, cook the linguine or spaghetti in boiling salted water just till tender; drain. Add the hot cooked pasta and cream to the vegetable mixture; toss to mix. Heat through. Transfer mixture to a serving platter. To serve, sprinkle with Parmesan cheese. If desired, garnish with fresh basil. Makes 6 side-dish servings.

Per serving: 237 calories, 7 g protein, 29 g carbohydrate, 9 g fat, and 187 mg sodium.

BAKED LETTUCE BUNDLES

- **12 large romaine *or* red-tipped lettuce leaves**
- **1 6-ounce package long grain and wild rice**
- **1 tablespoon olive *or* cooking oil**
- **3 beaten eggs**
- **½ cup ricotta cheese**
- **½ cup coarsely chopped walnuts**
- **¼ teaspoon fennel seed, crushed**
- **Olive *or* cooking oil**

Cut about 2 inches of the heavy center vein out of leaves. Cook in a large amount of boiling salted water about 30 seconds or just till limp. Drain well; pat dry with paper towels. Cool.

Meanwhile, for filling, cook rice according to package directions. In an 8-inch skillet heat the 1 tablespoon oil. Add eggs and cook over low heat, without stirring, till set. Invert over a baking sheet to remove eggs; cut into narrow strips. Reserve *one-third* of the egg strips. Coarsely chop remaining egg. Toss together rice, chopped egg, cheese, nuts, and fennel.

Arrange two leaves overlapping to form a cross. Place *½ cup* filling in center of cross. Fold leaves over rice to form a bundle. Place, seam side down, in an oiled 10x6x2-inch baking dish. Repeat with remaining leaves and filling.

Brush some oil over lettuce bundles. Bake, covered, in a 350° oven for 30 to 40 minutes or till heated through. Garnish with the reserved egg strips. Makes 6 side-dish servings.

Per serving: 278 calories, 11 g protein, 24 g carbohydrate, 16 g fat, and 492 mg sodium.

FILLED DUMPLING SQUASH

The combination of cream cheese, milk, and eggs forms the custard filling.

- **3 10- to 12-ounce dumpling *or* acorn squash**
- **1 3-ounce package cream cheese, cut up**
- **2 tablespoons milk**
- **3 slightly beaten eggs**
- **2 tablespoons sliced green onions**
- **¼ teaspoon salt**
- **⅛ teaspoon pepper**
- **3 tablespoons toasted, chopped almonds**
- **Fresh kale (optional)**
- **Slivered almonds (optional)**

Cut off the top of the squash; scoop out seeds. Lightly salt inside of squash. (Trim bottoms of acorn squash to allow them to stand.) Place squash, cut side down, in a shallow baking pan. Bake in a 375° oven for 30 to 35 minutes or till almost tender.

Meanwhile, for filling, in a mixer bowl beat the cream cheese with an electric mixer on medium speed till softened. Add milk; beat till fluffy. Add the eggs, green onions, salt, and pepper; beat till well combined.

Turn squash cut side up. Pour filling into the hot hollowed squash. Sprinkle with chopped almonds. Bake in a 375° oven about 20 minutes more or till a knife inserted near the center comes out clean. Let stand for 5 minutes. Place on a kale-lined serving platter. If desired, top the squash with slivered almonds. Halve squash before serving. Makes 6 side-dish servings.

Per serving: 198 calories, 8 g protein, 19 g carbohydrate, 12 g fat, and 159 mg sodium.

MEXICAN-STYLE PICKLED PEPPERS AND JICAMA

Use only pickling salt when preparing this zippy condiment. Regular table salt clouds the pickling liquid.

- ½ **pound banana peppers**
- 1½ **pounds jicama**
- 8 **cups water**
- ¼ **cup pickling salt**
- 2 **cups vinegar**
- 4 **teaspoons dried basil, crushed**
- 4 **or 5 cloves garlic**

Olive *or* cooking oil (optional)

Slice peppers crosswise into ½-inch strips; rinse and discard seeds and any interior pulp. Peel and slice jicama lengthwise into 4-inch-long sticks.

In a large mixing bowl combine *4 cups* of the water and the salt. Add peppers and jicama. Let stand overnight. Drain and rinse well.

In a large saucepan combine the remaining water, vinegar, and basil. Bring to boiling; reduce heat. Simmer, uncovered, for 10 minutes. Pack peppers and jicama into clean, hot pint jars, leaving ½-inch headspace. Add *one* clove of garlic to *each* jar.

Pour the hot vinegar solution over pepper mixture, stirring solution to keep herbs evenly distributed. Leave ½-inch headspace in each jar. Wipe rims. Adjust lids; process in boiling water bath for 10 minutes. (Start timing after the water comes to boiling.) Cover and chill overnight.

If desired, before serving, open jar and remove *2 tablespoons* of the vinegar solution and add *2 tablespoons* oil. Makes 4 pints, 16 servings.

Per serving: 21 calories, 0.4 g protein, 6 g carbohydrate, 0.06 g fat, and 801 mg sodium.

Note: Nutrition analysis was determined by assuming that *half* of the salt is rinsed off the chilled vegetable mixture before processing.

SCALLOPED GREENS AND KNACKWURST

Knackwurst, a German sausage seasoned with garlic, complements the robust flavor of the greens.

- 12 **ounces turnip greens, mustard greens, *or* spinach, torn into small pieces (8 to 9 cups)**
- 4 **ounces knackwurst *or* Polish sausage**
- 2 **beaten eggs**
- ½ **cup milk**
- ½ **cup shredded brick *or* Monterey Jack cheese (2 ounces)**
- 2 **tablespoons sliced green onions**

Dash pepper
- ¾ **cup soft whole wheat bread crumbs (1 slice)**
- 2 **teaspoons olive *or* cooking oil**

In a large saucepan cook greens, covered, in a small amount of simmering water for 3 minutes; drain well. Cool slightly. Meanwhile, cut a few slices from knackwurst for a garnish; set aside. Halve the remaining sausage lengthwise; cut into thin slices.

In a mixing bowl combine eggs, milk, *⅓ cup* of the cheese, green onions, pepper, and greens. Stir knackwurst into greens mixture. Turn the mixture into a greased 1-quart au gratin dish or a shallow casserole. Bake in a 350° oven for 20 minutes.

For topping, combine the remaining shredded cheese, bread crumbs, and oil; sprinkle over casserole. Bake about 5 minutes more or till a knife inserted near the center comes out clean. Let stand for 5 minutes before serving. Garnish with reserved knackwurst slices. Makes 6 servings.

Per serving: 163 calories, 9 g protein, 6 g carbohydrate, 12 g fat, 353 mg sodium.

HOT-SOUR SORREL AND RICE SOUP

When substituting turnip greens, add the 1 tablespoon vinegar to get the pleasant sour taste.

- 1 **recipe Rice Patties**
- 4 **cups chicken broth**
- 1 **tablespoon soy sauce**
- ⅛ **teaspoon pepper**
- 2 **cups packed, chopped sorrel leaves *or* turnip greens (with stems removed)**

Prepare the Rice Patties. In a 3-quart saucepan combine chicken broth, soy sauce, and pepper. Bring to boiling. Add chopped sorrel or turnip greens. Cover and cook for 1 to 2 minutes or just till sorrel is tender.

To serve, place *one* rice patty in *each* soup bowl. Stir soup and pour over patties. Makes 8 servings.

Note: Add 1 tablespoon *rice vinegar* or *vinegar* to the soup before cooking, if using turnip greens.

Rice Patties: Cook ¾ cup *short grain rice* according to package directions; cool. Using about *¼ cup* for *each*, form rice into eight patties about ½ inch thick, pressing rice together well. (Wet hands with water, if necessary.) Place on a well-greased baking sheet. Bake in a 300° oven about 30 minutes or till rice appears dry.

In a heavy skillet heat ¼ cup *cooking oil* and ½ teaspoon *sesame oil* over medium heat till a kernel of uncooked rice sizzles in the oil. Using a metal spatula, carefully transfer patties from baking sheet to skillet.

Cook patties, a few at a time, over medium heat for 30 to 45 seconds on each side or till light brown. Drain on paper towels. Keep warm in a 350° oven while cooking the remaining patties. Makes 8 servings.

Per serving: 130 calories, 6 g protein, 19 g carbohydrate, 4 g fat, and 923 mg sodium.

PEPPY AVOCADO AND CHILI DIP

Check the information on chili peppers on page 118 for a guide to choosing and using these fiery peppers. For a rim of red, dip the serving glass or bowl rim into water, then into chili powder.

- 3 fresh serrano *or* 2 Anaheim chili peppers
- 1 large avocado, seeded, peeled, and cut up
- ½ cup plain yogurt
- ½ cup mayonnaise *or* salad dressing
- 1 clove garlic, minced
- ½ teaspoon salt
- ¼ teaspoon pepper
- 1 recipe Fried Flour Tortilla Chips *or* purchased tortilla chips

Fresh cilantro (optional)

To peel fresh chili peppers, place them on an unheated broiler pan and broil 2 inches from heat about 10 minutes or till blistered on all sides, turning often. Place chili peppers in a paper bag. Close and let stand for 10 minutes. Hold peppers with a fork; peel and remove seeds using a knife. Discard seeds and finely chop peppers.

In a blender container or food processor bowl combine the chili peppers, avocado, yogurt, mayonnaise, garlic, salt, and pepper. Cover and blend till smooth. Spoon into a serving container. Use as a dip for Fried Flour Tortilla Chips. If desired, garnish with cilantro. Makes about 1½ cups.

Fried Flour Tortilla Chips: Cut a stack of five *flour tortillas* into eight wedges. In a heavy skillet heat ¼ inch *cooking oil.* Fry tortillas, a few wedges at a time, in hot fat for 1 to 1½ minutes or till crisp, turning once. Drain on paper towels. Keep warm. Makes 40.

Per tablespoon: 54 calories, 0.5 g protein, 2 g carbohydrate, 5 g fat, and 75 mg sodium.

CABBAGE AND MORE SLAW

For this salad, choose a combination of vegetables that will provide a variety of colors and textures.

- 4 cups desired vegetables (julienne-cut scallopini squash, coarsely shredded daikon, thin-sliced bok choy, shredded red cabbage, shredded carrot, julienne-cut pea pods, shredded jicama, *and/or* julienne-cut globe zucchini)
- ¾ cup broken walnuts
- 2 tablespoons sliced green onions
- 2 tablespoons salad oil
- 2 tablespoons lemon juice
- 2 tablespoons vinegar
- 1 tablespoon honey
- 1 teaspoon curry powder
- 1 teaspoon Dijon-style mustard
- ¼ teaspoon salt

Savoy cabbage leaves *or* other cabbage leaves (optional)

- 4 cups alfalfa sprouts
- 1 cup chopped unpeeled tart apple

In a large mixing bowl combine the desired vegetables, walnuts, and green onions. For dressing, in a screw-top jar combine salad oil, lemon juice, vinegar, honey, curry powder, mustard, and salt. Cover and shake well to mix. Drizzle dressing over mixture in bowl; toss well. Cover and chill for 2 to 24 hours.

To serve, line a serving platter with cabbage leaves, then with sprouts. Stir the chopped apple into the vegetable mixture. Spoon the mixture atop sprouts. Makes 6 servings.

Per serving: 191 calories, 4 g protein, 14 g carbohydrate, 14 g fat, and 124 mg sodium.

GARDEN SALAD FLAMBÉ

Turn to page 109 to see the attractive arrangement of this unusual salad.

- 2 small pattypan squash, sliced, cooked, and chilled
- 1 crookneck squash, crinkle cut, cooked, and chilled
- 1 cup fresh green beans
- 1 cup fresh pea pods
- 5 cups torn mixed greens (choose from fresh spinach, Bibb lettuce, Boston lettuce, red-tipped leaf lettuce, leaf lettuce, *and/or* Napa cabbage)
- 1 cup enoki mushrooms *or* other thinly sliced fresh mushrooms
- 1 small red onion, sliced and separated into rings
- 1 small carrot, cut into strips

Banana peppers (optional)
Radishes (optional)

- 1 recipe Tomato Ice Cups

Bacon curls (optional)

- 1 recipe Creamy Dijon Dressing
  Fresh basil (optional)
- 2 tablespoons brandy

Cook the pattypan and crookneck squashes, green beans, and pea pods in boiling salted water till tender; drain, cover, and chill.

Line a serving platter with greens. Top with vegetables, Tomato Ice Cups, and bacon curls. Prepare *Creamy Dijon Dressing;* pour atop vegetables. If desired, garnish with basil.

Before serving, in a saucepan heat the brandy. Using a long match, ignite the brandy. Pour atop vegetables. After flame subsides, toss the vegetables and serve immediately. Makes 8 servings.

Tomato Ice Cups: Prepare Savory Tomato Ice as directed on page 119. Halve four medium *tomatoes;* remove pulp, leaving ½-inch-thick shells. Using a melon baller, scoop the tomato ice into shells.

Creamy Dijon Dressing: Bring ¼ cup *vinegar* to boiling. Add 2 tablespoons *sugar;* cook and stir till sugar dissolves. Remove from heat. Combine ¼ cup *dairy sour cream,* 1 slightly beaten *egg yolk,* 1 tablespoon *Dijon-style mustard,* 1 tablespoon chopped *pimiento,* 1 teaspoon snipped *chives,* 1 teaspoon *all-purpose flour,* and ⅛ teaspoon *pepper.* Add to vinegar mixture. Return to heat. Cook and stir till bubbly.

SEPTEMBER

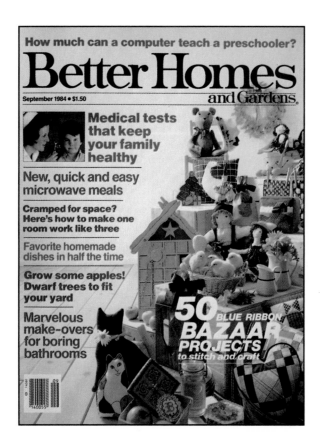

HOMEMADE
IN HALF THE TIME

Surprise your family with made-from-scratch flavor—even when you're pinched for time! It's a cinch with these home-style foods that fit today's busy times. You can even adapt the step-saving cooking methods used in these recipes to streamline the preparation of other family favorites. Also, learn more about ingredients—some new, others used in new ways—that minimize your minutes in the kitchen. On-the-go cooks never had it so easy and delicious!

By Joy Taylor

Photographs: Teri Sandison/Lightra. Food stylist: Judy Tills

DOUBLE-QUICK PEANUTTY COFFEE CAKE

Thanks to the new active dry yeast that raises bread dough doubly quick, your family can enjoy warm coffee cakes for breakfast any day of the week. Snipping the dough instead of rolling and shaping it saves time, too.

NO-MEASURE BEEF STEW

Lucky for you, none of the ingredients for this hearty entrée requires a measuring cup or spoon. Your only task is to cut the vegetables and combine them with a pound of stew meat, a can of tomato sauce, and an envelope of salad dressing mix for seasoning. Slip it into the oven to meld the flavors.

HOMEMADE *IN HALF THE TIME*

SKIP-SEVERAL-STEPS CHEESECAKE ROLL

Cake rolls once called for extra time and effort, but no more! Here, a filling bakes right along with the cake batter. After cooling, just roll the cake and orange-flavored cream cheese center together. Premelted chocolate in the cake batter and the icing simplifies this tempting dessert even more.

THIRTY-MINUTE TURKEY DINNER FOR TWO

The boneless turkey breast cutlets available at supermarkets offer convenient cooking plus superb taste. These thin serving-size portions sauté in seconds. For a complete meal reminiscent of special-occasion turkey dinners, serve the lean poultry pieces with seasoned tomato sauce and fast-cooking couscous.

FREEZER-TO-TABLE CHICKEN SUPPER

Your freezer probably houses the makings for a spur-of-the-moment dinner. This tempting example starts with frozen chicken pieces, vegetables, and rice. Separate the chicken and vegetables under running water, combine them with the package of frozen rice and teriyaki sauce, and then relax while supper simmers. No one will suspect that you assembled the meal in hurry-up fashion.

Note: Recipes were tested in countertop microwave ovens that operate on 600 to 700 watts. Times are approximations since microwave ovens vary by manufacturer.

NO-MEASURE BEEF STEW

- 1 15-ounce can tomato sauce
- 1 0.9-ounce envelope vintage herb salad dressing mix *or* one 1¾-ounce envelope stroganoff sauce mix
- 1 pound lean beef stew meat, cut into ½-inch cubes
- 2 large parsnips, thinly sliced
- 2 large sweet potatoes, peeled and cut into 1-inch pieces
- 1 medium onion, sliced and separated into rings
- 1 large green pepper, sliced

Celery tops (optional)

In a 3-quart casserole combine tomato sauce and salad dressing mix or sauce mix. Stir in beef, parsnips, potatoes, and onion. Bake, covered, in a 325° oven for 45 minutes. Stir in green pepper. Bake, covered, for 50 to 60 minutes more or till vegetables and meat are tender. Skim off fat; stir before serving. Garnish each serving with celery tops, if desired. Makes 6 to 8 servings.

Microwave directions: In a 3-quart nonmetal casserole combine the tomato sauce and salad dressing mix or sauce mix. Add beef, parsnips, sweet potatoes, and onion. Micro-cook, covered, on 100% power (HIGH) for 5 minutes. Reduce power to 50% (MEDIUM). Micro-cook, covered, for 45 minutes more or till the vegetables are almost tender, stirring once. Stir in green pepper. Micro-cook, covered, on 50% power (MEDIUM) for 5 minutes more or till vegetables and meat are tender. Skim off fat. Stir before serving.

FREEZER-TO-TABLE CHICKEN SUPPER

If you want to start with fresh chicken pieces, reduce the cooking time to just 20 minutes before adding the frozen rice and vegetables.

- 8 frozen chicken legs *or* thighs
- ¼ cup water
- 3 tablespoons teriyaki sauce *or* soy sauce
- 1 9-ounce package frozen Italian green beans
- 2 cups frozen crinkle-cut carrots
- 2 11-ounce packages frozen long grain and wild rice
- 2 tablespoons slivered almonds

Run warm water over frozen chicken and tap lightly on countertop to separate pieces. In a 12-inch skillet combine the frozen chicken pieces, water, and teriyaki or soy sauce. Bring to boiling; reduce heat. Cover and simmer about 30 minutes or till almost tender.

Meanwhile, transfer frozen vegetables to a colander and place under hot running water till separated. Add the vegetables and frozen rice to skillet. Return to boiling; reduce heat. Cook, covered, for 10 to 15 minutes more or till the chicken and vegetables are tender, stirring once or twice to break up rice. Before serving, sprinkle almonds atop. Makes 4 servings.

Microwave directions: To thaw chicken, place frozen pieces in a 3-quart nonmetal casserole. Micro-cook, covered, on 50% power (MEDIUM) for 2 minutes. Separate and rearrange pieces. Micro-cook, covered, for 6 to 8 minutes more or till thawed, rearranging pieces every 2 minutes. (Remove any thawed pieces.)

Arrange thawed chicken pieces so the meatiest portions are toward the outside of the casserole. Add *2 tablespoons* water and the teriyaki or soy sauce. Micro-cook, covered, on 100% power (HIGH) for 8 minutes.

Add the frozen beans, frozen carrots, and frozen rice. Micro-cook, covered, on 100% power (HIGH) for 8 minutes. Break up the rice and stir the mixture to distribute chicken pieces with the thawed rice and vegetables. Micro-cook, covered, 5 to 7 minutes more or till chicken and vegetables are tender, stirring once. Let stand, covered, for 3 minutes. Before serving, sprinkle slivered almonds atop.

THIRTY-MINUTE TURKEY DINNER FOR TWO

Turkey steaks usually come three or four to a package. Wrap the remaining steaks in moisture- and vaporproof wrap and freeze for up to six months.

- ⅓ cup boiling water
- ⅓ cup ready-to-cook couscous
- ½ teaspoon minced dried onion
- ¼ teaspoon dried oregano, crushed
- 1 8-ounce can stewed tomatoes, cut up
- 1 turkey breast steak (about 5 ounces)
- 1 tablespoon cooking oil
- 1 2½-ounce can whole mushrooms, drained

Snipped parsley (optional)
- ¼ cup shredded mozzarella cheese (1 ounce)

Cucumber slices (optional)
Sliced pitted ripe olives (optional)

In a small saucepan combine the boiling water and couscous. Cover and set aside. Stir the minced dried onion and the oregano into the *undrained* tomatoes. Halve the turkey steak crosswise.

In an 8-inch skillet cook the turkey pieces in hot oil for 2 to 4 minutes on each side. Drain off fat. Add the tomato mixture and the mushrooms to the skillet. Boil rapidly, uncovered, for 3 to 4 minutes or till liquid is slightly reduced and thickened.

To serve, fluff the couscous with a fork; spoon onto two dinner plates. Top with snipped parsley, if desired. Transfer the turkey and sauce to plates. Sprinkle the mozzarella cheese atop turkey and sauce. Garnish plates with cucumber slices and sliced olives, if desired. Makes 2 servings.

SKIP-SEVERAL-STEPS
CHEESECAKE ROLL

- 1 8-ounce container soft-style cream cheese
- ⅓ cup sugar
- 1 egg
- 1 tablespoon milk
- 1½ teaspoons finely shredded orange peel
- ½ cup all-purpose flour
- 1 teaspoon baking powder
- ¼ teaspoon salt
- 4 egg yolks
- ½ teaspoon vanilla
- ⅓ cup sugar
- 1 envelope (1 ounce) premelted unsweetened chocolate product
- 4 egg whites
- ½ cup sugar
- Powdered sugar
- 1 recipe Chocolate Glaze
- Orange peel curls (optional)
- Orange slices, halved (optional)
- Lemon leaves (optional)

Lightly grease a 15x10x1-inch baking pan. Line with waxed paper; grease paper. For filling, in a medium mixer bowl combine the cream cheese and the ⅓ cup sugar; beat with an electric mixer on medium speed till smooth. Add the whole egg, milk, and shredded orange peel; beat till combined. Spread filling in the prepared pan; set aside.

In a mixing bowl stir together the flour, baking powder, and salt; set aside. In a small mixer bowl beat the egg yolks and vanilla on medium speed about 5 minutes or till thick and lemon colored. Gradually add the ⅓ cup sugar, beating till sugar is dissolved. Add the premelted chocolate product; stir till combined.

Thoroughly wash the beaters. In a large mixer bowl beat the egg whites on medium speed till soft peaks form (tips curl). Gradually add the ½ cup sugar, beating on high speed till stiff peaks form (tips stand straight).

Fold yolk mixture into egg whites. Sprinkle the flour mixture evenly over egg mixture; fold in just till blended. Spread the batter evenly over the filling in the pan. Bake in a 375° oven about 15 minutes or till cake springs back when lightly touched.

Immediately loosen the cake from sides of pan and turn out onto a towel sprinkled with powdered sugar. Carefully peel off paper. Starting with narrow end, roll up cake. Cool. Drizzle Chocolate Glaze over cake roll. If desired, garnish with orange peel curls, orange slices, and lemon leaves. Makes 10 servings.

Chocolate Glaze: In a small mixing bowl combine one envelope of *premelted unsweetened chocolate product* and 2 tablespoons *butter* or *margarine,* melted. Stir in 1 cup *sifted powdered sugar* and ½ teaspoon *vanilla.* Add enough *boiling water* (1 to 2 tablespoons) to make a glaze of drizzling consistency. Makes about ⅔ cup.

DOUBLE-QUICK
PEANUTTY
COFFEE CAKE

When snipping the dough, dip your scissors into flour as necessary to prevent the dough from sticking to them.

- 2¾ cups all-purpose flour
- ¼ cup nonfat dry milk powder
- 3 tablespoons sugar
- ½ teaspoon salt
- 1 package quick-rising dry yeast
- ½ cup warm water (115° to 120°)
- ¼ cup cooking oil
- 2 eggs
- ½ cup peanut butter
- ¼ cup butter *or* margarine, softened
- ¼ cup honey
- 1 teaspoon ground cinnamon
- ¼ cup currant *or* other jelly
- Sugar-coated red grapes (optional)

In a large mixer bowl combine *1 cup* of the flour, the milk powder, sugar, salt, and quick-rising yeast. Add warm water, oil, and eggs. Beat with an electric mixer on low speed for 30 seconds, scraping sides of bowl constantly. Beat for 3 minutes on high speed. Using a spoon, stir in as much of the remaining flour as you can.

Turn the dough out onto a lightly floured surface. Knead in any remaining flour till dough is smooth and elastic. Divide dough in half. Cover and set aside *half* of the dough. Snip remaining dough into 1-inch pieces. Evenly scatter snipped dough pieces in the bottom of a greased 9x9x2-inch baking pan, leaving space between pieces. Cover dough and let rest while preparing filling.

For filling, combine the peanut butter, butter or margarine, honey, and cinnamon; stir till smooth. Spoon the filling over the dough in the pan. Snip the remaining dough into 1-inch pieces; scatter evenly over the filling. Cover dough. Let rise in a warm place till almost double (30 to 35 minutes).

Bake in a 350° oven about 30 minutes or till done. Turn out onto wire rack. In a small saucepan melt the desired jelly. Drizzle over warm coffee cake. Serve warm. Garnish with sugar-coated red grapes, if desired. Makes 1.

Magnificent MICROWAVE MEALS

Eggplant Relish

Greek-Style Manicotti

Nancy K. Wall/Joy Taylor

Salami-Vegetable Bake

Snowcapped Pork Burgers

Combine the convenience of cooking and serving one-dish meals with the speed of your microwave oven—that's shortcut cooking at its best! These meal-in-a-dish ideas are guaranteed to relieve the pan-juggling routine of preparing family meals. As a bonus, the whole-meal recipes offer easy after-dinner cleanup. If you don't have a microwave oven, just follow the conventional cooking directions for equally mouth-watering results. Tasty desserts to top off these specialties follow on the next pages.

Hearty One-Dish Entrées

Snowcapped Pork Burgers
Aside from turning out moist and juicy burgers, micro-cooking eliminates broiler-pan detail. Paper-thin radish slices brighten these soufflé-topped supper sandwiches.

Salami-Vegetable Bake
Micro-cooking enhances the flavors of cabbage, potatoes, and caraway in this hearty casserole. It also shaves 30 minutes from the conventional baking time and eliminates the need to precook the vegetables.

Greek-Style Manicotti with Eggplant Relish
The best part about making this recipe is that the pasta requires no precooking. The manicotti shells are filled with a mildly seasoned combination of beef or lamb and eggplant and laced with a creamy white sauce. The relish, a Mediterranean-inspired accompaniment served in an eggplant shell, micro-cooks during the manicotti's standing time.

Photograph: Mike Dieter
Food stylist: Fran Paulson

Simply Super Desserts

There's always time for homemade desserts with a microwave oven at hand. These four family-pleasing desserts streamline scratch cooking with spoon-licking results.

Creamy Cheesecake Ring

Don't bother with the beaters; this shortcut cheesecake owes its silky-smooth texture to the micro-cooked blend of cream cheese and custard dessert mix. (There's no fear of scorching the mixture in the microwave oven.) A nectarine sauce highlights the ring at serving time.

Marbled Cream Pie

The rich pie filling starts with a basic pudding recipe that you partially micro-cook in a mixing bowl. Then blend micro-melted unsweetened chocolate into half of the batch before filling the crisp cocoa crust—another microwave feat.

Carrot Cakes with Custard Sauce

For a dessert reminiscent of Grandma's good baking but made in a fraction of the time, try these tender mini-cakes—they micro-cook in less than three minutes! Granola, both inside and on top, adds color and crunch. When ready to serve, take another three minutes to stir and heat the complementary sauce.

Cranberry Sipper

Thanks to the microwave, you can warm mugfuls of cran-raspberry juice, apple slices, raisins, and spices while you enjoy dinner. Provide skewers so diners can nibble on the fruits.

Photograph: Scott Little
Food stylist: Janet Pittman

Marbled Cream Pie

Carrot Cakes with Custard Sauce

Cranberry Sipper

Creamy Cheesecake Ring

Note: To obtain the nutrition analysis of each recipe, the following guidelines were used:
- When ingredient options appear in a recipe, the analysis was calculated using the first ingredient choice.
- Optional ingredients were omitted in the analyses.
- The nutrition analyses for recipes calling for fresh ingredients were calculated using the measurements for raw fruits, vegetables, and meats.
- If a recipe gives two serving sizes (such as "Makes 6 to 8 servings"), the analysis was calculated using the first choice.

The United States Recommended Daily Allowances (USRDA) tell the amount of certain nutrients necessary to meet the dietary needs of most healthy people.

SALAMI-VEGETABLE BAKE

- 4 medium potatoes, peeled and sliced
- 2 medium carrots, sliced
- 1 medium onion, sliced
- ⅓ cup water
- 2 cloves garlic, minced
- 3 cups shredded cabbage
- ½ cup hot water
- 2½ teaspoons instant beef bouillon granules
- 1½ teaspoons caraway seed
- 2 tablespoons all-purpose flour
- 1 8-ounce carton plain yogurt or dairy sour cream
- 1 8-ounce package thin-sliced hard salami

Microwave directions: In a 2-quart nonmetal microwave-safe casserole combine potatoes, carrots, onion, the ⅓ cup water, and garlic. Micro-cook, covered, on 100% power (HIGH) about 10 minutes or till the vegetables are just tender, stirring after 5 minutes. Add the shredded cabbage.

Combine the ½ cup hot water, the bouillon granules, and the caraway; add to the vegetable mixture. Micro-cook, covered, for 4 to 5 minutes or till cabbage is tender, stirring once.

Stir the flour into yogurt or sour cream; stir into the cabbage mixture. Micro-cook, uncovered, about 2 minutes or till bubbly, stirring once. Stir the mixture again.

Fold the salami pieces into quarters; arrange around outer edges of casserole, pressing salami slightly into vegetable mixture. Micro-cook, uncovered, for 2 to 3 minutes. Spoon off fat. Makes 6 servings.

Conventional directions: In large saucepan cook the onion and garlic in 1 tablespoon *butter* or *margarine* till onion is tender but not brown. Stir in the potatoes, carrots, *1 cup* water, bouillon granules, and caraway seed. Bring to boiling; reduce heat. Cover and simmer about 20 minutes or till vegetables are just tender. Stir in the cabbage. Cover and cook for 10 minutes more.

Stir the flour into yogurt or sour cream; stir into the cabbage mixture. Cook and stir till bubbly. Transfer the mixture to a 2-quart casserole.

Fold the salami pieces into quarters; arrange around edge of casserole, pressing salami slightly into vegetable mixture. Bake in a 350° oven about 15 minutes or till heated through. Spoon off fat. Makes 6 servings.

Per serving: 293 calories, 14 g protein, 26 g carbohydrate, 15 g fat, 28 mg cholesterol, 707 mg sodium, 54% USRDA vitamin A, 64% USRDA vitamin C, 20% USRDA thiamine, 14% USRDA riboflavin, 19% USRDA niacin, 13% USRDA iron, and 22% USRDA phosphorus.

EGGPLANT RELISH

Accompany other pasta dishes with this versatile hot relish.

- 1 small eggplant
- 2 tablespoons finely chopped onion
- 2 tablespoons chopped pitted ripe olives
- 2 tablespoons finely snipped parsley
- 2 tablespoons tomato paste
- 2 tablespoons water
- 1 tablespoon butter or margarine
- ½ teaspoon sugar
- ¼ teaspoon salt
- ¼ teaspoon dried oregano, crushed
- ¼ teaspoon dried thyme, crushed

Microwave directions: Cut a thin slice off side of eggplant so it will sit flat. Using a grapefruit knife, remove all of the pulp to within ½ inch of skin. Chop eggplant pulp.

For filling, in a 1-quart nonmetal casserole combine *1½ cups* of the eggplant pulp and remaining ingredients. Micro-cook, covered, on 100% power (HIGH) for 3 to 4 minutes or till tender, stirring once.

Spoon the filling into hollowed eggplant shell. Place eggplant in a shallow nonmetal baking dish or pie plate. Micro-cook, covered, for 3 minutes. Let stand, covered, while preparing Cream Sauce. Serve with the Greek-Style Manicotti. Makes 4 servings.

Conventional directions: Cut thin slice off side of eggplant so it will sit flat. Using a grapefruit knife, remove all of the pulp to within ½ inch of skin. Chop eggplant pulp.

For filling, cook *1½ cups* of the eggplant pulp and onion, uncovered, in a small amount of boiling water for 8 to 10 minutes; drain well. In a mixing bowl combine eggplant mixture and remaining ingredients.

Spoon the filling into hollowed eggplant. Place eggplant in a shallow baking dish or pie plate; cover with foil. Bake in a 350° oven for 20 to 30 minutes or till tender. Serve with Greek-Style Manicotti. Makes 4 servings.

Per serving: 53 calories, 1 g protein, 5 g carbohydrate, 4 g fat, 9 mg cholesterol, 209 mg sodium, and 13% USRDA vitamin C.

GREEK-STYLE MANICOTTI WITH EGGPLANT RELISH

 1 slightly beaten egg
 ¼ cup cream-style cottage cheese
 ¼ cup tomato paste
 2 tablespoons fine dry seasoned bread crumbs
 2 tablespoons finely chopped celery
 2 tablespoons finely chopped onion
 ½ teaspoon garlic salt
 ¼ teaspoon ground cinnamon
 ½ pound lean ground beef *or* lamb
 8 manicotti shells
 1 recipe Cream Sauce
 1 recipe Eggplant Relish (see recipe, opposite) (optional)
 2 tablespoons grated Parmesan cheese
Ground cinnamon (optional)
Celery leaves

Microwave directions: For filling, in a medium mixing bowl combine the egg, cottage cheese, tomato paste, bread crumbs, celery, onion, garlic salt, and the ¼ teaspoon cinnamon. Add the beef or lamb; mix well.

Using a small spoon, generously fill the uncooked manicotti shells with meat mixture. Arrange filled manicotti shells in a 10x6x2-inch nonmetal microwave-safe baking dish. Add enough *hot water* to *completely* cover pasta.

Cover dish with vented heavy-duty clear plastic wrap; micro-cook on 100% power (HIGH) for 20 minutes, turning dish a quarter-turn every 5 minutes. Let stand, covered, for 15 minutes.

Meanwhile, prepare Cream Sauce. If desired, prepare Eggplant Relish. Use a wide spatula to transfer manicotti to a serving platter. Pour Cream Sauce atop. Sprinkle with Parmesan cheese and cinnamon, if desired. Serve with Eggplant Relish and garnish with celery leaves, if desired. Serves 4.

Cream Sauce: In a 4-cup glass measure micro-cook 2 tablespoons *butter* or *margarine,* uncovered, on 100% power (HIGH) for 30 to 50 seconds or till butter is melted. Stir in 2 tablespoons *all-purpose flour,* ⅛ teaspoon *salt,* and ⅛ teaspoon *pepper.* Stir in 1 cup *milk.* Micro-cook, uncovered, on 100% power (HIGH) for 2½ to 3 minutes or till thickened and bubbly, stirring after each minute. Makes 1 cup.

Conventional directions: For filling, in a medium mixing bowl combine egg, cottage cheese, tomato paste, bread crumbs, celery, onion, garlic salt, and cinnamon. Add beef or lamb; mix well.

Using a small spoon, generously fill the uncooked manicotti shells with meat mixture. Arrange filled manicotti in baking dish. Add enough *hot water* to *completely* cover pasta. Bake, covered, in a 350° oven for about 70 minutes or till manicotti shells are tender.

Meanwhile, prepare Cream Sauce. If desired, prepare the Eggplant Relish. Transfer the manicotti to serving platter. Pour Cream Sauce atop. Sprinkle with Parmesan cheese and cinnamon, if desired. Serve with Eggplant Relish and garnish with celery leaves, if desired. Makes 4 servings.

Cream Sauce: In a small saucepan melt 2 tablespoons *butter* or *margarine.* Stir in 2 tablespoons *all-purpose flour,* ⅛ teaspoon *salt,* and ⅛ teaspoon *pepper.* Add 1 cup *milk* all at once. Cook and stir till thickened and bubbly; cook and stir 1 minute more. Makes 1 cup.

Per serving: 480 calories, 26 g protein, 54 g carbohydrate, 17 g fat, and 134 mg cholesterol, 542 mg sodium, 16% USRDA vitamin A, 27% USRDA thiamine, 29% USRDA riboflavin, 28% USRDA niacin, 15% USRDA calcium, 24% USRDA iron, and 34% USRDA phosphorus.

SNOWCAPPED PORK BURGERS

 2 egg yolks
 2 tablespoons fine dry bread crumbs
 2 tablespoons milk
 ½ teaspoon pepper
 ¼ teaspoon dried thyme, crushed
 ½ pound ground fully cooked ham
 ½ pound ground pork
 ½ of a 3-ounce package cream cheese, softened
 1 tablespoon milk
 ½ teaspoon prepared mustard
 2 egg whites
 ⅛ teaspoon cream of tartar
 ¼ cup shredded cheddar *or* Swiss cheese (1 ounce)
 6 bagels, split and toasted, *or* hamburger buns
Radish slices (optional)
Shredded cheddar cheese (optional)

Microwave directions: In a large mixing bowl combine egg yolks, crumbs, the 2 tablespoons milk, pepper, and thyme. Add ham and pork; mix well. Shape into six 3½-inch-thick patties.

Place patties in a 12x7½x2-inch nonmetal microwave-safe baking dish. Micro-cook, uncovered, on 100% power (HIGH) for 3 minutes. Turn patties; give dish a half-turn. Micro-cook, uncovered, for 4 to 6 minutes more or till nearly done.

Meanwhile, stir together cream cheese, the 1 tablespoon milk, and mustard; set aside. In a small mixer bowl beat egg whites and cream of tartar with an electric mixer on high speed till stiff peaks form (tips stand straight). Fold cream cheese mixture and the ¼ cup shredded cheese into egg whites.

Spoon *one-sixth* of the egg white mixture over *each* patty. Micro-cook the patties, uncovered, on 100% power (HIGH) about 2 minutes or till egg mixture is soft-set and no longer glossy and patties are well-done, giving dish a half-turn once. Serve patties on bagels with radish slices and additional cheese, if desired. Makes 6 servings.

Conventional directions: In a large mixing bowl stir together the egg yolks, the 2 tablespoons milk, bread crumbs, pepper, and thyme. Add the ground ham and pork; mix well. Shape into six 3½-inch-thick patties.

Place patties on unheated rack of broiler pan. Broil 4 to 5 inches from heat for 7 minutes. Turn; broil about 6 minutes more or till nearly done.

Meanwhile, stir together cream cheese, milk, and mustard. In a small mixer bowl beat egg whites and cream of tartar with an electric mixer on high speed till stiff peaks form (tips stand straight). Fold the cream cheese mixture and the ¼ cup shredded cheese into the beaten egg whites.

Spoon *one-sixth* of the egg white mixture over *each* patty. Broil for 2 to 3 minutes more or till meat is well-done and egg mixture is soft-set and no longer glossy. Serve on bagels or buns with radish slices and additional shredded cheese, if desired. Makes 6 servings.

Per serving: 426 calories, 29 g protein, 29 g carbohydrate, 21 g fat, 171 mg cholesterol, 689 mg sodium, 45% USRDA thiamine, 27% USRDA riboflavin, 28% USRDA niacin, 18% USRDA calcium, 25% USRDA iron, and 34% USRDA phosphorus.

CRANBERRY SIPPER

To make this delicious beverage extra special, try spiking it with your favorite kind of rum.

- **4 tablespoons light raisins**
- **4 tablespoons rum (optional)**
- **4 apple slices**
- **4 cinnamon sticks**
- **Ground cloves**
- **3 cups cranberry-raspberry or cranberry-apple drink**

Microwave directions: In each of four 6-ounce nonmetal mugs place *1 tablespoon* of raisins, *1 tablespoon* of rum (if desired), an apple slice, a cinnamon stick, and a dash ground cloves. Pour *¾ cup* cranberry drink into *each* mug.

Place the four mugs in the center of the microwave oven. Micro-cook, uncovered, on 100% power (HIGH) for 6 to 8 minutes or just till mixture starts to boil. Micro-cook on 50% power (MEDIUM) for 2 minutes more. Cool the cranberry mixture slightly before serving. Makes 4 (6-ounce) servings.

Conventional directions: In a large saucepan combine raisins, rum (if desired), apple slices, cinnamon sticks, cloves, and cranberry drink. Cook mixture over medium heat for 8 to 10 minutes or till mixture starts to boil.

Ladle the hot beverage into four mugs, dividing the apple slices, raisins, and cinnamon sticks evenly among the four mugs. Cool the cranberry mixture slightly before serving. Makes 4 (6-ounce) servings.

Per serving: 157 calories, 0.5 g protein, 40 g carbohydrate, 0.3 g fat, 4 mg sodium, 52% USRDA vitamin C.

CREAMY CHEESECAKE RING

Ginger adds a peppy flavor to this updated recipe.

- **Butter *or* margarine**
- **2 tablespoons finely crushed graham crackers**
- **1 cup milk**
- **½ teaspoon ground ginger**
- **3 8-ounce packages cream cheese, cut up**
- **1 4½-ounce package custard dessert mix**
- **¼ cup sugar**
- **1½ teaspoons finely shredded lemon peel**
- **1 recipe Nectarine Sauce**
- **Fresh nectarine *or* peach slices (optional)**
- **Mint sprigs (optional)**

Microwave directions: Generously butter a 6-cup ring mold. Coat mold with graham cracker crumbs; set aside. In a 2-cup glass measure combine milk and ginger. Micro-cook, uncovered, on 100% power (HIGH) for 1½ to 2 minutes or till heated through.

In a 2½-quart nonmetal bowl micro-cook the cream cheese, uncovered, on 50% power (MEDIUM) for 2 to 3 minutes or till softened. Stir in the custard mix, sugar, and lemon peel. Gradually stir in the heated milk mixture.

Micro-cook, uncovered, on 100% power (HIGH) about 4½ minutes or till smooth and thick, stirring every 1½ minutes. Micro-cook, uncovered, on 100% power (HIGH) for 1½ minutes more. Cover surface with clear plastic wrap. Cool for 15 minutes.

Pour mixture into prepared mold. Cover and chill for 4 hours or overnight. Unmold onto serving platter. Spoon Nectarine Sauce over top. Garnish with nectarine or peach slices and mint, if desired. Makes 12 servings.

Nectarine Sauce: In a blender container or food processor bowl combine 2 cups *fresh* or *frozen (thawed) peeled nectarine* or *peach slices,* ½ cup *water,* 2 tablespoons *honey,* and 1½ teaspoons *cornstarch.* Cover and blend or process till very smooth.

Transfer mixture to a 4-cup glass measure. Micro-cook on 100% power (HIGH) for 1 minute; stir. Micro-cook for 3 to 4 minutes more or till thickened and bubbly, stirring every 30 seconds. Micro-cook for 30 seconds more. Cover sauce and chill thoroughly. Makes 1¾ cups sauce.

Conventional directions: Generously butter a 6-cup ring mold. Coat mold with the graham cracker crumbs; set aside. Cut up cheese; let stand at room temperature about 1 hour.

In a 3-quart saucepan combine the cream cheese, milk, ginger, custard mix, sugar, and lemon peel. Cook and stir over medium heat about 12 minutes or till mixture is smooth and thick. Remove from heat. Cover surface with clear plastic wrap. Cool 15 minutes.

Pour cheese mixture into prepared mold. Cover and chill 4 hours or overnight. Unmold onto a serving platter. Spoon Nectarine Sauce over top. Garnish with nectarine or peach slices and mint, if desired. Makes 12 servings.

Nectarine Sauce: In a blender container or food processor bowl combine 2 cups *fresh* or *frozen (thawed) peeled nectarine* or *peach slices,* ½ cup *water,* 2 tablespoons *honey,* and 1½ teaspoons *cornstarch;* cover and blend till smooth.

Transfer fruit mixture to a 2-quart saucepan. Cook and stir over medium heat till bubbly; cook and stir 2 minutes more. Cover and chill mixture thoroughly. Makes 1¾ cups sauce.

Per serving: 310 calories, 6 g protein, 24 g carbohydrate, 22 g fat, 66 mg cholesterol, 207 mg sodium, 26% USRDA vitamin A, and 11% USRDA riboflavin.

MARBLED CREAM PIE

If you're having trouble deciding on dessert tonight, try this luscious Marbled Cream Pie. This sweet sensation is a crispy chocolate crust that holds both a rich chocolate filling and a creamy vanilla filling. The team of chocolate and vanilla in this pie produces a dazzling duo of flavors.

- 1 recipe Chocolate Crust (see recipe, right)
- 1¼ cups sugar
- ⅓ cup cornstarch
- 4 cups milk
- 3 tablespoons butter *or* margarine, cut up
- 5 beaten egg yolks
- 1 teaspoon vanilla
- 2 squares (2 ounces) unsweetened chocolate

Fresh strawberry, halved (optional)

Microwave directions: Make Chocolate Crust; cool. In a 3-quart nonmetal mixing bowl stir together sugar and cornstarch. Stir in milk; add butter or margarine. Micro-cook, uncovered, on 100% (HIGH) 10 to 12 minutes or till mixture is bubbly, stirring once after 3 minutes and then stirring after every minute. Micro-cook 2 minutes more, stirring after every minute.

Gradually stir about *1 cup* of the hot mixture into the beaten yolks. Stir the egg yolk mixture into the remaining hot mixture in the bowl. Stir mixture till well blended. Stir in vanilla. Transfer *half* of the pudding mixture (about 2 cups) to another bowl.

Place wrapped chocolate squares in the microwave oven with folded side of wrapper up. Micro-cook on 100%

power (HIGH) for 2½ to 3 minutes or till melted. Lift wrappers by folded ends; stir the melted unsweetened chocolate into one portion of the pudding. Discard wrappers.

Turn chocolate mixture into the Chocolate Crust; gently spoon the vanilla mixture into the crust. (The filling mixtures will be very thick.) Draw a knife through the filling mixtures to form a pinwheel design. Cover and chill several hours. Garnish with a strawberry, if desired. Makes 8 servings.

Conventional directions: In a 2-quart saucepan combine the sugar and cornstarch. Gradually stir in the milk. Cook and stir over medium heat till mixture is thickened and bubbly; cook and stir 2 minutes more.

Gradually stir about *1 cup* of hot mixture into beaten yolks. Return all to saucepan. Cook and stir for 2 minutes more. Stir in the butter or margarine and vanilla.

Meanwhile, melt the unsweetened chocolate over low heat. Transfer *half* of the mixture to another bowl; stir in the melted chocolate.

Turn the chocolate mixture into crust; spoon the vanilla mixture into the chocolate crust. (The filling mixtures will be very thick.) Draw a knife through the filling mixtures to form a pinwheel design. Cover and chill pie for several hours. Garnish with a strawberry, if desired. Makes 8 servings.

Per serving: 484 calories, 9 g protein, 58 g carbohydrate, 26 g fat, 193 mg cholesterol, 204 mg sodium, 16% USRDA vitamin A, 13% USRDA thiamine, 21% USRDA riboflavin, 17% USRDA calcium, 10% USRDA iron, 23% USRDA phosphorus.

CHOCOLATE CRUST

- 1¼ cups all-purpose flour
- ¼ teaspoon salt
- ⅓ cup shortening
- 1 tablespoon butter *or* margarine
- 2 tablespoons sugar
- 2 tablespoons unsweetened cocoa powder

Microwave directions: In a mixing bowl stir together flour and salt. Cut in shortening and butter or margarine till mixture resembles coarse crumbs. Stir in sugar and cocoa powder.

Sprinkle 1 tablespoon *cold water* over part of the mixture. Gently toss with a fork; push to side of bowl. Repeat with 3 to 4 tablespoons *cold water* till all is moistened. Form into a ball.

On a lightly floured surface, flatten dough with hands. Roll dough from center to edge, forming a circle about ⅛ inch thick. Place the pastry in a 9-inch nonmetal microwave-safe pie plate, being careful not to stretch pastry. Trim the pastry ½ inch beyond edge. Fold pastry under and flute edge to form a high rim. Use a fork to prick bottom and sides of pastry.

Micro-cook, uncovered, on 100% power (HIGH) for 5 to 7 minutes or till done, rotating the dish a quarter-turn twice. Cool the crust on a wire rack. Makes one 9-inch crust.

Conventional directions: Prepare pastry as directed. On a lightly floured surface, flatten dough with hands. Roll dough from center to edge, forming a circle about ⅛ inch thick. Place the pastry in a 9-inch pie plate, trim and flute pastry edge as directed. Use a fork to prick bottom and sides of pastry.

Bake in a 450° oven for 10 to 12 minutes or till done. Cool on a wire rack. Makes one 9-inch crust.

CARROT CAKES WITH CUSTARD SAUCE

¼ cup hot water
⅓ cup granola
⅔ cup all-purpose flour
⅓ cup packed brown sugar
1 teaspoon baking powder
Dash salt
1 beaten egg
⅓ cup coarsely shredded carrot
2 tablespoons cooking oil
½ teaspoon shredded orange peel
3 tablespoons granola, crumbled
1 recipe Orange Custard Sauce
Finely shredded orange peel
(optional)

Microwave directions: Pour hot water over the ⅓ cup granola; set aside. In a mixing bowl stir together the flour, sugar, baking powder, and salt. Make a well in the center of dry ingredients.

Stir egg, carrot, oil, and ½ teaspoon orange peel into the moistened granola; add to the dry ingredients, stirring just till moistened (batter should be lumpy).

Spoon the batter into five lightly greased 6-ounce custard cups. Top each with some of the crumbled granola. Arrange the custard cups in a circle in the microwave oven. Micro-cook, uncovered, on 100% power (HIGH) for 2 to 2½ minutes or till a wooden toothpick inserted near the center comes out clean. Let cakes cool in cups for 3 to 4 minutes. Transfer cakes to a wire rack.

Meanwhile, prepare Orange Custard Sauce. Spoon sauce into dishes. Place one warm cake in each dish; spoon additional sauce over cakes. Garnish with orange peel, if desired. Serve immediately. Makes 5 servings.

Orange Custard Sauce: Melt 1 tablespoon *butter* or *margarine* on 100% power (HIGH) for 20 seconds. Stir in 2 tablespoons *sugar*, 1 teaspoon *cornstarch*, and ½ teaspoon *finely shredded orange peel*. Add ⅔ cup *milk* all at once.

Micro-cook for 1 to 1½ minutes or till bubbly. Gradually stir *half* of the hot mixture into 1 beaten *egg yolk;* return all to 2-cup glass measure. Micro-cook for 25 to 30 seconds more. Makes ¾ cup sauce.

Conventional directions: Pour hot water over the ⅓ cup granola; set aside. In a mixing bowl stir together the flour, sugar, baking powder, and salt. Make a well in the center of the dry ingredients.

Stir the egg, carrot, cooking oil, and orange peel into the moistened granola; add to the dry ingredients, stirring just till moistened (batter should be lumpy). Grease or line eight ½-inch muffin cups with paper bake cups. Spoon batter into cups. Sprinkle crumbled granola over each. Bake in a 375° oven for 20 minutes.

Remove from pans; cool on wire rack. Prepare Orange Custard Sauce. Spoon sauce into dishes. Place one cake in each dish; spoon additional sauce over cakes. Garnish each serving with orange peel, if desired. Serve immediately. Makes 5 servings.

Orange Custard Sauce: In a small saucepan melt 1 tablespoon *butter* or *margarine* over medium heat. Stir in 2 tablespoons *sugar*, 1 teaspoon *cornstarch*, and ½ teaspoon *finely shredded orange peel*. Add ⅔ cup *milk* all at once. Cook and stir over medium heat till thickened and bubbly; cook and stir for 2 minutes more.

Gradually stir *half* of the hot mixture into 1 beaten *egg yolk;* return all to saucepan. Cook and stir till bubbly. Makes ¾ cup sauce.

Per serving: 273 calories, 6 g protein, 38 g carbohydrate, 11 g fat, 113 mg cholesterol, 183 mg sodium, 23% USRDA vitamin A, 19% USRDA thiamine, 21% USRDA riboflavin, 12% USRDA niacin, and 12% USRDA phosphorus.

TONY'S MULTIGRAIN PIZZA

This recipe combines whole wheat flour, oat flour, and cornmeal to give an old-fashioned grain flavor to a traditional pizza crust.

1 cup whole wheat flour
1 cup oat flour*
¼ cup cornmeal
1 teaspoon baking powder
⅔ cup milk
¼ cup cooking oil
5 slices bacon
½ pound ground beef
2 8-ounce cans pizza sauce
½ green pepper, cut into rings
½ sweet red pepper, cut into rings
¼ cup sliced pitted ripe olives
1½ cups shredded mozzarella cheese (6 ounces)
1½ cups shredded cheddar cheese (6 ounces)
2 tablespoons grated Parmesan cheese

For crust, in a mixing bowl combine whole wheat flour, oat flour, cornmeal, and baking powder. Add milk and oil; mix well. Using greased hands, press dough into a greased 14-inch pizza pan. Build up the edges slightly; snip at 1-inch intervals. Bake in a 425° oven for 12 to 15 minutes or till done.

Meanwhile, for topping, cook bacon till crisp; remove. Drain on paper towels; crumble. Cook beef till brown; drain off fat.

Spread sauce over crust. Spoon cooked beef over sauce. Top with pepper rings, sliced olives, and bacon. Sprinkle pizza with mozzarella cheese, cheddar cheese, and Parmesan cheese. Return to oven. Bake for 10 to 15 minutes more. Makes 4 or 5 servings.

Note: To make oat flour, in a blender container or food processor bowl place 1¼ cups *rolled* or *quick-cooking oats*. Cover; blend till fine.

OCTOBER

20 tips to help you finance your child's college education

Better Homes
and Gardens.

October 1984 $1.50

PRIZE-WINNING DECORATING IDEAS TO PUT TO USE IN YOUR HOME

Parenting: Sensible answers to kids' questions about sex

How to cut home heating costs

TREND SETTING NEW HOUSES — STYLISH, EFFICIENT, AFFORDABLE

Money: Where to get good financial advice

FUN FOODS for festive fall get-togethers

Crafts: Knit the hot, new plaids for fall

Festive Fall Get-Togethers

R obust appetites go hand in hand with Indian-summer activities. So whatever work or play you share with family and friends, include hearty foods in the plans. Choose no-fuss recipes from the following pages to suit indoor and outdoor occasions—fancy picnic fare, hearty soup buffet, or pleasing party snacks.

Stage A Picnic

Cap an autumn outing with this savory spread of foods. Prepare the pack-and-carry feast the day before your fun begins. Then, follow the toting tips accompanying the recipes and the goods will arrive at your picnic site shipshape and ready to serve.

By Joy Taylor

MENU

CHICKEN ROLL WITH
CAPER SAUCE*

HARVEST GRAINS SALAD*

ASSORTED VEGETABLES

BREADSTICKS

CAKE-IN-A-TART*

BURGUNDY SUNSET*

Serve A Soup Buffet

After a busy day with friends, you'll appreciate the simplicity of this come-and-get-it meal. Invite everyone to concoct a bowl of soup from the fixed-ahead offerings—broth or cream soup base, meatballs, chicken livers, and vegetables. Guests help with dessert, too; they wrap pastry around apples and spices. While the dumplings bake, diners savor the soup.

Photographs: Left, Terri Sandison/Lightra; above, George Ceola

MENU

HOT CHEESE PUFFS*

CREATE-A-SOUP* with
CREAMY SOUP BASE*
BEEF BROTH BASE*
MINIATURE MEATBALLS*
STIR-FRIED LIVERS*
VEGETABLES / CROUTONS

STACKED BREAD LOAF*

GUACAMOLE SALAD*

AD-LIB APPLE DUMPLINGS*

ICED LEMONADE

Host An Open House

Gather your family and neighbors for an evening of home-brewed fun. Whether the party theme is Halloween or a simple celebration of autumn, decorate the party spot with seasonal colors. And for irresistible snacking, set out this tableful of nutritious finger foods.

Photographs: Left, Hedrich-Blessing; above, Hopkins Associates

MENU

FILL-A-PITA* with
NUTTY FRUIT SPREAD*
CHUNKY CHICKEN FILLING*
SUNNY SESAME BUTTER*

SPINACH NUGGETS*

SUGAR-AND-SPICE
POTATO BREAD*

INDIAN CARAMEL CORN*

NEAT WHEAT BROWNIES*

HOT APPLE CIDER

Note: Some nutrient information is given by gram weight per serving. The United States Recommended Daily Allowances (USRDA) for selected vitamins and minerals are given in the following recipes when the value exceeds 10 percent. The USRDA tell the amount of certain nutrients necessary to meet the dietary needs of most healthy people.

To obtain the nutrition analysis of each recipe, the following guidelines were used:
● When ingredient options appear in a recipe, the analysis was calculated using the first ingredient choice.
● Optional ingredients were omitted in the analyses.
● The nutrition analyses for recipes calling for fresh ingredients were calculated using the measurements for raw fruits, vegetables, and meats.
● If a recipe gives optional serving sizes (such as "Makes 6 to 8 servings"), the nutrition analysis was calculated using the first choice.

For good health, include a variety of foods from the Basic Food Groups in your daily diet. Follow your physician's advice if you are on a restricted diet.

Note: Microwave recipes were tested in countertop microwave ovens that operate on 600 to 700 watts. Cooking times are approximate because ovens vary by manufacturer.

Stage a Picnic
One day before serving:
● Roast Chicken Roll; chill.
● Mix the Caper Sauce; chill.
● Partially prepare the Harvest Grains Salad; chill.
● Bake Cake-in-a-Tart; cool and store.
Day of picnic:
● Slice Chicken Roll. Reassemble the slices; securely wrap in foil. Place the roll in a plastic bag; tie bag. Pack in a well-insulated cooler.
● Wrap assorted vegetables in plastic bags; pack in a cooler.
● Stir the oil and pear into Harvest Grains Salad; pack in a cooler.
● Frost Cake-in-a-Tart; replace side of springform pan around tart for transporting. Cover with foil.
● Prepare Burgundy Sunset; transfer to insulated beverage container.

CHICKEN ROLL WITH CAPER SAUCE

To bone the chicken, work slowly with a very sharp knife.

1 3½- to 4-pound whole roasting chicken
½ teaspoon dried thyme, crushed
½ of a 9-ounce package frozen whole green beans, thawed
2 to 3 ounces Swiss cheese, cut into two sticks (2½x1x¾ inches)
2 to 3 ounces cheddar cheese, cut into two sticks (2½x1x¾ inches)
8 slices (3 to 4 ounces) prosciutto *or* boiled ham
1 recipe Caper Sauce (see recipe, opposite)

To bone chicken, remove the chicken wings, leaving as much skin on chicken as possible. (Reserve wings for another use.) Remove tail. Place chicken, breast side down, with legs pointed away from you. With a sharp, short-blade knife, make a cut along the center of the backbone, the entire length of the bird (from the tail area to the neck). Working on one side of the chicken, use the knife and your fingers to scrape and push the meat away from the bone along the rib cage, working toward the breastbone. (Be careful not to cut through the skin at any point.) Sever thigh joint. Make a lengthwise cut along meaty side of leg

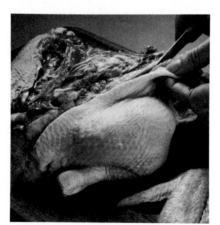

and thigh bones. Using knife and fingers, scrape and push meat from bones. Discard leg and thigh bones. Repeat boning steps on other side of chicken.

Place the boned chicken, skin side down, on a cutting board. Cut and discard any excess fat. Cover chicken with clear plastic wrap. Pound with meat mallet in thicker areas to form a 10-inch square of even thickness. Sprinkle chicken with the thyme and pepper.

Arrange the beans over the center of the chicken, perpendicular to where breastbone was removed and to within 1 inch from sides. Securely wrap each stick of cheese in two slices of the prosciutto. Lay wrapped cheese alongside beans, with Swiss cheese on one side and cheddar on the other.

Bring sides of chicken to the center, overlapping the edges and shaping the chicken roll to about 6 to 7 inches in

length. Tie crosswise and lengthwise with string to seal. If skin is broken, overlap and hold together with wooden toothpicks.

Place roll, seam side down, in a 13x9x2-inch baking pan. Roast, uncovered, in a 350° oven for 1½ hours. Cool. Cover; chill. To serve, remove strings and wooden toothpicks. Using a sharp knife, thinly slice the chilled chicken. Serve with Caper Sauce. Serves 8 to 10.

Per serving (with sauce): 835 calories, 74 g protein, 3 g carbohydrate, 57 g fat, 372 mg cholesterol, 797 mg sodium, 46% USRDA vitamin A, 22% USRDA thiamine, 44% USRDA riboflavin, 96% USRDA niacin, 24% USRDA calcium, 32% USRDA iron, and 73% USRDA phosphorus.

CAPER SAUCE

If you have leftover sauce, stir a few tablespoons of milk into it and use it as a salad dressing.

- ½ **cup dairy sour cream**
- ½ **cup mayonnaise *or* salad dressing**
- 3 **tablespoons milk**
- 2 **tablespoons capers, chopped**
- 1 **tablespoon snipped parsley**
- 1 **teaspoon Dijon-style mustard**

In a bowl combine all the ingredients. Transfer to a storage container. Cover and chill thoroughly. Makes 1⅓ cups.

Per tablespoon: 51 calories, 0.3 g protein, 0.5 g carbohydrate, 5 g fat, 6 mg cholesterol, and 47 mg sodium.

HARVEST GRAINS SALAD

Toss the cubed pear with a little lemon juice or ascorbic acid color keeper to prevent it from discoloring.

- ½ **cup wild rice**
- 2½ **cups chicken broth**
- ½ **cup bulgur wheat**
- ½ **of a 6-ounce package chopped mixed dried fruit (¾ cup)**
- 2 **tablespoons salad oil**
- 1 **pear, cored and cubed**

Rinse the uncooked wild rice. In a 2-quart saucepan combine the rice and broth. Bring to boiling; reduce heat. Cover and simmer 40 minutes. Remove from heat. *Do not drain.* Stir in bulgur wheat and dried fruit. Transfer to a storage container. Cover; chill. Before serving, stir in oil and pear. Serves 8.

Per serving: 160 calories, 4 g protein, 28 g carbohydrate, 5 g fat, 251 mg sodium, 11% USRDA vitamin A, and 10% USRDA niacin.

CAKE-IN-A-TART

- 1 **9-inch folded refrigerated unbaked piecrust**
- 1 **cup all-purpose flour**
- 1½ **teaspoons baking powder**
- ¼ **teaspoon salt**
- ⅔ **cup sugar**
- ½ **cup butter *or* margarine**
- 1 **teaspoon vanilla**
- 2 **eggs**
- ½ **cup milk**
- ½ **cup orange marmalade**
- 1 **recipe Confectioners' Icing**

Press pastry on bottom and 2 inches up sides of an 8-inch springform pan. Line pastry with foil. Bake in a 450° oven for 6 minutes; remove foil. Cool.

Stir together the flour, baking powder, and salt; set aside. In a mixer bowl beat together the sugar, butter or margarine, and vanilla. Beat in the eggs. Add the dry ingredients and milk alternately to the creamed mixture. (Batter may appear curdled.)

Spread marmalade over bottom of crust. Spoon cake batter into pan. Bake in a 375° oven about 45 minutes or till the cake tests done. Cool 10 minutes in pan on a wire rack. Remove the sides of pan; cool thoroughly. Drizzle Confectioners' Icing over cake. Slice to serve. Makes 8 servings.

Confectioners' Icing: Stir together 2 cups *sifted powdered sugar* and enough *milk* to make of drizzling consistency.

Per serving: 519 calories, 6 g protein, 79 g carbohydrate, 21 g fat, 101 mg cholesterol, 434 mg sodium, 13% USRDA vitamin A, 14% USRDA thiamine, and 11% USRDA riboflavin.

BURGUNDY SUNSET

You can prepare this beverage up to six hours before serving. To keep it hot, pour boiling water into two insulated containers and let stand, covered, for 5 minutes. Drain water. Pour hot Burgundy Sunset into heated containers and seal.

- 8 **whole cardamom seeds**
- 6 **inches stick cinnamon, broken**
- 5 **cups water**
- 2 **6-ounce cans frozen apple juice concentrate**
- 1 **750-ml bottle burgundy (about 4 cups)**

Cinnamon sticks (optional)

Tie cardamom and cinnamon in a cheesecloth bag; place in a Dutch oven. Add water. Bring to boiling; reduce heat. Cover and simmer for 10 minutes. Remove spice bag; discard. Add apple juice concentrate to saucepan; bring just to boiling. Add burgundy; heat through. Serve in mugs with cinnamon sticks. Makes 8 (8-ounce) servings.

Per serving: 217 calories, 0.3 g protein, 34 g carbohydrate, 8 mg sodium, and 11% USRDA iron.

HOT CHEESE PUFFS

Bake these puffs straight from the freezer and serve them piping hot.

- 1 **cup shredded Monterey Jack cheese with jalapeño peppers**
- 1 **3-ounce package cream cheese, cubed**
- ⅓ **cup butter *or* margarine**
- 2 **egg whites**
- 30 **1-inch cubes French bread (4 to 5 slices)**

In a medium saucepan combine the cheeses and butter or margarine. Cook and stir over low heat till melted; remove from heat. Beat egg whites till stiff peaks form (tips stand straight). Fold cheese mixture into egg whites.

Dip bread cubes into cheese mixture, scraping off the excess with a spatula. Place coated bread cubes on a baking sheet lined with waxed paper. Freeze till firm (30 to 60 minutes). Transfer to plastic bags; freeze.

At serving time, place frozen cubes on a lightly greased baking sheet. Bake in a 400° oven about 10 minutes or till puffed and golden brown. Serve immediately. Makes 30.

Per puff: 48 calories, 1 g protein, 3 g carbohydrate, 3 g fat, 10 mg cholesterol, and 71 mg sodium.

Serve a Soup Buffet

Two days before serving:
- Prepare and freeze Hot Cheese Puffs.
- Prepare and chill the Guacamole Salad.
- Mix dough for Ad-Lib Apple Dumplings; cut into squares, cover, and chill.

One day before serving:
- For Create-a-Soup: steam carrots and zucchini; cool. Place carrots, zucchini, ham, spinach, water chestnuts, croutons, and cheese in serving dishes or on a serving tray. Cover and chill.
- Prepare and chill Creamy Soup Base.
- Prepare and chill Beef Broth Base.
- Bake and chill Miniature Meatballs.
- Bake Stacked Bread Loaf; cover.
- Prepare and chill lemonade.

At serving time:
- Unmold and garnish the Guacamole Salad.
- Let vegetables, ham, and cheese for soup stand at room temperature.
- Let the pastry for dumplings stand at room temperature. Peel apples, brush with lemon juice or ascorbic acid color keeper, and set out remaining dessert ingredients.
- Bake Hot Cheese Puffs and heat Miniature Meatballs.
- Heat Creamy Soup Base.
- Heat Beef Broth Base, adding pasta, mushrooms, and onions as directed in recipe.
- Make Stir-Fried Livers; keep warm.
- Arrange foods and table service buffet style on kitchen counter.

GUACAMOLE SALAD

- 1 envelope unflavored gelatin
- 2 tablespoons sugar
- ½ cup water
- 1 large cucumber, peeled and chopped
- 2 tablespoons vinegar
- ½ cup bottled buttermilk salad dressing
- 1 envelope unflavored gelatin
- ¼ cup water
- 1¼ cups mashed avocado (2 large)
- 1 tablespoon lemon juice
- Several dashes bottled hot pepper sauce
- 1 cup vegetable juice cocktail
- Leaf lettuce (optional)
- Cherry tomatoes, sliced (optional)
- Cucumber slices, halved (optional)
- Avocado slices (optional)

Soften the first envelope gelatin and the 2 tablespoons sugar in the ½ cup water for 5 minutes. Place over hot water, stirring till dissolved.

In a blender container or food processor bowl combine the cucumber and vinegar. Cover and blend till pureed. If necessary, add enough *water* to puree to measure 1¼ cups.

Stir dissolved gelatin into cucumber mixture. Stir in buttermilk salad dressing. Set aside *¾ cup* of the cucumber mixture. Pour remaining cucumber mixture into a lightly oiled 8x4x2-inch loaf pan. Chill till almost firm.

Meanwhile, soften the second envelope of gelatin in the ¼ cup water for 5 minutes. Place over hot water, stirring till dissolved.

In a bowl stir together the mashed avocado, lemon juice, pepper sauce, *2 tablespoons* of the softened gelatin, and the reserved ¾ cup cucumber mixture; set aside at room temperature.

Combine remaining dissolved gelatin and vegetable juice cocktail; pour atop cucumber layer. Chill till almost firm (sticky to the touch).

Spread avocado mixture atop vegetable juice layer. Lightly press clear plastic wrap over avocado layer. Chill till firm. To serve, unmold salad onto a lettuce-lined platter. Garnish with cherry tomatoes, cucumber, and avocado. Makes 10 to 12 servings.

Per serving: 147 calories, 3 g protein, 9 g carbohydrate, 12 g fat, 6 mg cholesterol, 121 mg sodium, and 18% USRDA vitamin C.

AD-LIB APPLE DUMPLINGS

Let each person assemble his or her own apple dumpling.

- 3⅓ cups all-purpose flour
- ½ teaspoon salt
- 1 cup shortening
- ½ cup very finely chopped pecans
- ¾ cup water
- 12 small apples, peeled and cored
- Light raisins *or* miniature semisweet chocolate pieces
- Sugar (about ¾ cup)
- Ground cinnamon
- Ground nutmeg
- Light cream *or* ice cream (optional)

In a mixing bowl combine flour and salt; cut in shortening till pieces are the size of small peas. Stir in the pecans. Sprinkle *2 tablespoons* of the water over part of the mixture. Gently toss with a fork; push to side of bowl. Repeat with remaining water till all is moistened. Form the dough into a ball; divide dough into two portions.

On a lightly floured surface roll *half* of the dough into an 18x12-inch rectangle. (Trim rectangle to exact size; use any extra dough to cut out designs with a small cookie cutter, if desired.) Using a fluted pastry wheel, cut rectangle into six 6-inch squares.

Place dough squares in a stack, separating them with pieces of waxed paper. Repeat with remaining dough. Cover and chill dough.

For dumplings, remove the pastry dough squares from refrigerator. Let stand 30 minutes at room temperature. Place *one* cored apple in center of *each* dough square. Fill center of apple with raisins or chocolate pieces.

Sprinkle each with about *1 tablespoon* sugar and desired spices. Moisten edges of pastry with water. Fold corners to center; pinch edges to seal. Top with pastry cutouts, if desired.

Place in two shallow baking pans. Bake in a 375° oven for 40 to 45 minutes or till pastry is brown. Serve warm with light cream or ice cream. Makes 12 servings.

Per serving: 435 calories, 5 g protein, 60 g carbohydrate, 21 g fat, 93 mg sodium, 20% USRDA thiamine, 10% USRDA riboflavin, and 10% USRDA niacin.

CREATE-A-SOUP

Prepare these condiments to stir into Creamy Soup Base and Beef Broth Base. Be sure to cut the vegetables and ham into very small pieces. If cut too large, they won't heat through when added to the soup base.

- 2 **medium carrots, finely shredded**
- 2 **medium zucchini, finely shredded**
- ½ **pound fully cooked ham, cut into very thin strips**
- 2 **cups fresh spinach, cut into narrow strips**
- 1 **8-ounce can sliced water chestnuts, drained**
- **Grated Parmesan cheese (optional)**
- 1 **recipe Miniature Meatballs (see recipe, right)**
- 1 **recipe Stir-Fried Livers (see recipe, page 152)**
- **Herb-seasoned stuffing croutons (optional)**

Place carrots and zucchini in a steamer basket over, but not touching, boiling water. Cover; steam 4 minutes or just till tender. Cool. Cover and chill.

At serving time, let carrots, zucchini, ham, spinach, water chestnuts, and Parmesan cheese stand at room temperature. Stir the desired vegetables, ham, Miniature Meatballs, or Stir-Fried Livers into bowls of Creamy Soup Base or Beef Broth Base. Top each serving of soup with croutons or cheese. Makes 8 to 10 servings.

Note: The nutritional content of each soup serving will vary depending on the ingredients chosen.

CREAMY SOUP BASE

If this mixture seems too thick after reheating, stir in additional milk or water to thin it.

- 2 **10½-ounce cans condensed chicken broth**
- ½ **cup chopped onion**
- ½ **cup shredded carrot**
- ½ **cup chopped celery**
- ¼ **cup butter *or* margarine**
- ⅓ **cup all-purpose flour**
- ⅛ **teaspoon ground nutmeg**
- 4 **cups milk**
- **Water *or* milk (optional)**

In a 3- or 4-quart saucepan combine the chicken broth, onion, carrot, and celery. Bring to boiling; reduce heat. Cover and simmer about 15 minutes or till vegetables are very tender. Place the vegetable mixture in a blender container or food processor bowl; cover and blend till smooth. Set aside.

In a saucepan melt the butter or margarine. Stir in the flour and nutmeg. Add the pureed vegetable mixture and milk. Cook and stir till thickened and bubbly. Remove from heat; cover surface with waxed paper. Cool. Remove paper. Cover and chill.

At serving time, bring the soup base to boiling over medium-high heat, stirring occasionally. Serve hot. Makes about 7 cups.

Per cup: 208 calories, 9 g protein, 15 g carbohydrate, 13 g fat, 40 mg cholesterol, 731 mg sodium, 27% USRDA vitamin A, 17% USRDA riboflavin, 11% USRDA niacin, 18% USRDA calcium, and 15% USRDA phosphorus.

BEEF BROTH BASE

- 5 **14½-ounce cans beef broth**
- 1 **small onion, sliced**
- 1 **cup celery leaves**
- 6 **sprigs parsley**
- 2 **bay leaves**
- 4 **whole black peppercorns**
- 1 **teaspoon dried basil, crushed**
- ½ **cup tripolini (tiny bow-tie pasta)**
- 1½ **cups sliced fresh mushrooms**
- ½ **cup thinly sliced green onions**

In a 3- to 4-quart saucepan combine the beef broth, onion, celery leaves, parsley, bay leaves, peppercorns, and basil. Bring to boiling; reduce heat. Cover and simmer 20 minutes. Strain broth; discard vegetables and seasonings. Return broth to saucepan. Cool. Cover and refrigerate the mixture till serving time.

At serving time, bring broth to boiling over medium-high heat. Add the pasta; cook 10 minutes or till pasta is tender. Add the mushrooms and green onions; heat through. Serve immediately. Makes about 8 cups.

Per cup: 102 calories, 9 g protein, 14 g carbohydrate, 2 g fat, 24 mg cholesterol, and 1,713 mg sodium.

MINIATURE MEATBALLS

You can reheat these meatballs and bake the Hot Cheese Puffs in a conventional oven at the same time.

- 1 **beaten egg**
- ¼ **cup milk**
- 1 **tablespoon prepared mustard**
- ½ **teaspoon salt**
- **Several dashes bottled hot pepper sauce**
- 1 **cup soft bread crumbs**
- ½ **pound ground pork**
- ½ **pound ground veal**
- **Cherry tomato halves (optional)**
- **Celery leaves (optional)**

In a bowl combine egg, milk, mustard, salt, and hot pepper sauce. Stir in the bread crumbs. Add pork and veal; mix well. Shape meat mixture into 48 meatballs. Place in a 13x9x2-inch baking pan. Bake in a 375° oven for 15 to 20 minutes. Drain; cool. Transfer to a 2-quart casserole; cover and refrigerate till serving time.

To serve, heat meatballs, covered, in the 2-quart casserole in a 400° oven for 25 to 30 minutes or till meatballs are hot. Garnish with cherry tomato halves and celery leaves, if desired. Serve as a Create-a-Soup accompaniment. Makes 48.

Microwave directions: In a bowl combine egg, milk, mustard, salt, and hot pepper sauce. Stir in bread crumbs. Add pork and veal; mix well. Shape meat mixture into 48 meatballs.

Place meatballs in a 12x7½x2-inch nonmetal baking dish. Micro-cook, uncovered, on 100% power (HIGH) for 6 to 7 minutes or till no longer pink, rearranging meatballs and rotating the dish a quarter-turn after 4 minutes. Drain and cool. Transfer to a 2-quart nonmetal casserole; cover and refrigerate till serving time.

To serve, micro-cook meatballs in a covered 2-quart casserole on 50% power (MEDIUM) for 7 to 8 minutes or till meatballs are hot, stirring gently once. Garnish with cherry tomato halves and celery leaves, if desired. Serve as a Create-a-Soup accompaniment. Makes 48.

Per meatball: 28 calories, 3 g protein, 1 g carbohydrate, 1 g fat, 14 mg cholesterol, and 38 mg sodium.

STACKED BREAD LOAF

Let diners serve themselves by pulling off breadsticks.

1½ to 2 cups all-purpose flour
 1 package active dry yeast
 ¾ cup milk
 2 tablespoons butter *or* margarine
 1 tablespoon sugar
 ½ teaspoon salt
 2 tablespoons butter *or* margarine, melted
 2 to 3 teaspoons sesame seed, toasted, *or* poppy seed
 1 slightly beaten egg yolk
 1 tablespoon water

In small mixer bowl combine ¾ *cup* of the flour and the yeast. In a saucepan heat the milk, 2 tablespoons butter or margarine, sugar, and salt just till warm (115° to 120°) and butter is almost melted, stirring constantly. Add to flour mixture.

Beat the mixture with an electric mixer on low speed for 30 seconds, scraping sides of bowl constantly. Beat 3 minutes on high speed. With a wooden spoon, stir in as much of the remaining flour as you can.

Turn dough out onto a lightly floured surface. Knead in enough of the remaining flour to make a moderately stiff dough that is smooth and elastic (6 to 8 minutes total). Shape dough into a ball. Place in a lightly greased bowl; turn once. Cover; let rise in a warm place till double (45 to 60 minutes).

Punch dough down; turn out onto lightly floured surface. Divide into three portions. Divide each portion into six pieces. Cover; let rest 5 minutes. Roll each piece into an 8-inch-long rope.

On a greased baking sheet, place *seven* of the dough ropes parallel to each other, about ¼ inch apart. Lightly brush the ropes with a little of the melted butter or margarine; sprinkle lightly with a little of the sesame or poppy seed. Place *six* dough ropes atop; brush with more melted butter or margarine and sprinkle with more sesame or poppy seed. For the third layer, place the five remaining dough ropes atop.

Cover dough; let rise in a warm place till nearly double (about 40 minutes). Combine the egg yolk and water; brush over loaf and sprinkle with sesame seed or poppy seed. Bake in a 375° oven about 20 minutes or till done. Transfer loaf to wire rack; cool. Makes 1 loaf; 18 breadsticks.

Per breadstick: 89 calories, 2 g protein, 12 g carbohydrate, 4 g fat, 23 mg cholesterol, and 97 mg sodium.

STIR-FRIED LIVERS

These chicken livers are especially tasty with the Creamy Soup Base.

 1 small onion, sliced and separated into rings
 1 tablespoon cooking oil
 ½ pound chicken livers, halved
Parsley (optional)

In a skillet cook the onion in hot oil over high heat for 2 minutes. Add the chicken livers; cook and stir for 2 minutes or till barely pink. Transfer to a serving dish and garnish with parsley, if desired. Serve as a Create-a-Soup accompaniment. Makes 8 servings.

Per serving: 64 calories, 8 g protein, 1 g carbohydrate, 3 g fat, 212 mg cholesterol, 18 mg sodium, 70% USRDA vitamin A, 45% USRDA riboflavin, 17% USRDA niacin, and 14% USRDA iron.

Host an Open House

One to two days before serving:
● Bake pita bread for Fill-a-Pita.
● Prepare and chill the Nutty Fruit Spread, Chunky Chicken Filling, and Sunny Sesame Butter.
● Shape and freeze Spinach Nuggets.
● Bake, cover, and store Sugar-and-Spice Potato Bread.
● Bake Neat Wheat Brownies.
Day of the open house:
● Frost brownies.
● Prepare Indian Caramel Corn.
● Split each pita bread in half; place in serving container and cover.
● Slice and wrap potato bread.
At serving time:
● Heat apple cider; transfer to a self-serve insulated container.
● Bake Spinach Nuggets.
● Arrange foods buffet style.

SUNNY SESAME BUTTER

 ½ cup sunflower nuts
 ½ cup sesame seed, toasted
 1 10-ounce package frozen peas, cooked and drained
 1 cup mayonnaise *or* salad dressing
Few dashes bottled hot pepper sauce
 ¼ cup sunflower nuts
Sunflower nuts (optional)

In a blender container or food processor bowl combine the ½ cup sunflower nuts and sesame seed. Cover; blend till ground. Remove; set aside.

In the blender container or food processor bowl combine the cooked and drained peas, the mayonnaise or salad dressing, and the bottled hot pepper sauce. Cover; blend till smooth. Combine the pea mixture and the ground seed mixture. Stir in the ¼ cup sunflower nuts. Cover; chill.

Before serving, sprinkle the spread with additional sunflower nuts, if desired. Makes 2½ cups.

Per tablespoon spread: 70 calories, 1 g protein, 2 g carbohydrate, 7 g fat, 4 mg cholesterol, and 42 mg sodium.

FILL-A-PITA

Follow the rolling directions carefully; if you overwork the dough, it won't puff during baking.

    1 package active dry yeast
 1¼ cups warm water (110° to 115°)
 2¼ to 2¾ cups all-purpose flour
    ¼ cup shortening
 1½ teaspoons salt
    1 cup whole wheat flour
    1 recipe Nutty Fruit Spread
       (see recipe, right)
    1 recipe Chunky Chicken Filling
       (see recipe, right)
    1 recipe Sunny Sesame Butter
       (see recipe, opposite)

For pita bread, in a large mixer bowl soften yeast in warm water. Add *2 cups* of the all-purpose flour, the shortening, and salt. Beat with an electric mixer on low speed for 30 seconds, scraping sides of bowl. Beat 3 minutes on high speed. Using a spoon, stir in the whole wheat flour and as much of the remaining all-purpose flour as you can.

Turn the dough out onto a lightly floured surface. Knead in enough of the remaining all-purpose flour to make a moderately soft dough that is smooth and elastic (3 to 5 minutes total). Cover; let dough rest for 15 minutes.

Divide the dough into four equal portions. Wrap and refrigerate three of the portions. Divide the remaining portion into 10 pieces. Roll each piece between well-floured hands into a very smooth ball. Cover dough balls with plastic wrap or a damp cloth and let rest 10 minutes.

Using fingers, gently flatten the dough balls without creasing the dough. Cover and let rest for 10 minutes. (Keep the dough pieces covered till ready to use.)

On a well-floured surface, lightly roll one piece of dough at a time into a 3-inch round, turning the dough over once while rolling. (Do not stretch, puncture, or crease the dough.) Work with enough flour on the surface so that the dough does not stick.

Place three or four dough rounds at a time on a baking sheet. Bake in a 450° oven about 3 minutes or till the dough is puffed and softly set. Turn dough over with a spatula; bake 3 minutes more or till light brown. Cool on a wire rack. Immediately place cooled bread in an airtight container to store.

Shape the remaining dough portions, baking one batch before rolling and baking the next batch.

To serve, halve each pita crosswise. Fill as desired with Nutty Fruit Spread, Chunky Chicken Filling, or Sunny Sesame Butter. Makes about 40.

Per pita bread: 53 calories, 1 g protein, 9 g carbohydrate, 1 g fat, and 80 mg sodium.

CHUNKY CHICKEN FILLING

 ⅔ cup water
 ⅓ cup bulgur wheat
 ½ cup chopped cooked chicken
 ¼ cup finely chopped jicama
 ¼ cup finely chopped green pepper
 ¼ cup orange yogurt
 ¼ cup mayonnaise *or* salad
    dressing
    4 teaspoons chutney
 ½ teaspoon curry powder
 ½ teaspoon dry mustard
 ¼ teaspoon salt

In a saucepan combine the water and bulgur wheat. Bring to boiling; reduce heat. Simmer, covered, for 15 minutes. Drain well, pressing out excess liquid.

Combine bulgur, chicken, jicama, and green pepper. Combine the yogurt, mayonnaise or salad dressing, chutney, curry powder, dry mustard, and salt; stir into the bulgur mixture. Cover and chill. Makes 2 cups.

Per tablespoon filling: 26 calories, 1 g protein, 2 g carbohydrate, 2 g fat, 3 mg cholesterol, and 32 mg sodium.

NUTTY FRUIT SPREAD

    1 8-ounce carton soft-style cream
       cheese with pineapple
    1 cup crunchy peanut butter
 ½ cup shredded carrot
 ½ cup shredded zucchini
 Pineapple juice *or* water
    (about 2 tablespoons)
 Shredded carrot *or* zucchini
    (optional)

In a small mixer bowl beat cream cheese and peanut butter till smooth. Stir in the ½ cup shredded carrot and the ½ cup shredded zucchini. If necessary, add pineapple juice or water to make of spreading consistency. Cover; chill till serving time.

Garnish with shredded carrot or zucchini, if desired. Makes 2½ cups.

Per tablespoon spread: 61 calories, 2 g protein, 2 g carbohydrate, 5 g fat, 6 mg cholesterol, and 54 mg sodium.

SPINACH NUGGETS

If you skip the freezing step, bake the appetizers a few minutes less.

- 2 10-ounce packages frozen chopped spinach
- 1 tablespoon minced dried onion
- 2 cups herb-seasoned stuffing croutons
- 1 cup grated Parmesan cheese
- 2 beaten eggs
- 3 tablespoons butter *or* margarine, melted

In a saucepan cook the spinach and the dried onion according to spinach package directions. Drain well. In a mixing bowl combine the spinach mixture, croutons, and Parmesan cheese. Stir in beaten eggs and melted butter or margarine. Shape into 1-inch balls. Place the balls in a shallow pan. Cover and freeze. Transfer to freezer storage containers; return to freezer.

At serving time, place frozen nuggets in a shallow baking pan. Bake in a 375° oven for 15 to 20 minutes or till heated through. Makes about 48.

Microwave directions: Place the frozen spinach and minced dried onion in a 1-quart nonmetal casserole with 2 tablespoons *water*. Micro-cook, covered, on 100% power (HIGH) for 7 to 9 minutes, stirring once. Let stand for 3 minutes. Drain well.

In a mixing bowl combine spinach, croutons, and the Parmesan cheese. Stir in beaten eggs and melted butter or margarine. Shape into 1-inch balls. Place in a shallow pan. Cover and freeze. Transfer to freezer storage containers; return to freezer.

At serving time, place *half* of the nuggets in a 12x7½x2-inch nonmetal baking dish. Micro-cook, uncovered, on 100% power (HIGH) for 3 to 4 minutes or till heated through. Repeat with remaining frozen nuggets. Makes 48.

Per nugget: 37 calories, 2 g protein, 4 g carbohydrate, 2 g fat, 15 mg cholesterol, 62 mg sodium, and 16% USRDA vitamin A.

SUGAR-AND-SPICE POTATO BREAD

- 2 cups all-purpose flour
- 2 teaspoons baking powder
- ½ teaspoon ground ginger
- ½ teaspoon ground nutmeg
- ¼ teaspoon baking soda
- ¼ teaspoon salt
- ⅔ cup packed brown sugar
- ⅓ cup shortening
- 2 eggs
- 1 8-ounce can sweet potatoes, drained and mashed
- ¼ cup orange juice

Lightly grease a 9x5x3-inch loaf pan; set aside. In a mixing bowl stir together the flour, baking powder, ginger, nutmeg, baking soda, and salt; set aside.

In a large mixer bowl beat together the sugar and shortening till combined; beat in eggs. Add the mashed sweet potatoes and orange juice to beaten mixture (mixture may appear curdled); mix well. Gradually add the flour mixture, beating till combined.

Turn the batter into prepared loaf pan. Bake in a 350° oven for 40 minutes or till a wooden toothpick comes out clean. Cool 10 minutes in pan. Remove from pan; cool on wire rack. Wrap and store overnight before slicing. Makes 1 loaf; 18 servings.

Per serving: 140 calories, 2 g protein, 22 g carbohydrate, 4 g fat, 28 mg cholesterol, 98 mg sodium, and 23% USRDA vitamin A.

NEAT WHEAT BROWNIES

- 1¼ cups whole wheat flour
- 1 teaspoon baking powder
- ½ teaspoon salt
- 1 cup shortening
- 2 cups sugar
- ¾ cup unsweetened cocoa powder
- 4 eggs
- 1 teaspoon vanilla
- ¾ cup chopped pecans
- 1 recipe Chocolate Frosting
- ¼ cup chopped pecans (optional)

Grease a 13x9x2-inch baking pan; set aside. Stir together flour, baking powder, and salt; set aside.

In a saucepan melt shortening. Remove from heat; stir in sugar and cocoa powder. Add eggs and vanilla; stir till blended. Stir in dry ingredients and the ¾ cup pecans.

Spread the batter in prepared pan. Bake in a 350° oven for 25 to 30 minutes or till done. Cool on a wire rack.

Frost with Chocolate Frosting. Top with the ¼ cup pecans, if desired. Cut into squares. Makes 18.

Chocolate Frosting: Beat together 2 cups *sifted powdered sugar*, 3 tablespoons *unsweetened cocoa powder*, 2 tablespoons *softened butter* or *margarine*, 2 tablespoons *milk*, and 1 teaspoon *vanilla*. If necessary, add 1 tablespoon *milk* to make of spreading consistency.

Per serving: 340 calories, 4 g protein, 45 g carbohydrate, 18 g fat, 61 mg cholesterol, and 109 mg sodium.

INDIAN CARAMEL CORN

- 2½ quarts popped popcorn (about ½ cup unpopped corn)
- 1 cup packed brown sugar
- ¾ cup water
- ¼ cup light corn syrup
- ¾ teaspoon vinegar
- ½ cup dried apricots, finely snipped
- ½ cup raisins

Put popped popcorn in a large roasting pan; keep warm in a 300° oven. In a 1-quart saucepan combine sugar, water, corn syrup, and vinegar. Cook and stir till mixture boils; continue cooking to hard-ball stage (250°). Pour over popcorn; add apricots and raisins, stirring till all is coated.

Using buttered hands, quickly shape the popcorn mixture into twelve 3½-inch sticks, resembling corn on the cob. Insert wooden skewers into one end of each. Store up to several hours in a tightly covered container. Serve the same day. Makes 12.

Per serving: 151 calories, 1 g protein, 37 g carbohydrate, 0.5 g fat, 13 mg sodium, and 12% USRDA vitamin A.

NOVEMBER

FAMILY CAR BREAKTHROUGH: THE NEW MINIVANS

Better Homes
and Gardens

November 1984 • $1.50

MAKE-AHEADS FOR CHRISTMAS:
*Enchanted Cottage and Dolls
to Stitch, Craft, Enjoy!*

Decorating Contest Winners
Family-Designed Ideas to
Work Wonders in Your Home

**YOUR MEDICAL RIGHTS:
SURPRISING FACTS
YOU SHOULD KNOW**

**Look What's New in
American Cooking!
15 Outstanding
Regional Recipes**

**Popular Diets:
How Safe Are
They?**

**Building:
STORAGE PROJECTS
for Every Room
in Your House**

By Diana McMillen

Cooks from coast to coast express a new pride in American foods. They combine native ingredients and locally produced foods with American ingenuity to spawn an array of new tastes and traditions.

To celebrate, we're honoring some of America's best foods—Southern sweet potatoes, Midwest pork chops, West Coast salmon—in recipes that boast freshness. These wonderful regional ingredients are available countrywide, ready to sample in the recipes on the following pages.

S OURDOUGH CHOCOLATE CAKE probably never occurred to prospectors who journeyed west with their sourdough starter. Originally, the starter was used as leavening for breads. Here, the famous San Francisco sourdough adds tang to America's favorite cake.

WESTERN SAMPLER creates a naturally splashy show of color for a festive appetizer plate. This taste of the West overflows with ingredients representing the coastal states—artichokes, goat cheese, salmon, avocados, and dates.

IOWA CHOPS WITH BLUE CHEESE SAUCE combines two Midwest specialties—the extra-thick-cut pork chop and blue cheese. The piquant sauce adds a simple elegance.

WHITE SANGRIA capitalizes on the award-winning wines from California vineyards. The familiar Mexican beverage typically starts with red wine. Here the spritely taste of oranges and lemons mixes with dry white wine.

Photographs: de Gennaro Studios. Food stylist: Mable Hoffman

As with most things American, there are no complicated techniques or special equipment needed for the honest-to-goodness, great-tasting dishes on these pages.

SAVORY RACK OF LAMB is an American favorite on many holiday tables. A spunky wine and lemon marinade is the basis of the rich sauce served with the roasted lamb and the vegetables.

SCALLOPS IN BREAD CUPS features tiny bay scallops from the coasts dressed in a light vinaigrette. Serve the cups as luncheon salads or dinner party appetizers.

CALIFORNIA FRUITCAKE gets its sweetness from dried figs, golden raisins, and apricot nectar. This recipe makes two cakes—one for holiday gift-giving and one for you.

BLUEBERRY BRAN MUFFINS and ANADAMA BREADSTICKS are inspirations from the New England bread basket. For a twist on tradition, bake the muffin batter in a spoked iron skillet. As in the original Anadama loaf, molasses accents these braided cornmeal breadsticks.

MADE IN ·AMERICA·

The beauty of American cooking is the abundance of foods available and the freedom to experiment unencumbered by the rules of older cuisines.

CRISPY PAN-FRIED LAKE FISH proves that the coasts aren't the only source of delicious fresh fish. The Midwest favorite, trout, pictured here, and other lake fish such as perch and white fish now are available nationwide.

CHORIZO CHILI is a tribute to the popular spicy cuisine of the Southwest. Hot chorizo sausage, beef round steak, hominy, and plenty of peppers are the heart of this long-simmering chili.

SWEET POTATO SPOON BREAD typifies two Southern favorites—spoon bread and sweet potatoes. Serve this soufflélike quick bread with butter and, as the name says, with a spoon.

MINT JULEP CREAM PIE is a glamorous takeoff on the bourbon-based mint julep, a classic drink served at the Kentucky Derby. This extra-creamy dessert blends distinctive bourbon whiskey with crème de menthe.

Note: Some nutrient information in these recipes is given by gram weight per serving. To obtain the nutrition analysis of each recipe, the following guidelines are used:

● When ingredient options appear in a recipe, the analysis is calculated using the first ingredient choice.

● Optional ingredients are omitted in the analyses.

● The nutrition analyses for recipes calling for fresh ingredients are calculated using the measurements for raw fruits, vegetables, and meats.

● If a recipe gives optional serving sizes (such as "Makes 6 to 8 servings"), the nutrition analysis is calculated using the first choice.

For good health, include a variety of foods from the Basic Food Groups in your daily diet. Follow your physician's advice if you are on a restricted diet.

SMOKED TURKEY WITH CREOLE STUFFING

- 1 **pound fresh *or* frozen shelled shrimp**
- ½ **cup finely chopped celery**
- 1 **medium onion, chopped (½ cup)**
- ¼ **cup butter *or* margarine**
- ½ **teaspoon salt**
- ¼ **to ⅛ teaspoon ground red pepper**
- 6 **cups dry French bread cubes**
- ¾ **cup coarsely chopped pecans**
- 1 **slightly beaten egg**
- ¼ **to ½ cup chicken broth *or* water**

Hickory chips
- 1 **10- to 12-pound turkey**

Cooking oil
- 1 **recipe Roux Gravy**

Hot cooked okra

Thaw shrimp, if frozen. Halve large shrimp. In a saucepan cook the celery and onion in butter or margarine till tender. Add shrimp; cook and stir just till shrimp turn pink. Remove from heat. Stir in the salt and ground red pepper. Place the dry bread cubes in a large mixing bowl. Add the shrimp mixture; add the pecans. Stir in the

egg. Drizzle with enough broth or water to moisten, tossing gently. Press about ½ *cup* of the stuffing firmly into measuring cup and unmold onto a greased baking sheet. Repeat with remaining stuffing to make 12 mounds. Cover and refrigerate.

About 1 hour before cooking turkey, soak 6 cups of hickory chips in enough water to cover. Rinse turkey; pat bird dry with paper towels. Skewer the turkey neck skin to back; tie legs securely to the tail with cord. Twist wing tips under back.

In a covered grill arrange *medium-slow* coals around a 13x9-inch foil drip pan in the firebox. Add 2 cups *water* to the pan. Drain hickory chips; sprinkle about *half* of the chips over the coals. Place the turkey, breast side up, on grill rack over the drip pan. Brush turkey with cooking oil. Lower grill hood. Grill the turkey for 2½ to 3 hours or till a meat thermometer inserted inside thigh muscle registers 180° and the leg moves easily in the socket. Brush turkey occasionally; add additional dampened hickory chips every 30 minutes. Let stand 15 minutes before carving.

Meanwhile, bake stuffing, uncovered, in a 325° oven for 25 to 30 minutes or till heated through. Serve turkey with stuffing, Roux Gravy, and okra. Makes 12 servings.

Oven Roasting Variation: Prepare the shrimp-pecan dressing as above. Place the turkey, breast side up, on a rack in a shallow roasting pan. Brush stuffed turkey with some cooking oil. Insert meat thermometer in center of inside thigh muscle, making sure bulb of thermometer does not touch bone.

Roast, uncovered, in a 325° oven for 3½ to 4 hours or till thermometer registers 180°. When turkey is two-thirds done, cut band of skin or string between legs so turkey will cook evenly. Let turkey stand 15 minutes before carving. Meanwhile, bake stuffing for 25 to 30 minutes or till heated through. Makes 10 to 12 servings.

Roux Gravy: In a small saucepan stir together ¼ cup *all-purpose flour* and ¼ cup *cooking oil.* Cook and stir over medium-low heat for 20 to 25 minutes or till a very dark reddish brown. Stir in ½ cup *chicken broth* and ¼ cup *light cream* or *milk.* Season with salt and pepper. Cook and stir till thickened and bubbly. Cook and stir 1 minute more. Makes 1 cup gravy.

Per serving: 632 calories, 64 g protein, 26 g carbohydrate, 30 g fat, 308 mg cholesterol, and 427 mg sodium.

IOWA CHOPS WITH BLUE CHEESE SAUCE

Blue cheese is the American version of French Roquefort cheese.

- 4 **pork chops, cut 1 to 1¼ inches thick**
- 2 **medium carrots, cut into julienne strips**
- 1 **small rutabaga (8 ounces), cut into julienne strips**
- 1 **small tomato, peeled, seeded, and chopped**
- ¼ **teaspoon sugar**
- 1 **clove garlic, minced**
- 2 **tablespoons butter *or* margarine**
- 4 **teaspoons all-purpose flour**
- ¾ **cup milk**
- 1 **tablespoon snipped parsley**
- ½ **cup crumbled blue cheese**

Fresh sage (optional)

Place chops on rack of unheated broiler pan; broil chops 3 to 4 inches from heat for 14 minutes. Season with pepper. Turn meat; broil for 12 to 14 minutes more or till done. Meanwhile, cook carrots and rutabaga in a small amount of boiling salted water for 10 minutes.

For sauce, sprinkle tomato with sugar; set aside. In a small saucepan cook garlic in butter or margarine for 1 minute. Stir in flour. Add milk; cook and stir till thickened and bubbly. Cook and stir for 1 minute more. Stir in tomato and parsley. Heat through. Stir in ¼ *cup* blue cheese. Serve sauce over chops. Sprinkle remaining cheese atop. Serve with carrots and rutabaga. Garnish with sage. Makes 4 servings.

Per serving: 474 calories, 22 g protein, 17 g carbohydrate, 35 g fat, 95 mg cholesterol, and 286 mg sodium.

SOURDOUGH CHOCOLATE CAKE

1 cup Sourdough Starter
2 cups all-purpose flour
1½ teaspoons baking soda
1 teaspoon ground cinnamon
½ teaspoon salt
½ cup shortening
1¼ cups sugar
1 teaspoon vanilla
2 eggs
3 squares (3 ounces) unsweetened chocolate, melted and cooled
1 cup milk
1 recipe Cocoa Cream Cheese Filling (see recipe, right)
1 recipe Sweet Chocolate Glaze (see recipe, right)
2 White Chocolate Leaves (optional)
White confectioners' coating, milk chocolate, and semisweet chocolate curls (optional)

Bring Sourdough Starter to room temperature. Grease and flour two 9x1½-inch round cake pans; set aside. Stir together the flour, baking soda, cinnamon, and salt. In a large mixer bowl beat the shortening with an electric mixer on medium speed for 30 seconds. Add sugar and vanilla; beat till fluffy. Add eggs, one at a time, beating for 1 minute after each addition. Beat in the melted chocolate.

Combine the Sourdough Starter and milk. Add dry ingredients and milk mixture alternately to beaten mixture, beating till well combined. Turn batter into prepared pans. Bake in a 350° oven about 30 minutes or till done. Cool 10 minutes on wire racks. Remove from pans; cool thoroughly on wire racks.

Spread Cocoa Cream Cheese Filling onto one cake layer; top with remaining cake layer. Glaze cake with Sweet Chocolate Glaze. Drizzle a design atop with the reserved cream cheese icing and top with White Chocolate Leaves, if desired. Garnish plate with confectioners' coating curls and chocolate curls, if desired. Makes 12 servings.

Sourdough Starter: Dissolve 1 package *active dry yeast* in ½ cup *warm water* (110° to 115°). Stir in 2 cups additional *warm water,* 2 cups *all-purpose flour,* and 1 tablespoon *sugar* or *honey.* Beat till smooth. Cover with cheesecloth. Let stand at room temperature for 5 to 10 days or till bubbly, stirring two or three times each day.

To store, transfer the Sourdough Starter to a jar and cover with cheesecloth; refrigerate. *Do not cover the jar with a metal lid.* To use starter, bring desired amount to room temperature.

To replenish Starter after each use, stir ¾ cup *all-purpose flour,* ¾ cup *water,* and 1 teaspoon *sugar* or *honey* into remaining amount. Cover; let stand at room temperature at least 1 day or till the mixture is bubbly. Refrigerate for later use. (If starter isn't used within 10 days, stir in 1 teaspoon *sugar* or *honey.* Repeat every 10 days or till used.)

White Chocolate Leaves: To make a white chocolate leaf, use a small paintbrush to brush melted white confectioners' coating on the underside of a small silk-cloth leaf. Chill to harden. Carefully peel away the silk leaf before using the chocolate leaf as a garnish. Rechill chocolate leaf on waxed paper before using.

Per serving (with glaze and filling): 479 calories, 7 g protein, 76 g carbohydrate, 19 g fat, 53 mg cholesterol, and 278 mg sodium.

COCOA CREAM CHEESE FILLING

1 cup sifted powdered sugar
1 3-ounce package cream cheese
¼ teaspoon vanilla
Milk
2 tablespoons unsweetened cocoa powder
½ cup sifted powdered sugar

In a mixer bowl combine the 1 cup powdered sugar and cream cheese; beat till fluffy. Beat in the vanilla. If necessary, beat in enough milk (about 2 teaspoons) to make of pouring consistency.

For icing, reserve ¼ *cup* of the mixture to decorate the top of the cake. For filling, stir the cocoa powder into the remaining mixture in bowl. Add the remaining ½ cup powdered sugar and beat till smooth. Use the cocoa mixture to spread between cake layers. Makes ⅔ cup filling; ¼ cup icing.

SWEET CHOCOLATE GLAZE

¾ cup sugar
2 tablespoons cornstarch
Dash salt
1 cup water
2 squares (2 ounces) German sweet cooking chocolate, cut up
1½ teaspoons vanilla

In a small saucepan combine the sugar, cornstarch, and salt. Stir in water and sweet cooking chocolate. Cook and stir till chocolate is melted and mixture is thickened. Cook and stir 2 minutes more. Remove from heat; stir in vanilla. Cover surface with clear plastic wrap or waxed paper. Let stand 10 to 15 minutes or till slightly cooled and of spreading consistency. Spread the glaze over top and sides of cake. Chill cake till set. Makes 1½ cups glaze.

WESTERN SAMPLER

- 2 **medium artichokes**
- 4 **ounces goat cheese (chèvre)**
- 1 **3-ounce package cream cheese, softened**
- 1 **tablespoon olive oil** *or* **cooking oil**
- ½ **teaspoon dried basil, crushed**

Dash bottled hot pepper sauce
- 3 **tablespoons pine nuts, toasted**
- 2 **avocados, seeded, peeled, and cut into thin wedges**

Lemon juice
- 4 **ounces thin-sliced smoked salmon**
- 3 **pita bread rounds, cut into wedges and toasted**

Leaf lettuce (optional)
Desired fresh fruit (tangerines, dates, *and/or* strawberries)
Blanched whole almonds (optional)

Wash artichokes, trim stems, and remove loose outer leaves. Place artichokes in a saucepan; add water to a 1½-inch depth. Bring to boiling; reduce heat. Cover and simmer for 20 to 30 minutes or till an artichoke leaf pulls out easily. Drain upside down; chill.

Meanwhile, in a small mixer bowl combine the goat cheese, cream cheese, oil, basil, and hot pepper sauce. Beat with an electric mixer till fluffy. Chop *2 tablespoons* of the pine nuts; stir into cheese mixture.

Halve artichokes lengthwise. Using a spoon, remove choke. Fill each hollowed artichoke half with cheese mixture. Sprinkle with the remaining 1 tablespoon pine nuts. Brush avocado with some lemon juice. Cut salmon into strips and wrap around avocado. Arrange artichokes, salmon-wrapped avocado, pita bread wedges, lettuce, fruit, and almonds on serving platter. Makes 10 to 12 appetizer servings.

Per serving: 195 calories, 8 g protein, 11 g carbohydrate, 14 g fat, 15 mg cholesterol, and 770 mg sodium.

WHITE SANGRIA

Serve this drink as an accompaniment to the Western Sampler.

- 3 **oranges**
- 2 **lemons**
- 4 **cups dry white wine**
- ¼ **cup brandy**
- 2 **tablespoons honey**
- 1 **10-ounce bottle carbonated water, chilled**

Halve *one* orange and *one* lemon. Slice one half of each to use as garnish; wrap and chill. Squeeze juice from remaining oranges and lemons. Stir together the juices, dry white wine, brandy, and honey; cover and chill.

Just before serving, pour chilled mixture into a large pitcher or serving bowl. Slowly add the chilled carbonated water. Add reserved orange and lemon slices. Makes 14 (4-ounce) servings.

Per serving: 139 calories, 0.5 g protein, 14 g carbohydrate, 0.1 g fat, and 3 mg sodium.

SAVORY RACK OF LAMB

A rack of lamb is a line of ribs from one side of the animal.

- 1 **7- to 9-rib rack of lamb (1¼ to 1½ pounds)**
- 1 **cup dry white wine**
- 4 **green onions, sliced**
- 2 **tablespoons lemon juice**
- 2 **tablespoons olive oil** *or* **cooking oil**
- 1 **tablespoon Worcestershire sauce**
- ½ **teaspoon sugar**
- ½ **teaspoon dried oregano, crushed**
- ¼ **teaspoon pepper**
- 1 **tablespoon cornstarch**

Hot cooked new potatoes (optional)
Hot cooked broccoli (optional)
Lemon wedges (optional)

Have butcher loosen backbone from the rack of lamb. Trim fat from meat. Place a large plastic bag in a large bowl; place meat in bag. Combine the wine, green onions, lemon juice, oil, Worcestershire sauce, sugar, oregano, and pepper; add to bag. Close bag tightly. Refrigerate overnight, turning bag several times to distribute marinade.

Drain meat, reserving marinade. Pat excess moisture from meat with paper towels. Place meat, bone side down, in a shallow roasting pan. Roast lamb in a 450° oven for 15 minutes. Reduce heat to 400°; roast meat about 20 minutes more for rare or 25 minutes for medium. Transfer meat from pan to serving platter; keep warm.

For sauce, in a small saucepan combine the reserved marinade mixture and the cornstarch. Cook and stir till thickened and bubbly. Cook and stir for 2 minutes more.

To serve, arrange lamb on platter with hot cooked new potatoes, broccoli, and lemon wedges, if desired. Serve with the hot sauce. Makes 4 servings.

Per serving: 512 calories, 17 g protein, 7 g carbohydrate, 41 g fat, 81 mg cholesterol, and 114 mg sodium.

SCALLOPS IN BREAD CUPS

- 8 **ounces fresh or frozen bay scallops**
- ½ **cup water**
- 2 **teaspoons lemon juice**
- ¼ **teaspoon salt**
- 1 **bay leaf**
- 1 **small tomato, peeled, seeded, and chopped**
- ¼ **cup bias-sliced celery**
- 2 **tablespoons sliced green onion**
- 2 **tablespoons white wine vinegar**
- 1 **tablespoon olive oil or salad oil**
- ½ **teaspoon honey**
- ⅛ **teaspoon salt**

Dash pepper
- 6 **large Bread Cups (see recipe, right)**

Leaf lettuce

Thaw scallops, if frozen. In saucepan bring water, lemon juice, ¼ teaspoon salt, and bay leaf to boiling. Add scallops and return to boiling; reduce heat. Simmer for 30 seconds or till scallops turn opaque. Drain and cool. Discard bay leaf. In a mixing bowl combine scallops, tomato, celery, and onion.

For marinade, in a screw-top jar combine vinegar, oil, honey, ⅛ teaspoon salt, and pepper. Cover and shake well. Pour over scallop mixture; toss. Cover; refrigerate for 3 hours.

To serve, use a sharp knife to cut out top of each Bread Cup. Hollow each, leaving a bread shell about ½ inch thick. Place shells and tops on individual serving plates. Line each shell with leaf lettuce. Drain scallop mixture, reserving marinade. Spoon into lettuce-lined cups. Drizzle each with some of the reserved marinade. Serve immediately. Makes 6 appetizer servings.

Microwave directions: Thaw scallops, if frozen. In a 1-quart nonmetal casserole combine scallops, water, lemon juice, ¼ teaspoon salt, and bay leaf. Micro-cook, covered, on 100% power (HIGH) for 2½ to 3½ minutes or till scallops turn opaque. Drain and cool. Discard the bay leaf. Marinate scallops and vegetables as directed above and serve in lettuce-lined Bread Cups.

Per serving: 257 calories, 14 g protein, 29 g carbohydrate, 11 g fat, 93 mg cholesterol, and 381 mg sodium.

BREAD CUPS

Start the dough a day ahead.

- 1 **package active dry yeast**
- ¼ **cup warm water (110° to 115°)**
- ½ **cup butter or margarine**
- ⅓ **cup sugar**
- ½ **teaspoon salt**
- ½ **teaspoon dried dillweed**
- 4 **cups all-purpose flour**
- ½ **cup milk**
- 4 **eggs**
- 1 **tablespoon water**

Soften yeast in the ¼ cup warm water. In a large mixer bowl beat together butter or margarine, sugar, salt, and dillweed. Add *1 cup* of the flour and the milk. Separate *one* of the eggs; set egg white aside. Blend yolk with remaining 3 eggs; add to beaten mixture. Add softened yeast; beat well. Stir in remaining flour till smooth. Turn into a greased bowl. Cover; let dough rise till double (about 2 hours). Refrigerate overnight.

Stir dough down; turn out onto a lightly floured surface. Divide dough into quarters; set one portion aside. Divide each of the remaining quarters into six pieces, making a total of 18.

With floured hands, form each piece into a ball, tucking under edges. Place each in a greased individual brioche pan. Divide reserved dough into 18 pieces; shape into balls. (To bake in muffin cups, divide each of the three quarters of dough into eight pieces, making a total of 24. Place in greased muffin cups. Divide remaining dough into 24 pieces.)

With a floured finger, make an indentation in the top of each large ball. Press a small ball into each indentation. Blend reserved egg white and 1 tablespoon water; brush over rolls. Cover; let rise till double (40 to 45 minutes). Bake in a 375° oven for 12 to 15 minutes for either pan option, brushing again with egg white mixture after 7 minutes. Makes 18 large or 24 muffin-size rolls.

Per roll (1/18 of recipe): 184 calories, 5 g protein, 25 g carbohydrate, 7 g fat, 73 mg cholesterol, and 139 mg sodium.

CALIFORNIA FRUITCAKE

- 3 **cups all-purpose flour**
- 1 **teaspoon baking powder**
- 1 **cup butter or margarine**
- 1 **cup sugar**
- 4 **eggs**
- ½ **cup apricot nectar or orange juice**
- ¼ **cup light corn syrup**
- 1 **teaspoon finely shredded lemon peel**
- 1 **12-ounce package (2 cups) dried figs, snipped**
- 1½ **cups chopped almonds**
- 1 **cup light raisins**

Corn syrup (optional)
Whole dried figs, halved (optional)

Grease one 5½-cup ovenproof ring mold and one 10x3½x2½-inch loaf dessert pan; set aside. Stir together the flour and baking powder. In a mixer bowl beat the butter or margarine for 30 seconds. Add the sugar and beat till fluffy. Add the eggs, one at a time, beating 1 minute after each. Combine the apricot nectar, ¼ cup corn syrup, and lemon peel.

Add dry ingredients and apricot nectar mixture alternately to beaten mixture, beating after each addition. Combine the snipped figs, chopped almonds, and light raisins; fold into batter. Divide batter evenly between the prepared pans.

Bake cakes in a 300° oven for 50 to 60 minutes for ring mold, 70 minutes for large loaf pan, or till done. Cool in pans on wire racks. Remove from pans.

Wrap cakes in cheesecloth moistened with apricot brandy or fruit juice. Overwrap with foil or clear plastic wrap, or place in an airtight container. Store fruitcake in the refrigerator at least 1 week. Remoisten cheesecloth as needed if storing longer than 1 week.

Before serving, glaze tops of cakes with additional corn syrup, if desired. Garnish with the dried fig halves. Makes 2 fruitcakes; 30 servings.

Note: You also can prepare this recipe using three 8x4x2-inch loaf pans. Prepare the batter as directed. Divide among the three greased pans. Bake in a 300° oven for 50 to 55 minutes or till done. Continue as directed.

Per serving: 228 calories, 4 g protein, 32 g carbohydrate, 11 g fat, 53 mg cholesterol, and 98 mg sodium.

BLUEBERRY BRAN MUFFINS

    1 cup fresh *or* frozen blueberries
  1½ cups whole bran cereal
    1 cup buttermilk *or* sour milk
    1 beaten egg
   ¼ cup cooking oil
    1 cup all-purpose flour
   ⅓ cup sugar
    2 teaspoons baking powder
   ½ teaspoon baking soda
   ½ teaspoon salt

Thaw blueberries, if frozen; drain. In a mixing bowl combine cereal and buttermilk or sour milk; let stand 3 minutes. Stir in egg and oil; set aside.

In a large mixing bowl stir together flour, sugar, baking powder, baking soda, and salt; make a well in the center. Add the bran mixture all at once, stirring just till moistened (batter will be *thick*). Gently fold in the blueberries.

Grease muffin cups and fill two-thirds full *or* pour the batter into a well-greased cast-iron corn bread skillet, filling two-thirds full. Bake in a 400° oven for 20 to 25 minutes or till done. If using skillet, cut bread into wedges. Makes about 12 muffins or 6 to 8 wedges.

Microwave directions: Prepare the Blueberry Bran Muffin batter as directed. Line a microwave cupcake dish or 6-ounce custard cups with paper bake cups. Fill cups two-thirds full with batter. Place dish in the microwave oven or arrange cups in a circle in the oven. Micro-cook, uncovered, on 100% power (HIGH) for 2½ to 3 minutes for six muffins. Remove from cupcake dish or custard cups. Let stand on wire rack for 5 to 10 minutes. Repeat with remaining batter.

Per muffin: 135 calories, 3 g protein, 20 g carbohydrate, 5 g fat, 22 mg cholesterol, and 247 mg sodium.

ANADAMA BREADSTICKS

  1¾ to 2¼ cups all-purpose flour
   ¼ cup cornmeal
    1 package active dry yeast
   ⅔ cup milk

    3 tablespoons molasses
    2 tablespoons shortening
   ½ teaspoon salt
    1 egg white
    1 tablespoon water
  Sesame seed *or* poppy seed

In a mixer bowl combine ¾ *cup* flour, cornmeal, and yeast. In a saucepan heat the milk, molasses, shortening, and salt just till warm (115° to 120°), stirring constantly. Add to flour mixture. Beat with an electric mixer on low speed for 30 seconds, scraping sides of bowl constantly. Beat 3 minutes on high speed. Using a spoon, stir in as much remaining flour as you can.

Turn out onto a lightly floured surface. Knead in enough of the remaining flour to make a stiff dough that is smooth and elastic (8 to 10 minutes total). Shape into a ball. Place in a lightly greased bowl; turn once. Cover; let rise in a warm place till nearly double (about 45 to 60 minutes).

Punch dough down. Turn out onto a lightly floured surface. Divide dough into two portions. Cover; let rest 10 minutes. Roll each portion into a 10-inch square. Cut off 36 strips of dough about 10 inches long and ¼ inch wide. Using three strips for each breadstick, braid the strips of dough and secure ends. Place on a greased baking sheet.

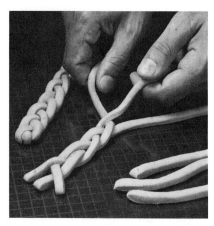

Cover and let rise in a warm place till nearly double (about 30 minutes). Brush with a mixture of egg white and water. Sprinkle with sesame seed or poppy seed. Bake in a 375° oven for 10 to 15 minutes or till golden. Makes 24.

Per breadstick: 62 calories, 2 g protein, 10 g carbohydrate, 2 g fat, 11 mg cholesterol, and 51 mg sodium.

CRISPY PAN-FRIED LAKE FISH

When buying fresh fish, look for shiny, taut skin and bright colors that indicate freshness. A fresh fish will smell sweet, not fishy.

    4 8- to 10-ounce fresh *or* frozen pan-dressed trout, lake perch, *or* other white fish
   ¾ cup finely crushed saltine crackers (21 crackers)
   ¼ cup grated Parmesan cheese
    1 tablespoon snipped parsley
   ⅓ cup all-purpose flour
   ⅛ teaspoon pepper
    3 tablespoons lemon juice
    1 beaten egg
    3 to 4 tablespoons shortening *or* cooking oil
  Lemon slices, halved (optional)
  Fresh parsley, rosemary, and dill (optional)

Thaw fish, if frozen. In a shallow bowl combine the crushed crackers, grated Parmesan cheese, and snipped parsley. In another shallow bowl combine the flour and pepper. Place lemon juice and egg in separate bowls. Dip fish in lemon juice, then in flour mixture, then in egg, and finally in the cracker mixture.

In a 12-inch skillet heat shortening or cooking oil. Add fish in a single layer. Fry over medium heat for 5 to 7 minutes or till brown. Turn fish; fry for 5 to 7 minutes more or till fish flakes easily when tested with a fork. Drain on paper towels. If desired, serve fish with lemon and garnish with parsley, rosemary, and dill. Makes 4 servings.

Per serving: 443 calories, 36 g protein, 19 g carbohydrate, 24 g fat, 120 mg cholesterol, and 704 mg sodium.

CHORIZO CHILI

Chorizo, a Mexican pork sausage, gets its hot and spicy flavor from garlic, cayenne, and chili powder.

 8 **ounces chorizo *or* Italian**
   sausage links, sliced
 8 **ounces beef round steak, cut**
   into ½-inch cubes
 2 **tablespoons cooking oil**
 1 **medium onion, chopped**
   (½ cup)
 1 **small green pepper, chopped**
 1 **clove garlic, minced**
 2 **cups beef broth**
 1 **tablespoon paprika**
1½ **teaspoons dried oregano,**
   crushed
1½ **teaspoons cumin seed, crushed**
 ¼ **to ½ teaspoon ground red**
   pepper
 1 **15-ounce can hominy, drained**
 1 **4-ounce can chopped green**
   chili peppers
 3 **flour tortillas, cut into wedges**
 ½ **cup shredded cheddar cheese**
   (2 ounces)
Cilantro (optional)
Chili peppers (optional)

In a 12-inch skillet cook sliced chorizo and beef cubes in hot oil till brown. Remove meat; set aside. Reserve *2 tablespoons* drippings in skillet. Cook onion, green pepper, and garlic in drippings till tender but not brown.

Stir meat mixture, beef broth, paprika, oregano, cumin, and red pepper into onion mixture. Bring to boiling; reduce heat. Simmer, covered, for 1½ hours, stirring occasionally. If necessary, spoon off fat. Stir in hominy and *undrained* chili peppers. Simmer, uncovered, for 20 minutes more, stirring occasionally.

Meanwhile, in each serving bowl arrange four or five tortilla wedges, points up, around edge of bowls. Spoon chili into each bowl. Sprinkle with cheese. Garnish with cilantro and chili peppers. Makes 5 servings.

Microwave directions: In a 2-quart nonmetal casserole micro-cook the chorizo and beef, covered, in oil on 100% power (HIGH) for 4 minutes. Remove meat, reserving *2 tablespoons* drippings in the casserole; set meat aside. Micro-cook the onion, green pepper, and garlic in drippings, covered, on 100% power (HIGH) for 2 to 4 minutes or till tender.

Stir in the meat mixture, *1½ cups* beef broth, paprika, oregano, cumin, and red pepper. Micro-cook, covered, on 100% power (HIGH) for 5 minutes or till bubbly. Micro-cook, covered, on 50% power (MEDIUM) about 35 minutes or till the meat is tender, stirring every 15 minutes.

Stir in hominy and *undrained* chili peppers. Micro-cook, covered, on 50% power (MEDIUM) for 10 minutes more; stir once. Spoon off fat. In each serving bowl arrange tortilla wedges, points up, around edge of bowls. Spoon chili into each bowl. Sprinkle with cheese. If desired, garnish with cilantro and chili peppers. Makes 5 servings.

Per serving: 549 calories, 21 g protein, 30 g carbohydrate, 39 g fat, 70 mg cholesterol, and 997 mg sodium.

SWEET POTATO SPOON BREAD

Sweet potatoes and spoon bread are traditional staples in Southern cooking. They're combined here for an attractive and hearty side dish.

 1 **cup milk**
 ½ **cup yellow cornmeal**
 1 **cup mashed, cooked sweet**
   potatoes *or* one 8-ounce can
   sweet potatoes, drained and
   mashed
 1 **tablespoon butter *or* margarine**
 ½ **teaspoon baking powder**
 ¼ **teaspoon salt**
 1 **egg yolk**
 1 **stiff-beaten egg white**
Butter *or* margarine

In a medium saucepan stir the milk into the cornmeal. Cook, stirring constantly, about 5 minutes or till mixture is very thick and pulls away from the sides of the pan. Remove from heat. Stir in the mashed sweet potatoes, the 1 tablespoon butter or margarine, baking powder, and salt. Beat in egg yolk. Gently fold in the beaten egg white.

Turn mixture into four greased 8- to 10-ounce baking dishes or one greased 1-quart casserole. Sprinkle with additional cornmeal. Bake in a 325° oven for 30 to 40 minutes for the individual baking dishes or 50 to 60 minutes for the casserole, or till knife inserted near the center comes out clean. Serve immediately with butter or margarine. Makes 4 servings.

Microwave directions: In a 1-quart nonmetal casserole combine milk and cornmeal. Micro-cook, uncovered, on 100% power (HIGH) for 3 to 5 minutes or till mixture is very thick and all the liquid is absorbed, stirring every minute. Stir in the mashed sweet potatoes, the 1 tablespoon butter or margarine, baking powder, and salt. Beat in the egg yolk. Gently fold in the beaten egg white.

Spoon mixture into four greased 8- to 10-ounce nonmetal baking dishes. Sprinkle the tops with additional cornmeal. Micro-cook, uncovered, on 100% power (HIGH) for 6 to 8 minutes or till a knife inserted near the center comes out clean, rearranging baking dishes after 4 minutes. Serve spoon bread immediately with butter or margarine. Makes 4 servings.

Per serving: 220 calories, 6 g protein, 34 g carbohydrate, 7 g fat, 81 mg cholesterol, and 261 mg sodium.

MINT JULEP CREAM PIE

A real mint julep should be made with bourbon whiskey, first made in Bourbon County, Kentucky. However, for this pie, other whiskeys are acceptable, too.

⅔ cup sugar
¼ cup cornstarch
Dash salt
2¼ cups milk
2 3-ounce packages cream cheese, cut into ½-inch cubes
3 slightly beaten eggs
3 tablespoons bourbon *or* other whiskey
2 tablespoons green crème de menthe
1 teaspoon vanilla
Vanilla Nut Crust (see recipe, right)
Whipped cream (optional)
Mint leaves (optional)

In a 2-quart saucepan stir together the sugar, cornstarch, and salt. Gradually stir in the milk. Add the cubed cream cheese. Cook and stir over medium heat till mixture is thickened and bubbly. Cook and stir for 2 minutes more.

Gradually stir about *1 cup* of the hot mixture into the beaten eggs; return all to saucepan. Return mixture to heat; cook and stir for 2 minutes more. Do not boil. Remove from heat. Stir in bourbon or other whiskey, green crème de menthe, and vanilla.

Turn the mixture into prepared Vanilla Nut Crust. Cool. Chill for 4 to 6 hours or till set. If desired, dollop or pipe whipped cream atop and garnish with mint leaves. Makes 8 servings.

Microwave directions: In a small nonmetal bowl micro-cook the cream cheese on 50% power (MEDIUM) for 1 to 1½ minutes or till softened; set aside.

In a microwave-safe mixing bowl stir together the sugar, cornstarch, and salt. Gradually stir in the milk. Add the cream cheese. Micro-cook, uncovered, on 100% power (HIGH) for 7 to 10 minutes or till the mixture starts to boil, stirring every minute. Micro-cook, uncovered, for 2 minutes more, stirring every minute.

Gradually stir *1 cup* of the hot mixture into the eggs; return all to mixing bowl. Micro-cook, uncovered, on 100% power (HIGH) for 45 to 60 seconds or just till the mixture boils. Stir in the bourbon, crème de menthe, and vanilla.

Turn the mixture into Vanilla Nut Crust. Cool. Chill for 4 to 6 hours or till set. If desired, dollop or pipe whipped cream atop and garnish with fresh mint. Makes 8 servings.

Per serving: 416 calories, 9 g protein, 38 g carbohydrate, 24 g fat, 137 mg cholesterol, and 267 mg sodium.

VANILLA NUT CRUST

The crushed wafers add sweetness and the chopped nuts provide a speckled appearance. You also can use this unique pastry for favorite pie recipes that call for a baked pastry shell.

1 cup all-purpose flour
¼ cup finely crushed vanilla wafers
½ teaspoon salt
⅓ cup lard *or* shortening
3 tablespoons finely chopped pecans
3 to 4 tablespoons water

In a mixing bowl combine the flour, crushed vanilla wafers, and salt. Cut in lard or shortening till pieces are the size of small peas. Stir in the finely chopped pecans. Sprinkle *1 tablespoon* water over part of the mixture; gently toss with a fork. Push to side of bowl. Repeat, using 2 to 3 tablespoons more water, till all is moistened. Form dough into a ball.

On a lightly floured surface flatten dough with hands. Roll into a 12-inch circle; transfer to a 9-inch pie plate. Trim pastry to ½ inch beyond edge of pie plate. Flute edge. Prick bottom and sides with tines of a fork. Bake in a 450° oven for 10 to 12 minutes or till pastry is golden. Cool thoroughly on a wire rack. Continue as directed in pie recipe. Makes 1 crust; 8 servings.

Microwave directions: In a mixing bowl combine flour, crushed vanilla wafers, and salt. Cut in lard or shortening till pieces are the size of small peas. Stir in the finely chopped pecans. Sprinkle *1 tablespoon* water over part of the mixture; gently toss with fork. Push to side of bowl. Repeat, using 2 to 3 tablespoons more water, till all is moistened. Form dough into a ball.

On a lightly floured surface flatten dough with hands. Roll into a 12-inch circle; transfer to a 9-inch nonmetal pie plate. Trim pastry to ½ inch beyond edge of pie plate. Flute the edge. Prick bottom and sides with tines of a fork.

Micro-cook, uncovered, on 100% power (HIGH) for 5 to 7 minutes or till crust is dry, rotating the dish a quarter-turn twice. Continue as directed in the pie recipe. Makes 1 crust; 8 servings.

Note: Microwave recipes were tested in countertop microwave ovens that operate on 600 to 700 watts. Cooking times are approximate since microwave ovens vary by manufacturer.

DECEMBER

COOKS WHO MAKE
CHRISTMAS SPECIAL

By Diana McMillen, Joy Taylor, and Nancy K. Wall

Christmas is a cooking holiday! Bread-bakers, candy-makers, and folks who cook to preserve traditions give loved-ones more than delicious dishes; they spread the yuletide spirit, too. On the pages that follow, you'll learn how some of the cheeriest Christmas cooks around sweeten their own seasonal celebrations. Let their spirit-lifting ideas enrich your festivities.

NURTURING FRIENDSHIPS

As part of their Christmastime festivities, the Scottish/American Pflanz family of Des Moines, Iowa, hosts a High Tea. Their guests include "holiday orphans"—other immigrants without local relatives.

"It's very rewarding personally to share my heritage with my family and friends," says Anne Marie Pflanz, a native of Scotland.

Mincemeat Plait (pronounced pleat—it's Scottish for braid) shares the tray with **Scottish Shortbread**, a cookielike treat that can be shaped either in wood or clay molds or freehand. Savory tidbits like pastry-wrapped **Sausage Rolls** (front left) often are included on the menu. Liqueur-flavored **Drambuie Cake** and cream-filled **Yule Log** are traditional and expected sweets.

"It also gives me the opportunity to prepare and serve many of the foods that I loved when I was a child growing up in Scotland.

"High Tea is traditionally the most formal tea. This special tea is usually served late in the afternoon," Anne Marie explains. The sumptuous spread typically includes a variety of irresistible foods, both savory and sweet and is comparable to a light meal.

A must on Anne's tea menu is shortbread— shaped in a mold that she hand-carried from Scotland 16 years ago. Her four children, ages 8 through 14, help with the baking. "Our baking lessons teach them

valuable cooking skills and an appreciation for their family roots."

Photographs: Jim Hedrich

PROVIDING A HOLIDAY HOME

Foreign travelers enjoy a home-for-the-holidays feeling when they stay at La Maida House in North Hollywood, California. On Christmas Eve, innkeeper Megan Timothy hosts a "family" meal for the inn guests who may be thousands of miles from their homelands.

(*Opposite*) **Smoked Trout with Horseradish Sauce** (front left), **Vegetable Chartreuse** (front right), **Zanzibar Duck with Wild Rice** (center back), and **Lemon-Mint Sherbet** (back left).
(*Below*) **Apple Butter Charlotte.**

Knowing the importance of holiday food traditions, Megan plans and prepares the yuletide feast. "Everyone talks about his favorite foods and I start getting ideas for the recipes. I try to re-create the food traditions so my guests will really feel at home," she says.

Since many of Megan's guests live outside the United States, the menu takes on wonderful international flavors. The foods for last year's feast had origins as far away as Africa.

Megan's face lights up as she recalls dinners of former years. "I think I get more out of these events than my guests! After this kind of heartwarming holiday occasion, you're faced with the hardest part of hosting—saying good-bye to your newfound friends."

Photographs: de Gennaro Studios

PRESERVING A FOOD CRAFT

The spirit of Christmas thrives 12 months a year in Northumberland, Pennsylvania. That's because Paulette and Bill Rishel, along with their four children, prepare for the holiday season nearly every day.

"I could keep busy for a lifetime just making things for others to enjoy," says Paulette, to explain the one reason she embarks on numerous crafts and cooking adventures throughout the year. Equally important to Paulette and Bill is their desire to pass on talents, values, and traditions to their children. All of the creative projects they undertake emphasize family involvement.

The one project dearest to the Rishel family is "The Candy Cottage," named in honor of their quaint 80-year-old home nestled in the woods. The Rishels launched their candy venture four years ago when Paulette was determined "to make candy the old-fashioned way—with lots of love." After a series of trials and errors, the family mastered a variety of confections. "Now, with much patience and endurance we start making pounds and pounds of assorted creams, caramels, fudge, brittle, toffee, lollipops, and molded candies four months before Christmas," explains Paulette. By December 25, none of the goodies is left.

Everyone helps in the small, cozy kitchen, but the children also design and decorate the candy bags and boxes throughout the year. Susie, aged 15, learned calligraphy to address the bags, boxes, and tags; 13-year-old Billy and 11-year-old Amy stencil the labels and boxes with festive artwork. And all agree that Jeremy, aged 10, "is a great little all-around helper." Bill's personal pleasure comes from finding antique candy molds to add to the family collection.

Candies fill the home before Christmas, including: **Raisin-Cashew Clusters** (front right); **Sour Cream Fudge** (in red bucket); **Cottage Brittle** (on board) and **Peanut Brittle** (in jars); **Lollipops** (in tea tin); **Cherry-Almond Creams, Orange-Pecan Creams,** and **Northumberland Creams** (in doily-lined box).

Photographs: Jim Hedrich

SHARING HOLIDAY SPECIALTIES

During November and December, it's common to find six or more men and women cooking energetically in Madelaine Bullwinkel's classroom kitchen. But what they stir together and bake is deliciously uncommon: Madelaine's personal versions of fresh tarts and pastries, buttery cookies, delicate steamed puddings, tender breads, and more. The sugarplum treats they turn out rely on Madelaine's cooking expertise and fail-proof recipes. "I emphasize recipe *technique* in these classes and see to it that everyone has hands in on the fun," explains Madelaine. As a result, the eager students acquire both the skills and the confidence to produce the same mouth-watering results for their families.

The waiting list for Madelaine's cooking classes in west-suburban Chicago is proof positive that many share her holiday baking enthusiasm. Sample her A-rated recipes in your home.

Photographs: Jim Hedrich

Some of Madelaine's classroom cookie favorites include (on rack): pecan-rich **Holiday Triangles; Filbert Cookies** sandwiched with preserves; and star-shaped **Swedish Butter Cookies.** Extra-special desserts such as **Christmas Bread Pudding** (left), **Cranberry Orange Tart** (right), and **Kugelhof Mold** (back center) served with jam, are especially popular with her student bakers.

Note: Nutrition information is given by gram weight per serving. To obtain the nutrition analysis of each recipe, the following guidelines are used:
● When ingredient options appear in a recipe, the analysis is calculated using the first ingredient choice.
● Optional ingredients are omitted in the analyses.
● The nutrition analyses for recipes calling for fresh ingredients are calculated using the measurements for raw fruits, vegetables, and meats.
● If a recipe gives optional serving sizes (such as "Makes 6 to 8 servings"), the nutrition analysis is calculated using the first choice.

For good health, include a variety of foods from the Basic Food Groups in your daily diet. Follow your physician's advice if you are on a restricted diet.

The Pflanzs

SCOTTISH SHORTBREAD

1½ cups all-purpose flour
¼ cup sugar
½ cup butter *or* margarine

In a medium mixing bowl stir together the flour and the sugar. Cut in butter or margarine till the mixture resembles fine crumbs. Form the mixture into a ball; knead till smooth. Press dough into an 8-inch shortbread mold. (Or, on a baking sheet pat dough into an 8-inch circle. Using fingers, press to make a scalloped edge. With fork, prick dough to make 8 to 16 pie-shape wedges.) Bake in a 300° oven for 50 to 60 minutes or till done. Makes 8 to 16.

Per serving: 211 calories, 3 g protein, 24 g carbohydrate, 12 g fat, 36 mg cholesterol, and 141 mg sodium.

YULE LOG

This Scottish dessert is similar to the French dessert, Bûche de Noël, except Scottish cooks use a coffee-flavored center instead of a chocolate-rum filling.

1 cup all-purpose flour
¼ teaspoon salt
5 egg yolks
2 tablespoons dry sherry
1 tablespoon finely shredded orange peel
1 cup sugar
5 egg whites
¼ teaspoon cream of tartar
1 recipe Coffee Cream Filling
1 recipe Chocolate Frosting
Marzipan Holly (optional)

Grease a 15x10x1-inch jelly-roll pan. Line with waxed paper. Grease waxed paper; set aside. Stir together flour and salt. In a small mixer bowl beat egg yolks, sherry, and orange peel with an electric mixer on high speed 5 minutes or till thick and lemon colored. Gradually add ½ cup of the sugar, beating till sugar dissolves. Wash beaters.

In a large mixer bowl beat egg whites and cream of tartar on medium speed till soft peaks form. Gradually add the remaining ½ cup sugar, beating on high speed till stiff peaks form. Fold yolk mixture into egg whites. Sprinkle flour mixture over egg mixture; fold in lightly with a spatula. Spread batter in pan. Bake in a 375° oven for 12 to 15 minutes or till done.

Turn cake onto a towel sprinkled with powdered sugar. Remove the waxed paper. Starting with the narrow end, roll warm cake and towel together; cool on a wire rack. Unroll cake; spread cake with Coffee Cream Filling to within 1 inch of edges. Roll up cake. Frost with Chocolate Frosting. Score with tines of a fork to resemble tree bark. Garnish with Marzipan Holly, if desired. Makes 10 servings.

Coffee Cream Filling: Stir together 1 cup *whipping cream*, ¼ cup *sifted powdered sugar*, and 1½ teaspoons *instant coffee crystals*. Cover and chill while cake cools. Beat mixture to soft peaks just before filling cake.

Chocolate Frosting: In a saucepan melt together 2 squares (2 ounces) *unsweetened chocolate*, cut up, and 2 tablespoons *butter* or *margarine*. Remove saucepan from heat.

Stir in 1¾ cups *sifted powdered sugar*, ¼ cup *whipping cream*, ¾ teaspoon *vanilla*, and dash *salt* till combined. If necessary, stir in additional *powdered sugar*, 1 tablespoon at a time, to make of spreading consistency.

Per serving: 396 calories, 6 g protein, 53 g carbohydrate, 19 g fat, 173 mg cholesterol, and 138 mg sodium.

MARZIPAN HOLLY

1 cup whole blanched almonds (6 ounces) *or* 1⅓ cups slivered almonds
1⅓ cups sifted powdered sugar
3 tablespoons water
½ teaspoon almond extract
2¼ cups sifted powdered sugar
1 tablespoon slightly beaten egg white
Few drops red food coloring
Few drops green food coloring

Place almonds in a blender container or a food processor bowl. Cover and blend till ground. In a mixer bowl beat together the ground almonds, the 1⅓ cups powdered sugar, the water, and the extract till mixture forms a ball. Stir in the 2¼ cups powdered sugar. Stir in enough egg white to form a clay-like mixture. Divide in half. Wrap and chill *one-half* for another use.

Tint *one-fourth* of the remaining half red (knead in food coloring). Shape into 72 small balls. Press three balls together to make berry clusters. Repeat with remaining small balls. Allow marzipan balls to dry.

Meanwhile, tint remaining portion of marzipan green. On a powdered sugar-dusted surface, roll the green-tinted marzipan portion to about ⅛-inch thickness. Using a small knife or cutter, cut the green marzipan to make 48 ½-inch holly leaves.

Press two leaves and one berry cluster together to make holly. Repeat with the remaining leaves and berries. Shape the chilled marzipan as desired. Store in a covered container at room temperature. Makes 24 holly candies.

Per serving: 104 calories, 1 g protein, 19 g carbohydrate, 3 g fat, 0 mg cholesterol, and 1 mg sodium.

DRAMBUIE CAKE

2½ cups all-purpose flour
  1 teaspoon baking powder
  1 teaspoon baking soda
  1 cup butter *or* margarine
  1 cup sugar
  1 tablespoon finely
      shredded orange peel
  3 egg yolks
  1 tablespoon Drambuie
1¼ cups dairy sour cream
  ½ cup chopped walnuts
  3 egg whites
  1 recipe Drambuie Sauce
Shredded orange peel (optional)

Stir together flour, baking powder, and baking soda. In a large mixer bowl beat butter or margarine for 30 seconds. Add ⅔ cup of the sugar and the 1 tablespoon finely shredded orange peel. Beat till fluffy. Add the egg yolks, one at a time, beating for 1 minute after each; scrape bowl frequently, guiding mixture to beaters. Add Drambuie. Beat till well combined. Add dry ingredients and sour cream alternately to beaten mixture, beating after each addition. Stir in walnuts. Wash beaters.

In a small mixer bowl beat egg whites with electric mixer on medium speed till soft peaks form (tips curl). Gradually add the remaining ⅓ cup sugar, 1 tablespoon at a time, beating till stiff peaks form (tips stand straight). Gently stir some egg white into flour mixture to lighten the batter. Gently fold remaining egg whites into flour mixture. Turn batter into an ungreased 10-inch tube pan. Bake in a 325° oven about 80 minutes or till cake tests done.

Place cake on wire rack; cool for 20 minutes. Remove from pan; place on wire rack over a baking sheet or waxed paper. Using a long-tine fork, prick top of hot cake deeply in several places. Gradually spoon hot Drambuie Sauce over cake. Spoon any sauce that drips onto pan over cake again. Cool completely. Garnish with shredded orange peel and cedar, if desired. To serve, cut into slices. Serves 12.

Drambuie Sauce: In a small saucepan combine ½ cup *sugar* and ½ cup *orange juice.* Cook and stir till sugar dissolves and mixture boils; boil for 1 to 2 minutes. Stir in ¼ cup *Drambuie.*

Per serving: 450 calories, 6 g protein, 48 g carbohydrate, 25 g fat, 121 mg cholesterol, and 334 mg sodium.

MINCEMEAT PLAIT

  ½ of a 17¼-ounce package
      (1 sheet) frozen puff pastry
  1 9-ounce package instant
      condensed mincemeat
  ½ cup light raisins
  ¼ cup chopped candied cherries
  1 beaten egg
  1 recipe Powdered Sugar Icing
Seedless red *or* green grapes
      (optional)
Grape leaves (optional)

Thaw pastry according to package directions. Remove one sheet; return remaining pastry to the freezer. Prepare mincemeat according to package directions, using 1½ cups *water.* Stir in raisins and cherries. On a floured surface, roll pastry into a 14x12-inch rectangle. Transfer to a greased baking sheet.

Spoon fruit mixture, lengthwise, down center of rectangle. Make 4-inch cuts at 1-inch intervals on both sides of filling. Fold strips over filling at an angle, overlapping and pinching at center. Seal ends to hold in filling. Brush with beaten egg. Bake in a 425° oven for 15 to 20 minutes or till golden brown. Drizzle icing over warm pastry. Garnish platter with grapes and grape leaves, if desired. Serves 10 to 12.

Powdered Sugar Icing: Combine 1 cup *sifted powdered sugar,* ¼ teaspoon *vanilla,* and enough *milk* (about 4 teaspoons) to make mixture of drizzling consistency.

Per serving: 288 calories, 3 g protein, 46 g carbohydrate, 12 g fat, 26 mg cholesterol, and 137 mg sodium.

SAUSAGE ROLLS

  1 beaten egg
  ⅓ cup fine dry bread crumbs
  ¼ cup finely chopped onion
  1 pound bulk pork sausage
  1 17½-ounce package (2 sheets)
      frozen puff pastry, thawed

In a bowl combine egg, bread crumbs, and onion. Add pork sausage; mix well. Shape mixture into eight 5-inch-long rolls. Place sausage rolls in a shallow baking pan. Bake in a 400° oven about 20 minutes or till no longer pink. Drain and cool on paper towels. Cut each puff pastry sheet into quarters.

For each pastry roll, place one sausage roll near one long side of a pastry quarter. Roll up jelly-roll style. Seal edges and ends. Place in an ungreased 15x10x1-inch baking pan. Repeat with remaining sausage and pastry. Bake in a 425° oven about 20 minutes or till brown. To serve, cut each roll crosswise into 1-inch slices. Makes about 40.

Per serving: 127 calories, 2 g protein, 5 g carbohydrate, 11 g fat, 13 mg cholesterol, and 156 mg sodium.

The Timothys

LEMON-MINT SHERBET

Preparing the sherbet in an ice-cream freezer results in a softer mixture that pipes easily. Use a pastry bag fitted with a large star tip and pipe the sherbet immediately after removing it from the ice-cream freezer. Serve ¼-cup portions as an intermezzo before the entrée; serve ½ cup portions as a refreshing dessert.

1½ teaspoons unflavored gelatin
  ¼ cup water
1½ cups milk
  1 cup light cream
  ½ cup sugar
  2 tablespoons snipped fresh mint
      or 2 teaspoons dried mint,
      crushed
  1 tablespoon finely shredded
      lemon peel
  ½ cup lemon juice
Shredded lemon peel (optional)

In a custard cup soften gelatin in the water; dissolve over hot water. In a bowl combine milk, cream, sugar, mint, the 1 tablespoon lemon peel, lemon juice, and gelatin mixture.

Freeze sherbet in an ice-cream freezer following manufacturer's directions. (Or, to prepare the sherbet using your refrigerator freezer, turn the mixture into an 8x8x2-inch pan. Cover and freeze till firm. Break up mixture; place in a large chilled mixer bowl. Beat with an electric mixer till fluffy. Return to pan. Cover; freeze till firm.) Scoop or pipe the sherbet to serve. Sprinkle with additional shredded lemon peel, if desired. Makes 4 cups.

Per ½-cup serving: 147 calories, 3 g protein, 17 g carbohydrate, 8 g fat, 26 mg cholesterol, and 36 mg sodium.

APPLE BUTTER CHARLOTTE

- 18 ladyfingers
- ⅓ cup apple brandy *or* brandy
- 1 envelope unflavored gelatin
- 3 tablespoons lemon juice
- 2 tablespoons water
- 2 tablespoons apple brandy *or* brandy
- 1½ cups apple butter
- 1 envelope unflavored gelatin
- ¼ cup water
- 2¾ cups milk
- 2 tablespoons cornstarch
- ¼ cup honey
- 3 beaten egg yolks
- 1 teaspoon vanilla
- 3 egg whites

Whipped cream (optional)
Candied rose petals *or* violets (optional)
- 1 recipe Crystal Apple Balls (optional) (see recipe, right)

Line the bottom of an 8-inch spring-form pan with a circle of waxed paper. Sprinkle cut side of ladyfingers with the ⅓ cup brandy. Line sides of pan with ladyfingers, cut side facing center of pan. Arrange remaining ladyfingers, cut side up, spoke-fashion in bottom of pan and trim ends at center to fit tightly. Trim additional ladyfingers to fill open spaces. Set aside lined pan while preparing filling.

For apple filling, in a custard cup soften one envelope gelatin in lemon juice and 2 tablespoons water; dissolve over hot water. Stir in the 2 tablespoons brandy. Stir gelatin mixture into apple butter. Chill till partially set.

Meanwhile, for vanilla filling, soften one envelope gelatin in the ¼ cup water; set aside. In a saucepan stir the milk into the cornstarch. Add the honey. Cook and stir mixture till thickened and bubbly. Gradually stir about *1 cup* of the hot mixture into the yolks. Return all to saucepan; cook and stir for 2 minutes. Remove from heat. Add the softened gelatin; stir till dissolved. Stir in the vanilla. Chill mixture till partially set; beat till fluffy. Beat egg whites till soft peaks form (tips curl); fold into the gelatin mixture.

To assemble charlotte, pour *half* of the vanilla filling into the prepared pan. Chill till nearly set (surface should be sticky). Keep the remaining vanilla filling at room temperature. Spoon the apple butter filling over the vanilla fill-ing in the pan; spread evenly. Pour the remaining vanilla filling over the apple butter mixture. Cover; chill overnight.

Trim ladyfingers even with the top of the filling. Using a narrow spatula, loosen the charlotte from the pan. Invert onto a serving platter; gently peel off waxed paper. Garnish with whipped cream, rose petals, and the Crystal Apple Balls, if desired. Makes 12 servings.

Per serving: 231 calories, 6 g protein, 37 g carbohydrate, 5 g fat, 130 mg cholesterol, and 56 mg sodium.

CRYSTAL APPLE BALLS

The apples should be glazed just before serving. Follow directions carefully.

- 3 large apples
- 1 cup sugar

Peel the apples. Using a melon baller, make 12 apple balls. Pat dry with paper towels. Cover the floor near the work area with newspapers. In a heavy 1-quart saucepan heat the sugar over medium-low heat without stirring. When sugar begins to melt, heat and stir constantly till mixture is a caramel color. Stir in ¼ to ½ teaspoon *hot water.*

Skewer each apple ball on the end of a buttered bamboo skewer. Working quickly, dip the apple balls into the caramel, remove and weight the ends of the skewers on the counter so the balls hang over the edge and drip excess caramel. If mixture thickens, stir in additional water. Break off the caramel drips to desired length. Garnish cake immediately (apples weep upon standing). Makes 12.

Per serving: 91 calories, 0.1 g protein, 24 g carbohydrate, 0.2 g fat, and 0.7 mg sodium.

VEGETABLE CHARTREUSE

The beauty of this side dish is the arrangement of the vegetables. Try your hand at creating your own artful vegetable arrangement, or use the photograph on page 172 and the directions below as a guide.

- 3 whole green beans
- 3 medium carrots
- 1 crookneck squash (optional)

Butter *or* margarine
- 1 cup frozen peas, thawed
- 6 medium potatoes (2 pounds)
- 2 eggs
- ¼ cup butter *or* margarine
- ½ teaspoon salt
- ⅛ teaspoon white pepper

Trim ends off beans. Split lengthwise in half. Cut a few slices from the carrot. Using a potato peeler, cut lengthwise strips from the remaining carrot. If using squash, peel so squash peel comes off in large pieces. Reserve pulp for another use. Cut squash peel into 2-inch triangular shapes.

In a large saucepan or skillet cook green beans in a small amount of boiling water, covered, for 10 minutes. Add carrot strips and squash peel; cover and cook 5 minutes more or till vegetables are crisp-tender. Remove the vegetables from the heat; drain.

Generously butter a 1½-quart ovenproof bowl. Trim and arrange the beans, carrots, peas, and squash in a spokelike fashion to cover bottom and sides of bowl, trimming ends ½ inch below edge of bowl. If you're preparing this dish in advance, cover bowl and place in refrigerator for 3 to 24 hours. Or, continue as directed.

Peel and cube potatoes. In a medium saucepan cook potatoes, uncovered, in boiling water for 10 to 15 minutes or till tender; drain. In a mixer bowl mash the potatoes. Add the eggs, the ¼ cup butter or margarine, salt, and pepper; beat till combined. Carefully spoon the mashed potatoes into vegetable-lined bowl, spreading smooth. Cover with foil. Bake in a 350° oven for 40 to 45 minutes or till just slightly puffed and center is hot. Remove from oven; let stand 5 minutes. Unmold onto serving plate. Serve at once. Makes 8 servings.

Per serving: 174 calories, 5 g protein, 23 g carbohydrate, 7 g fat, 81 mg cholesterol, and 258 mg sodium.

SMOKED TROUT WITH HORSERADISH SAUCE

Smoke the trout with the bone in and then remove the bone, head, and tail before serving.

- 2 tablespoons salt
- 2 8- to 10-ounce fresh *or* frozen dressed trout, with head and tail intact
- Cooking oil
- Fresh tarragon sprigs *or* dried tarragon
- Hickory chips
- Lemon slices
- Lemon leaves (optional)
- Radicchio (optional)
- 1 recipe Horseradish Sauce

In a large mixing bowl make a brine by combining 8 cups *water* and salt. Soak trout in brine overnight in the refrigerator. Rinse with water; pat dry with paper towels. Lightly brush the trout skin and cavity with oil. Stuff the cavity with tarragon.

Smoker directions: About 1 hour before cooking, soak *2 cups* hickory chips in enough water to cover. Arrange a full pan of coals in smoker and ignite. When coals are hot, drain the hickory chips; sprinkle some over coals. Fill water pan of smoker with water; set in place. Place stuffed fish on grill over water pan. Cover and cook for 1 to 1¼ hours or till done, replenishing coals, hickory chips, and water, if necessary, every 30 minutes. Skin trout; remove head and tail. Arrange on serving plate with lemon slices, lemon leaves, and radicchio, if desired. Serve with Horseradish Sauce. Makes 4 appetizer servings.

Covered grill directions: About 1 hour before cooking, soak *2 cups* hickory chips in enough water to cover. In covered grill arrange *medium-slow* coals around a foil drip pan in the firebox. Add 1 cup *water* to drip pan. Drain hickory chips; sprinkle *half* of the chips over coals. Place stuffed fish on grill rack over drip pan; brush with oil. Lower the grill hood and cook for 20 to 30 minutes or till done. Skin trout; remove head and tail. Arrange trout on serving plate with lemon slices, lemon leaves, and radicchio, if desired. Serve with Horseradish Sauce.

Horseradish Sauce: In a small mixer bowl beat ½ cup *whipping cream* just till soft peaks form (tips curl). Gently fold in 2 teaspoons *prepared horseradish* and 1 teaspoon *tarragon vinegar*. Makes about 1 cup sauce.

Per serving: 206 calories, 12 g protein, 1 g carbohydrate, 17 g fat, 71 mg cholesterol, and 586 mg sodium.

ZANZIBAR DUCK WITH WILD RICE

You can buy roasted cashews and skip the step for toasting the nuts.

- 2 tablespoons coarsely chopped raw cashews
- 1 orange
- 1 lime
- 1 sweet red *or* green pepper
- 1½ cups cooked wild rice (about ½ cup uncooked)
- 2 tablespoons finely chopped onion
- 1 tablespoon finely chopped celery
- ¼ teaspoon salt
- ⅛ teaspoon pepper
- Dash ground cloves
- 1 5- to 5½-pound domestic duckling
- Ground red pepper
- 1 cup chicken broth
- 1 medium onion, cut into wedges
- 12 whole cloves
- ⅓ cup orange juice
- 2 tablespoons lime juice
- Watercress (optional)

Place raw cashews in a shallow baking pan. Toast in a 350° oven for 6 to 7 minutes or till golden. Finely shred ¼ *teaspoon* of orange or lime peel for the stuffing; cut two 2x1½-inch strips of orange peel and one 2x1½-inch strip of lime peel for the cooking liquid; cut remaining orange peel into strips for garnish. (Reserve lime for another use.)

Finely chop *2 tablespoons* of the red or green pepper and cut the remainder into strips to use for garnish. In a medium mixing bowl combine the toasted cashews, shredded citrus peel, chopped pepper, wild rice, chopped onion, celery, salt, pepper, and ground cloves. Set aside.

Rinse the bird and pat dry with paper towels. Rub cavity with additional salt and ground red pepper. Spoon the prepared stuffing into body cavity. Skewer neck skin to back; tie legs to tail. Tie wings to body. Prick duck skin all over with a fork. Sprinkle outside of duck with additional salt and ground red pepper. Place bird, breast side up, in a roasting pan. Combine chicken broth, onion wedges, whole cloves, orange juice, lime juice, reserved 2x1½-inch orange peel strips, and 2x1½-inch lime peel strip; pour over duck.

Insert a meat thermometer into thigh. Cover and bake in a 375° oven about 2 hours or till meat thermometer registers 185°. Drain pan juices and discard. Increase oven temperature to 450°. Bake, uncovered, for 15 to 20 minutes more or till golden. Transfer duck to a serving platter. Garnish with watercress, if desired; orange peel strips; and red pepper strips. Serves 3 or 4.

Per serving: 424 calories, 41 g protein, 23 g carbohydrate, 19 g fat, 167 mg cholesterol, and 323 mg sodium.

The Rishels

RAISIN-CASHEW CLUSTERS

You'll find confectioners' coating in several flavors: chocolate, butterscotch, and vanilla (sometimes called white chocolate). These products have had the cocoa butter replaced with another fat.

- 1 cup raisins
- 1 pound raw cashews *or* dry roasted unsalted cashews
- 1 pound milk chocolate confectioners' coating

Place raisins in a steamer basket. Place over, but not touching, boiling water. Steam, covered, for 5 minutes. Let raisins stand at room temperature about 2 hours or till completely dry.* To roast raw cashews, spread in a shallow baking pan. Bake in a 350° oven about 15 minutes or till light brown.

In a large heavy saucepan melt the confectioners' coating over low heat. Remove from heat. Stir in cashews. Add raisins; mix well. Drop from a teaspoon onto waxed paper. Let stand till firm. Store, tightly covered, in a cool place. Makes about 64.

Note: Steaming softens the raisins. For a chewier Raisin-Cashew cluster, omit this step.

Per piece: 75 calories, 1 g protein, 9 g carbohydrate, 4 g fat, 15 mg sodium.

COTTAGE BRITTLE

Butter the sides of the saucepan for candy making to prevent the mixture from climbing the sides of the pan and boiling over—

¾ **cup whole blanched almonds**
¾ **cup filberts**
¾ **cup broken pecans**
¾ **cup walnuts**
1½ **cups sugar**
1 **cup light corn syrup**
½ **cup butter *or* margarine**
1 **teaspoon vanilla**
1 **teaspoon orange extract**

Place all of the nuts in an 8x8x2-inch baking pan. Toast nuts in a 325° oven for 15 minutes, stirring twice. Butter a baking sheet; set aside. Butter a heavy 3-quart saucepan. In the saucepan stir together the sugar, corn syrup, and butter or margarine. Cook over medium heat to boiling, stirring constantly with a wooden spoon. Clip a candy thermometer to the side of the pan.

Cook over medium heat, without stirring, till mixture reaches 290° (soft-crack stage). Mixture should boil at a moderate, steady rate over entire surface. Remove from heat; remove thermometer. Stir in the vanilla and orange extract. Stir in the warm nuts. Immediately turn candy mixture out onto a buttered baking sheet; spread evenly. Cool completely. Break the brittle into pieces. Store in a tightly covered container at room temperature. Makes about 2¼ pounds candy.

Per half-ounce candy: 75 calories, 1 g protein, 9 g carbohydrate, 4 g fat, 4 mg cholesterol, and 20 mg sodium.

LOLLIPOPS

Prepare two or more batches of Lollipops or Hard Candy Drops, making each batch a different flavor and color. Use these bright candies as a holiday decoration or gift.

2 **cups sugar**
⅔ **cup light corn syrup**
½ **cup water**
¼ **teaspoon oil of cinnamon, cloves, anise, peppermint, *or* wintergreen**
Few drops food coloring

If using lollipop molds, oil molds or spray with nonstick vegetable coating; attach lollipop sticks. (Place sticks approximately halfway up the mold.)

Butter the sides of a heavy 2-quart saucepan. In the saucepan combine sugar, corn syrup, and water. Cook over medium-high heat to boiling, stirring constantly with a wooden spoon. Cover with a lid for 1 minute. Remove the lid and reduce the heat to medium. Clip candy thermometer to side of pan.

Continue cooking the mixture over medium heat, stirring occasionally, till the thermometer registers 300° (hard-crack stage). Mixture should boil at a moderate, steady rate over entire surface. Remove saucepan from heat. Remove the thermometer. Stir in desired oil and food coloring.

Immediately spoon mixture into molds. Let stand about 10 minutes or till firm. Invert the molds; twist to remove candies. Cool completely. Store tightly covered. Makes 1¼ pounds.

Per ounce: 109 calories, 0 g protein, 28 g carbohydrate, 0 g fat, 0 mg cholesterol, and 8 mg sodium.

Hard Candy Drops: Lightly grease two cookie sheets. Prepare Lollipops as directed above *except* omit molds and spoon the hot candy mixture onto cookie sheets. Cool completely.

ROYAL CREAM FONDANT

If you want to make Northumberland Creams, Orange-Pecan Creams, and Cherry-Almond Creams, you'll need to make three separate batches of fondant. Never double or triple any candy recipe; you won't have successful results.

2½ **cups sugar**
½ **cup milk**
½ **cup whipping cream**
½ **cup butter *or* margarine**

Butter the sides of a heavy 3-quart saucepan. In the saucepan combine sugar, milk, cream, and butter or margarine. Cook mixture over medium-high heat to boiling, stirring constantly with a wooden spoon. Clip the thermometer to the side of the pan. Reduce heat to medium and cook, stirring once or twice, till the thermometer reaches 240° (soft-ball stage). Mixture should boil at a moderate, steady rate over entire surface.

Immediately pour into a 15x10x1-inch baking pan or onto a marble surface. *Do not scrape pan.* Cool, without stirring, about 25 minutes or till just slightly warm. (For Cherry-Almond Creams, add the extract, flavoring, and coloring; for Orange-Pecan Creams, add the extract and coloring.)

Use a wooden spoon to scrape candy from edge to center, then beat vigorously for 4 to 8 minutes, till fondant is creamy and stiff. (Butter may seep out, but will blend in after beating.)

Knead fondant with hands for 10 to 15 minutes or till free of lumps. Wrap in waxed paper or clear plastic wrap; place in plastic storage bags. Refrigerate for at least 7 days or up to 1 month to ripen. Use Royal Cream Fondant for Cherry-Almond Creams, Northumberland Creams, or Orange-Pecan Creams. Makes 1¼ pounds.

DIPPING INSTRUCTIONS

It's important that the creams stand at room temperature long enough to form a "crust." This hard outer coating prevents the cream from dissolving when it's dipped into the warm confectioners' coating. Follow the directions on the package for melting the confectioners' coating or use the directions that follow.

Break the confectioners' coating into small pieces; place coating pieces into a large heavy saucepan. Melt coating over low heat, stirring constantly with a wooden spoon till smooth. Do not allow steam or water to drip into the confectioners' coating. Remove coating from the heat. (Do not overheat or the coating will appear gray.)

Drop cream centers, one at a time, into the melted confectioners' coating; turn centers to coat. Lift the candy out of the coating with a long-tined fork, being careful not to pierce the candy center. Hold over pan, letting excess coating drip off the fork.

Draw the bottom of the fork across the rim of the saucepan to remove excess coating from it and the dipped candy. Invert the dipped candy onto a waxed-paper-lined baking sheet. To swirl the coating on the top of the candy, twist the fork slightly as the candy falls. (If a large amount of chocolate coating pools at the base, next time allow more chocolate coating to drip off the fork before inverting the candy.)

CHERRY-ALMOND CREAMS

Try milk chocolate confectioners' coating on this candy, too.

 1 **recipe Royal Cream Fondant (see recipe, left)**
 ¼ **teaspoon almond extract**
 4 **drops cherry flavoring**
Few drops red food coloring (optional)
 ½ **cup chopped almonds, toasted**
 ¼ **cup finely chopped candied red cherries**
 1 **pound dark chocolate confectioners' coating**

Prepare Royal Cream Fondant as directed, *except* after fondant has cooled till slightly warm make indentation in fondant and add the almond extract; cherry flavoring; and food coloring, if desired. Continue beating and allow to ripen as directed.

Knead almonds and cherries into ripened fondant. (If mixture is sticky, add sifted powdered sugar to fondant, 1 tablespoon at a time, and coat hands with powdered sugar.) Shape candy into 1-inch balls. Place on baking sheet lined with waxed paper. Let stand at room temperature, uncovered, for at least 1 hour or till a "crust" forms over surface of the candies.

Dip candies in melted confectioners' coating (see the dipping instructions at left). Place dipped candies on baking sheets lined with waxed paper or on a marble slab till dry and set. Makes about 1¾ pounds (70 pieces).

Per piece: 73 calories, 0.4 g protein, 12 g carbohydrate, 3 g fat, 7 mg cholesterol, and 27 mg sodium.

NORTHUMBERLAND CREAMS

The Rishel family fondly named this brandied candy after their hometown in Pennsylvania.

 1 **recipe Royal Cream Fondant (see recipe, left)**
 ½ **cup chopped raisins**
 ¼ **cup brandy**
 ½ **cup chopped walnuts**
 1 **pound dark chocolate confectioners' coating**
Finely chopped walnuts (optional)

Prepare Royal Cream Fondant and allow it to ripen as directed. Stir together raisins and brandy; cover and let stand for 24 hours. Drain well. Pat raisins dry on paper towels.

Knead the raisins and walnuts into the ripened fondant. (If mixture is sticky, add sifted powdered sugar to fondant, 1 tablespoon at a time, and coat hands with additional powdered sugar.) Shape candy into 1-inch balls. Place on baking sheets lined with waxed paper. Let candies stand at room temperature, uncovered, for at least 1 hour or till a "crust" forms over the surface of candies.

Dip the candies in melted confectioners' coating (see dipping instructions at left). Place the dipped candies on the baking sheets lined with waxed paper or on a marble slab till dry and set. If desired, sprinkle finely chopped walnuts over tops of candies before the chocolate coating is set. Makes about 1¾ pounds (70 candies).

Per piece: 76 calories, 0.4 g protein, 12 g carbohydrate, 3 g fat, 7 mg cholesterol, and 27 mg sodium.

ORANGE-PECAN CREAMS

The delicate orange flavor complements the pecans.

  1 **recipe Royal Cream Fondant (see recipe, page 182)**
  ¼ **teaspoon orange extract**
  3 **drops yellow food coloring (optional)**
  2 **drops red food coloring (optional)**
  ½ **cup finely chopped pecans**
  1 **pound milk chocolate confectioners' coating**

Prepare Royal Cream Fondant as directed, *except* after cooling make indentation in fondant and add the orange extract. If desired, add food coloring. Continue beating and allow to ripen as directed.

Knead pecans into ripened fondant. Shape candy into 1-inch balls. Place balls on baking sheets lined with waxed paper. Let stand at room temperature, uncovered, for at least 1 hour or till a "crust" forms over the surface of the candies.

Dip candies in melted confectioners' coating (see dipping instructions, page 183). Place dipped candies on baking sheets lined with waxed paper or on a marble slab till dry and set. Makes about 1¾ pounds (70 pieces).

Per piece: 72 calories, 0.3 g protein, 11 g carbohydrate, 3 g fat, 7 mg cholesterol, and 27 mg sodium.

SOUR CREAM FUDGE

The butter or margarine may separate from the cooked mixture, but beating the mixture reblends it.

1½ **cups sugar**
  ⅔ **cup dairy sour cream**
  ½ **cup butter *or* margarine**
  8 **ounces white confectioners' coating, finely chopped**
  1 **teaspoon vanilla**
  ¾ **cup broken walnuts, toasted**

Butter an 8x8x2-inch baking pan; set aside. Butter the sides of a heavy 2-quart saucepan. In the saucepan combine the sugar, sour cream, and butter or margarine. Cook over medium-high heat to boiling, stirring constantly with

a wooden spoon. Clip a candy thermometer to the side of the pan.

Reduce heat to medium. Continue cooking to 238° (soft-ball stage), stirring occasionally. Mixture should boil at a moderate, steady rate over entire surface. Remove from heat. Stir in confectioners' coating and vanilla, stirring till coating is melted. Add walnuts; stir till smooth and creamy and mixture starts to thicken (about 3 minutes). Pour into the prepared pan. Score candy while warm into 1-inch pieces. Cool till firm. Cut into pieces. Store tightly covered. Makes 2 pounds (64 pieces).

Per piece: 59 calories, 0.4 g protein, 8 g carbohydrate, 3 g fat, 6 mg cholesterol, and 26 mg sodium.

PEANUT BRITTLE

Humidity makes brittle sticky, so it's important to store it tightly covered.

  2 **cups sugar**
  1 **cup light corn syrup**
  ⅔ **cup water**
  ½ **teaspoon salt**
  1 **pound raw peanuts**
  1 **tablespoon butter *or* margarine**
  1 **teaspoon vanilla extract**
  2 **teaspoons baking soda**

Butter a 15x10x1-inch baking pan; set aside. Butter the sides of a heavy 3-quart saucepan. In the saucepan combine sugar, corn syrup, water, and salt. Cook over medium-high heat to boiling, stirring constantly with a wooden spoon. Clip candy thermometer to side of pan.

Cook over medium-low heat, stirring occasionally, till thermometer registers 240°. Stir in peanuts. Continue cooking over medium-low heat, stirring till thermometer registers 295° (hard-crack stage). Mixture should boil at a moderate, steady rate over entire surface. Remove from heat; stir in butter or margarine and vanilla, stirring just till butter is melted. Immediately stir in baking soda. (Mixture will foam.) Pour candy into prepared pan. Do not spread candy. Cool completely. Break candy into pieces. Store in an airtight container at room temperature. Makes 2¼ pounds.

Per half-ounce: 101 calories, 3 g protein, 12 g carbohydrate, 5 g fat, 1 mg cholesterol, and 54 mg sodium.

The Bullwinkels

FILBERT COOKIES

Filberts also are called hazelnuts.

1¼ **cups blanched filberts (5 ounces)**
  2 **cups unbleached flour**
  ¼ **cup sugar**
  ⅛ **teaspoon salt**
  1 **cup unsalted butter (at room temperature)**
  ¼ **cup preserves**

Place filberts in a shallow baking pan. Toast in a 350° oven for 10 minutes. Grind the nuts using a food processor or blender.

In a mixing bowl combine the filberts, flour, sugar, and salt. Cut in the butter till mixture forms a soft ball. Knead dough with hands to form a smooth ball.

Food processor directions: Place steel blade in work bowl. Add the filberts, flour, sugar, and salt. Process with three or four on/off turns till combined. Add butter. Process with on/off turns till a ball of dough forms.

If dough is soft, chill for 1 hour or till firm enough for rolling. Divide dough into thirds. On a lightly floured surface, roll each portion of dough to ⅛-inch thickness; cut with a 1½-inch fluted round cutter.

Place dough rounds on an ungreased cookie sheet. Bake in a 350° oven for 10 to 12 minutes or till edges are just golden. Cool on a baking sheet for 3 minutes; transfer to a wire rack. Cool thoroughly. To make sandwich cookies, spread *half* of the cookies with ¼ *teaspoon* preserves; top with second cookie. Makes about 54.

Per serving: 62 calories, 1 g protein, 6 g carbohydrate, 4 g fat, 8 mg cholesterol, and 6 mg sodium.

KUGELHOF MOLD

Enjoy this bread the same day you bake it, when it is the most tender and moist. Or, seal the bread in moisture- and vaporproof wrap; label and freeze.

- 3 **packages active dry yeast**
- 1¼ **cups warm milk (110° to 115°)**
- 2 **cups bread flour** *or* **all-purpose flour**
- 2 **cups light raisins**
- 1½ **cups warm water**
- 1¼ **cups unsalted butter, softened**
- ½ **cup sugar**
- 10 **egg yolks (at room temperature)**
- 1 **tablespoon finely shredded lemon peel**
- ¾ **teaspoon salt**
- ½ **teaspoon vanilla**
- 3½ **cups unbleached flour** *or* **all-purpose flour**
- **Powdered sugar (optional)**
- **Orange marmalade** *or* **cranberry jam (optional)**

In a medium mixing bowl soften yeast in warm milk. Add the 2 cups flour; beat with a wooden spoon for 1 minute. Cover; let rise in a warm place till double (40 to 60 minutes).

Soak raisins in warm water for 30 minutes; drain. In mixing bowl beat the butter and sugar till fluffy. Add the egg yolks, one at a time, mixing well after each. Stir in the lemon peel, salt, and vanilla. Stir yeast mixture into egg yolk mixture. Stir in raisins. Gradually add the 3½ cups flour, stirring till combined to make a moderately soft dough.

Generously grease two 7-cup kugelhof molds or one 12-cup fluted tube pan and one 9x5x3-inch loaf pan; divide the dough in half. Spread dough into the two prepared pans. Cover; let rise in a warm place till almost double (about 1 hour). Bake in a 350° oven; allow 40 minutes for the kugelhof mold and 35 minutes for other pans. If necessary, cover with foil during the last 15 minutes of baking time to prevent overbrowning. Remove from pans. Cool on wire racks. If desired, sift powdered sugar over each. Serve at room temperature with marmalade or jam, if desired. Makes 2 cakes, 16 servings each.

Per serving: 202 calories, 4 g protein, 28 g carbohydrate, 8 g fat, 97 mg cholesterol, and 62 mg sodium.

CHRISTMAS BREAD PUDDING

- 4 **beaten egg yolks**
- 2 **cups light cream**
- ½ **cup sugar**
- ¼ **teaspoon salt**
- 2 **teaspoons vanilla**
- ¾ **cup light raisins**
- ¾ **cup dark raisins**
- ½ **cup whole red candied cherries, halved**
- 1 **cup cream sherry**
- 10 **slices whole wheat bread**
- 11 **slices white bread**
- 1 **recipe Caramel Raisin Sauce**

For custard, in a heavy medium saucepan combine the egg yolks, cream, sugar, and salt. Cook and stir over medium heat. Continue cooking till the mixture coats a metal spoon. Remove from heat; cool at once by placing pan in a sink of ice water and stirring for 1 to 2 minutes. Stir in vanilla. Cover surface with clear plastic wrap.

In a small mixing bowl combine the raisins; place the cherries in another bowl. Heat the sherry till warm. Pour about ⅔ *cup* of the sherry over the raisins and the remaining sherry over the cherries; set aside. Remove crusts from bread slices; wrap and store crusts for another use. Cut bread into ½-inch cubes; toss the cubes together. (You should have about 13½ cups bread cubes.)

Grease a 2½- or 3-quart heatproof mold (with or without tube). Drain raisins and cherries, reserving sherry. Reserve ½ *cup* of the raisins for sauce. Arrange *2 tablespoons* cherries in bottom of mold; sprinkle about ¼ *cup* raisins in mold. Add *3 cups* bread cubes. Sprinkle with *3 tablespoons* sherry; drizzle with ½ *cup* custard. Repeat layers three more times, arranging cherries and raisins near edge of mold. Press last layer with back of a spoon.

Cover mold tightly with foil. Place mold on rack in deep kettle; add boiling water to kettle to a depth of 1 inch. Cover kettle. Steam pudding for 1¼ to 1½ hours or till puffed slightly and pudding springs back when touched; add more water to kettle as needed. Remove mold and let stand for 10 minutes. Carefully unmold pudding onto platter. Serve warm with Caramel Raisin Sauce. Or, cover and chill pudding. At serving time, return steamed pudding to same mold. Cover and resteam for 30 to 45 minutes or till warm. Let stand for 10 minutes; unmold and serve with sauce. Serves 12.

Caramel Raisin Sauce: In a 1-quart saucepan bring 1 cup *sugar* and ½ cup *water* to boiling, stirring to dissolve the sugar. Cook about 15 minutes or till mixture turns a light caramel color. Remove from heat. Cool for 2 minutes. Add ½ cup *water*. Stir over low heat till smooth. Add the ½ cup reserved raisins from the Christmas Bread Pudding plus 3 tablespoons *cream sherry;* heat through. Makes about 1⅓ cups.

Note: The sauce continues to cook and darken after it is removed from the heat; stop cooking the sauce when it is still a light caramel color.

Per serving: 434 calories, 7 g protein, 73 g carbohydrate, 11 g fat, 112 mg cholesterol, and 328 mg sodium.

SWEDISH BUTTER COOKIES

In place of the vanilla sugar, you can use ½ cup sugar plus ½ teaspoon vanilla.

- 1 **cup unsalted butter (at room temperature)**
- ½ **cup Vanilla Sugar**
- 4 **teaspoons finely shredded lemon peel**
- 2½ **cups sifted cake flour** *or* **2¼ cups all-purpose flour**
- 1 **recipe Double Chocolate Dip (see recipe, page 186)**

In a mixer bowl beat butter for 30 seconds. Add Vanilla Sugar and lemon peel; beat till fluffy. Add flour, ½ *cup* at a time, beating well. Cover; chill 1 hour. Halve dough. On a lightly floured surface, roll each half to ¼-inch thickness; cut into stars using 2-inch cookie cutters. Place stars on buttered parchment-lined cookie sheets. Bake in a 375° oven for 10 to 12 minutes or till light brown. Let cool for 1 minute. Transfer to a wire rack. Cool. Dip half of each cookie in Double Chocolate Dip. Let dry on wire rack for 30 minutes. Makes 42.

Per serving: 83 calories, 1 g protein, 8 g carbohydrate, 6 g fat, 10 mg cholesterol, and 1 mg sodium.

Vanilla Sugar: Snip one 7-inch *vanilla bean* into ¼-inch segments. In a blender container or food processor bowl combine vanilla with 1 cup *sugar.* Cover and blend till smooth. Store Vanilla Sugar in an airtight container. Use Vanilla Sugar in recipes using sugar and vanilla. Makes 1 cup.

HOLIDAY TRIANGLES

- ¾ cup unsalted butter
  (at room temperature)
- 3 tablespoons sugar
- 1 beaten egg
- ½ teaspoon vanilla
- 2 cups all-purpose flour
- ½ cup orange marmalade
- 5 egg whites
- 1½ cups sugar
- 3 tablespoons all-purpose flour
- 1 tablespoon light corn syrup
- 1 teaspoon ground cinnamon
- 2⅔ cups broken pecans
- ½ teaspoon orange extract
- ¼ teaspoon baking powder
- 1 recipe Double Chocolate Dip
  (see recipe, right)

Line a 15x10x1-inch pan with foil; butter foil. Set aside.

In a large mixer bowl beat the butter for 30 seconds. Add the 3 tablespoons sugar and beat till fluffy. Add egg and vanilla; beat well. Add the 2 cups flour, ½ cup at a time, beating just till combined.

Food processor directions: Place steel blade in work bowl. Add the 2 cups flour and 3 tablespoons sugar; process 5 seconds to mix. Cut the butter into chunks. Add butter to work bowl; process with on/off turns till mixture is crumbly. Add egg and vanilla; process just till dough forms a ball.

Press dough into the foil-lined pan. Chill 1 hour. Spread marmalade over dough. In a 1½-quart saucepan combine the egg whites, 1½ cups sugar, 3 tablespoons flour, corn syrup, and cinnamon. Bring to boiling over medium-high heat. Reduce heat to medium-low. Stir constantly till the mixture reaches 200°. (Mixture will be brown and may appear overcooked.) Stir in the pecans, orange extract, and baking powder. Spread hot mixture over marmalade. Bake in a 350° oven about 30 minutes or till golden. Cool in pan on wire rack. Lift foil to remove baked mixture from pan. Cut into 24 squares. Diagonally cut each square in half to form 48 triangles. Dip edges of each triangle in warm Double Chocolate Dip. Let dry on rack. To store, place cookies between layers of waxed paper in an airtight container. Store in a cool place. Makes 48.

Per serving: 145 calories, 2 g protein, 16 g carbohydrate, 9 g fat, 12 mg cholesterol, and 9 mg sodium.

DOUBLE CHOCOLATE DIP

- 3 squares (3 ounces) semisweet chocolate
- 1 square (1 ounce) unsweetened chocolate
- 2 tablespoons shortening

In the top of a double boiler combine the semisweet chocolate, unsweetened chocolate, and shortening. Place chocolate mixture over, but not touching, hot water. Cook and stir over medium heat till chocolate is melted. Remove from heat to dip cookies. If necessary, rewarm chocolate over water. Use to make Holiday Triangles.

FRENCH PASTRY

- 1½ cups unbleached flour
- 2 tablespoons sugar
- ⅛ teaspoon salt
- ½ cup cold unsalted butter
- 3 tablespoons ice water

In a mixing bowl stir together the flour, sugar, and salt. Cut in cold butter till the mixture resembles coarse crumbs. Sprinkle *1 tablespoon* of the water over part of the mixture; gently toss with a fork. Push to side of bowl. Repeat till all is moistened. Form dough into a ball. Wrap and chill dough for 1 hour. Roll out and bake as directed for Cranberry-Orange Tart.

CRANBERRY-ORANGE TART

- 1 recipe French Pastry
  (see recipe, left)
- 2 tablespoons currant jelly, melted
- 1 cup currant jelly
- ¼ cup water
- 2 cups cranberries
- ¼ of an orange, cut up
- 1 envelope unflavored gelatin
- ¼ cup water
- 3 tablespoons orange liqueur

On a lightly floured surface roll French Pastry dough into a 13-inch circle. Line an 11-inch flan pan with removable bottom with dough, being careful not to stretch dough. Trim edges. Fold any excess dough under. Prick the bottom and sides; line dough in pan with foil and fill with dry beans.

Bake pastry in a 400° oven for 15 minutes. Remove foil and beans; continue baking for 10 to 15 minutes more or till pastry is light brown. Brush melted currant jelly over the bottom of the crust. Cool on a wire rack.

In a 10-inch skillet bring the 1 cup currant jelly and ¼ cup water to boiling. Add cranberries; cook, uncovered, over low heat for 3 to 5 minutes or till berries pop. With slotted spoon, transfer cranberries to a bowl; set aside. In a blender container or food processor bowl combine the orange and ¼ cup of the jelly liquid; cover and blend till smooth. Return mixture to the skillet.

Combine gelatin and ¼ cup water; let stand for 5 minutes. Add gelatin mixture and orange liqueur to the skillet. Heat and stir till gelatin is dissolved. Pour gelatin mixture over the cranberries in bowl. To cool, place the skillet in a bowl or sink of ice about 15 minutes or till the mixture is partially set, stirring occasionally. Spoon mixture into pastry shell; spread evenly. Chill 2 hours or till firm. To serve, cut into wedges. Serves 10.

Per serving: 263 calories, 3 g protein, 43 g carbohydrate, 8 g fat, 22 mg cholesterol, and 36 mg sodium.

Turkey Roasting Guide

You can count on roasting this year's turkey to perfection using the techniques below. You'll also find tips for thawing and stuffing the bird.

Thawing the turkey

Refrigerator thawing: Leave the original wrap on the frozen bird; place the bird on a tray. Refrigerate 3 to 4 days, about 24 hours for each 5 pounds.

Cold-water thawing: Place the frozen turkey in its original wrap in a sink filled with cold water. Change water every 30 minutes. Allow 30 minutes thawing time for each pound of turkey.

Preparing the turkey for roasting

After thawing: Remove the wrap, free legs and tail, then remove giblets and neck piece from the cavities. Rinse bird; pat dry. *Do not stuff the bird till just before it is to be cooked.*

To stuff the turkey: Spoon some stuffing loosely into neck cavity; pull neck skin over stuffing and fasten the skin securely to back of bird with a skewer. Place turkey, neck side down, in large bowl. Lightly spoon stuffing into the body cavity; do not pack the stuffing or the mixture will not cook properly. If turkey has a band of skin across its tail, tuck drumsticks under the band. Otherwise, securely tie legs to tail. Twist wing tips under the back.

Roasting the turkey

Open roasting pan directions: Place bird, breast side up, on rack in shallow roasting pan. Brush with cooking oil. Insert meat thermometer in center of inside thigh muscle, making sure that the bulb does not touch a bone. Cover turkey loosely with a foil "cap" that barely touches bird. Press foil lightly at ends of drumsticks and neck. Roast in 325° oven. Baste occasionally with drippings or oil. Remove foil last 30 minutes for final browning.

Covered roasting pan directions: Place turkey, breast side up, on a rack in roasting pan; brush with cooking oil. Insert meat thermometer. Do not add water. Roast, covered with vent open, in 325° oven 20 to 25 minutes per pound. Uncover; drain reserving pan juices. Raise the oven temperature to 475°. Continue roasting for 20 minutes more or till turkey is brown.

For a foil-wrapped turkey: Wrap the turkey, breast side up, in a piece of greased, heavy foil. Place in large shallow roasting pan. Insert meat thermometer in the thigh muscle through the foil. Place pan in a 450° oven. Roast turkey till done. Open foil for the last 20 to 30 minutes of cooking time.

For frozen prestuffed turkey: Remove wrap from the frozen turkey. Do not thaw turkey. Place the frozen turkey on a rack in a shallow roasting pan; brush bird with oil. Place in 325° oven. Baste turkey occasionally with pan drippings or oil. Cover entire turkey loosely with foil to prevent overbrowning, if necessary. After 3 hours, insert meat thermometer in center of inside thigh muscle. Roast till done.

Testing doneness: For the above methods, roast the turkey till the meat thermometer registers 180° to 185° or till the thickest part of drumstick is soft and the drumstick twists in the socket. Make sure the turkey juices are no longer pink when skin is pricked with fork. Remove the turkey from oven; loosely cover with foil. Let the turkey stand 15 minutes before slicing. If bird is stuffed, the temperature of the stuffing should read 165° to be sufficiently cooked.

TURKEY ROASTING TIMES

Since birds differ in size, shape, and tenderness, use these roasting times as a general guide.

Type of Turkey	Ready-to-Cook Weight	Oven Temp.	Guide to Roasting Time
Stuffed Whole Turkey	6–8 lbs.	325°	3–3½ hrs.
	8–12 lbs.	325°	3½–4½ hrs.
	12–16 lbs.	325°	4–5 hrs.
	16–20 lbs.	325°	4½–5½ hrs.
	20–24 lbs.	325°	5–6½ hrs.
Foil-Wrapped Turkey (unstuffed)	8–10 lbs.	450°	1¼–1¾ hrs.
	10–12 lbs.	450°	1¾–2¼ hrs.
	12–16 lbs.	450°	2¼–3 hrs.
	16–20 lbs.	450°	3–3½ hrs.
	20–24 lbs.	450°	3½–4½ hrs.
Frozen Prestuffed Turkey	7–9 lbs.	325°	5–5½ hrs.
	9–11 lbs.	325°	5½–6 hrs.
	11–14 lbs.	325°	6–6½ hrs.
	14–16 lbs.	325°	6½–7 hrs.
Boneless Turkey Roast	3–4 lbs.	325°	2¼–2¾ hrs.
	4–5 lbs.	325°	2¾–3¼ hrs.
	5–6 lbs.	325°	3¼–3¾ hrs.

Servings: For turkey weighing 12 lbs. or less, allow 1 lb. per serving; over 12 lbs. allow ¾ lb. per serving.

Netted boneless turkey roast: Remove outer wrap from the turkey roast. Do not remove the inside netting. Thaw according to package directions. Place thawed turkey roast on rack in shallow roasting pan. Insert a meat thermometer. Brush with oil. Roast, uncovered, in 325° oven. Baste occasionally with oil. Cover turkey loosely with foil to prevent overbrowning. Roast till thermometer registers 170° to 175°. To serve the turkey, remove netting.

INDEX

D-H

Index

Q-S

Index

T-Z

Have BETTER HOMES AND
GARDENS® magazine delivered to
your door. For information, write to:
MR. ROBERT AUSTIN,
P.O. BOX 4536,
DES MOINES, IA 50336.